The Anthem Companion to Raymond Boudon

Edited by
Christian Robitaille and Robert Leroux

ANTHEM PRESS

Anthem Press
An imprint of Wimbledon Publishing Company
www.anthempress.com

This edition first published in UK and USA 2024
by ANTHEM PRESS
75–76 Blackfriars Road, London SE1 8HA, UK
or PO Box 9779, London SW19 7ZG, UK
and
244 Madison Ave #116, New York, NY 10016, USA

British Library Cataloguing-in-Publication Data
A catalogue record for this book is available from the British Library.

Library of Congress Cataloging-in-Publication Data
A catalog record for this book has been requested.
2024930074

ISBN-13: 978-1-83999-145-5 (Hbk)
ISBN-10: 1-83999-145-3 (Hbk)

Cover Credit: Stéphane Boudon

This title is also available as an e-book.

ANTHEM COMPANIONS TO SOCIOLOGY

The Sociology program takes a fresh and challenging sociological look at the interactions between politics, society, history, and culture. Titles transcend traditional disciplinary boundaries. This program includes a variety of book series.

Anthem Companions to Sociology offers authoritative and comprehensive assessments of major figures in the development of sociology from the last two centuries. Covering the major advancements in sociological thought, these companions offer critical evaluations of key figures in the American and European sociological tradition and will provide students and scholars with an in-depth assessment of the makers of sociology and chart their relevance to modern society.

Series Editor
Bryan S. Turner—City University of New York, USA/Australian Catholic University, Australia/University of Potsdam, Germany

Titles in the Series
The Anthem Companion to Erving Goffman
The Anthem Companion to Niklas Luhmann
The Anthem Companion to Ferdinand Tönnies
The Anthem Companion to Karl Mannheim
The Anthem Companion to Philip Selznick
The Anthem Companion to Talcott Parsons
The Anthem Companion to Alexis de Tocqueville
The Anthem Companion to Max Weber
The Anthem Companion to Georg Simmel
The Anthem Companion to Pierre Bourdieu
The Anthem Companion to Hannah Arendt
The Anthem Companion to Raymond Boudon
The Anthem Companion on David Riesman

To the memory of Robert Leroux (1964–2022).

CONTENTS

LIST OF CONTRIBUTORS

Massimo Borlandi was a professor of sociology at the University of Turin. He has worked extensively on the history of French social thought. He is currently the editor of the *Revue européenne des sciences sociales*.

Nathalie Bulle is a sociologist and a research director at the National Center for Scientific Research in France. She has notably coedited *The Palgrave Handbook of Methodological Individualism* and published *Methodological Individualism: Introduction and Founding Texts* with Routledge. She is coeditor of *Philosophy of the Social Sciences*.

Pierre Demeulenaere is a professor of sociology at Sorbonne University, France.

Francesco Di Iorio is an associate professor of philosophy at Nankai University, China.

Enzo Di Nuoscio is a professor of logic and epistemology at the University of Molise and Luiss University, Italy.

Renaud Fillieule is a professor of sociology at the Institute of Social Sciences of the University of Lille, France, and a member of the CLERSÉ research unit (CNRS UMR 8019). He received his Habilitation to direct research in 2006 from the University of Lille and his PhD in sociology in 1994 from Paris-Sorbonne University, under the supervision of Raymond Boudon. His research interests include the question of rationality in the social sciences, the epistemology of the social sciences, the sociology of delinquency, the economic sociology of prices, and the Austrian School of Economics. He can be contacted at renaud.fillieule@univ-lille.fr.

Jean-Michel Morin is a senior lecturer in sociology at Université de Paris Cité. He also teaches at the École Professorale de Paris, the Collège des Bernardins, and the Institut de Philosophie Comparée. He is notably the author of *Boudon, un sociologue classique*, 2nd edition published in 2020.

Emmanuel Picavet is a professor of philosophy (applied ethics) at Paris 1 Panthéon-Sorbonne University. He is the author of *Approches du concret* (Ellipses, 1995), *Choix rationnel et vie publique* (PUF, 1996), and *La Revendication des droits* (Classiques Garnier, 2011, 2021). He is the coeditor of *Revue de philosophie économique / Review of Economic Philosophy* (Vrin) and is the director of the *Centre de Philosophie Contemporaine at the Sorbonne*. He is a member of the Bureau of the *Société Française de Philosophie*, in charge of the international relations, and France's delegate to the Bureau of the *Fédération Internationale des Sociétés de Philosophie* (FISP).

Alexander Riley has written extensively on social theory and the history of the social sciences over the past 25 years. His work on the nature and legacy of the Durkheimian tradition is internationally recognized. Riley is the author of *Toward a Biosocial Science: Evolutionary Theory, Human Nature, and Social Life*, *Angel Patriots: The Crash of United Flight 93 and the Myth of America*, and *Godless Intellectuals? The Intellectual Pursuit of the Sacred Reinvented*.

Christian Robitaille is a lecturer (assistant professor) in sociology at Liverpool Hope University. His research focuses on theories of rationality, epistemology, the sociology of action, and the history of social scientific thought. He can be contacted at robitac@hope.ac.uk.

INTRODUCTION

Christian Robitaille

Raymond Boudon's (1934–2013) contributions to the social sciences demonstrate both depth and breadth. From the beginning of his career to the very end of his life, he tackled topics such as the use of mathematics in sociology, educational outcomes and social mobility, the social origins of values, the reasons for adhering to an ideology, the antiliberal attitudes of most intellectuals (in the classical meaning of the term "liberal"[1]), as well as many other social phenomena. This apparent curiosity for a wide range of topics does not only reflect a desire to provide explanations for social phenomena he found intriguing but is also indicative of a more profound and ambitious quest. In fact, Raymond Boudon wanted to discover and systematize the foundations of a properly *scientific* sociology. In his mind, these foundations would allow for sociology to become a *general* science that would be able to shed light on a large range of social phenomena, thus explaining why he himself studied such a wide variety of topics. If he could find the commonalities between the successful analyses of a large range of topics, he thought he would get closer to discovering a *general* and *scientific* way to conduct sociological studies.

To achieve this, he developed an interest in the critical study of successful social thinkers of the past and of his time. His analysis of classical sociologists such as Durkheim, Weber, Simmel, Tocqueville, and even elements from Marx or of some of his most famous contemporaries such as James Coleman and Mancur Olson allowed him to put forward a sociological theory that was sufficiently general to become the grounds on which, in his mind, social scientific inquiries on a broad variety of topics could rest.

In this introduction, I wish to present an outline of the main threads of Boudon's resolutely complex course of thought, which has greatly contributed

---

[1] Which differs from what Americans nowadays consider to be "liberal." Boudon's understanding of liberalism was rooted in individual autonomy and sharply opposed to any form of Marxism, neo-Marxism, "critical" theory, or poststructuralism. On Boudon's understanding of liberalism, see Leroux (2022, Ch. 7).

to the development of a general and scientific sociology. As Boudon remains a relatively unknown figure in anglophone intellectual circles, I will take an approach that is somewhat biographical to contextualize this course of thought. I will then show how this book can help interested readers to both understand and apply Boudon's many insights in the spirit of participating in his project of building a scientific sociology.

Boudon's Early Career: From Mathematical Sociology to the Analysis of Educational Outcomes and Social Mobility

During his studies in philosophy, mathematics, and social sciences at the famous *École normale supérieure* in Paris as well as during his military service, Boudon read Paul Lazarsfeld's work, known for its empirical studies in mathematical sociology (Jeřábek 2001, 236–237), and then spent a year at Columbia University (1961–1962) under his direction. Under his impulsion, he became interested in the mathematical analysis of social facts and in the limits of the structuralist approach to social analysis (Boudon and Leroux 2003, 34–41). As such, once he came back to France, these interests were then respectively systematized in his main doctoral dissertation on the use of mathematics in sociology (Boudon 1967) and in his complementary dissertation on the notion of structure in the social sciences (Boudon 1971 [1968]). These early considerations stemmed from Boudon's idea that the mathematical formalization of sociological thought could become a possible solution to sociology's notorious lack of cumulativity and eclecticism. A scientific sociology could perhaps, in his mind, be built on the basis of the use of a clear language such as mathematics. Likewise, he perceived structuralism as an improper theoretical stance to allow for the acquisition of cumulative knowledge, as the notion of structure is often vague and diffuse, while foundational theories and concepts must be clear and strong. It was clear, then, that sociology must either clarify or abandon such a notion in order to become scientific and cumulative.

Quickly after the publication of his two doctoral dissertations, however, Boudon became increasingly skeptical about mathematical sociology's potential claim to become the foundation of a *general* sociology (Boudon 1980 [1971], 23). Although useful for the elucidation of some empirical topics or for the creation of social indices, mathematics limits the scope of sociological investigations to narrow areas of the social world that are simple enough to be translated into mathematical equations and relationships. If mathematics has the advantage of defining society in a clear language, the risk is that such a foundation for sociological studies would make social scientists put aside topics that are not easily described in these terms. And, indeed, most of the social world is too complex to be reduced to simple mathematical formulations. This does not mean, in Boudon's mind, that mathematics must be abandoned entirely; they remain important but must be relegated to a more modest role than in, for instance, disciplines such as physics (Boudon and Leroux 2003, 41). The fact that his next books, while focusing on empirical topics such as educational outcomes and opportunities or relative frustration, relied on game theory and mathematical simulation models demonstrates that he still considered mathematics to be useful in *some* sociological investigations.

It is his work with André Davidovitch on the criminal justice system and the abandonment of judicial cases that marked the beginning of Boudon's use of experimental simulation models for the understanding of empirical phenomena (Davidovitch and Boudon 1964). From then on, he defended the method both theoretically (Boudon 1965) and in the context of his own topical analyses. His most famous work, *Education, Opportunity, and Social Inequality*, published in French in 1973 (and translated into English in 1974), indeed relies on both the analysis of empirical statistical data and the use of simulation models to make sense of educational decision-making processes. If Bourdieu and Passeron (1990 [1970]) sought to demonstrate that educational inequalities were rooted in *habitus* and class reproduction, as the structural effects of quite rigid cultural dispositions, Boudon argued, on the contrary, that it was socially influenced *decisions* made by individual actors that are the most important factors in explaining such inequalities. This can explain why, in spite of contemporary efforts to "democratize" education, there seems to be a lack of "improvement" in terms of social mobility, as individuals from lower social classes tend to be satisfied with a lesser educational attainment than individuals from higher social classes (assuming comparable abilities).

This focus on socially located individuals will be at the forefront of Boudon's future work, as he believed that this conception of the social world could be key to find general foundations for a scientific sociology. The foundations on which the social sciences rest are not always mathematical, in Boudon's mind, but they seemed to be always based on a proper understanding of contextualized individual features and actions.

Methodological individualism, henceforth seen as the only appropriate approach to find ultimate social explanations, made Boudon seek to study various paradoxes which are based on the social effects of individual action. This led to his book *The Unintended Consequences of Social Action*, published in French in 1977 and translated into English in 1982 (Boudon 1982 [1977]). It assembles chapters on topics already addressed by Boudon such as the perverse effects of educational decisions, but also treats new topics such as social change, relative frustration, conceptions of justice, and social scientific paradigms. Their common theme is that they can often be seen as the unintended consequences of particular actions or policies. Understanding them requires a focus on individual purposes, as unintended consequences still spring from intentional desires, that is, from actors who *intend* to achieve some purpose. As Carl Menger argued, one can understand the unintended only by focusing on what was indeed intended by the actors, as the meaning of their action had an impact on the action taken and, therefore, on its *unintended* consequences (Robitaille 2022, 66–67). Methodological individualism is of utmost importance, then, to make sense of social phenomena which cannot, at first, be easily understood.

Simply put, *even if* these phenomena are not the result of any particular intention, one must go back to individual decision-making to reconstruct them intelligibly. The intentions of individuals involved *can* be understood, and the unintended consequences of their actions then become more easily understandable (Boudon 1990 [1979], 23, 51–52). Nobody wishes, for instance, to create a traffic jam. Hence, to understand why traffic jams occur, one must go back to typical individual decision-making; socially influenced individual purposes led a large proportion of car owners to choose to take the road at the same time, thus creating the jam and explaining it. The traffic jam is not the result of obscure social forces imposing themselves on individuals, but rather the undesirable consequence of rational deliberations by individuals.

Although Boudon did realize that methodological individualism is the key to understand intriguing social phenomena while studying education inequalities, it is in his book on the unintended consequences of social action that his focus becomes somewhat more theoretical and where epistemological considerations seem to guide the topical analyses presented much more explicitly (Boudon 1982 [1977], 7–10).

Indeed, Boudon then started to put forward his sociological program as a study of the interrelations between human "autonomy" and the structures which actors perceive as constraining their action (Boudon 1990 [1979], 296). It is merely through the microsocial analysis of the actor's decision-making and reasoning processes that one can make sense of macrosocial topics such as social change (Boudon 1986 [1984], 224–225). The notion of structure only makes sense (and is only operative) *through* the individual and his or her thinking and acting. A scientific sociology, then, must only focus on structures insofar as they are conceived as being constraining action *by the individual actors themselves*. This scientific program focusing on individual actors remained to be explored in more depth in the 1980s. This is something that Boudon attempted to do, both alone, as we will see next, and in collaboration with others, such as when he collaborated with François Bourricaud to create a dictionary delineating the main debates and objects of sociological inquiries (Boudon and Bourricaud 1982).

Beliefs and Values: Complex Topics Requiring a Sociological Explanation

Boudon mentioned that one of the reasons why he stopped focusing on the study of education was linked to his realization that, in education as well as in other fields, the result of rigorous research did not seem any more likely to win in the public competition of ideas than ideologically oriented research (Boudon and Leroux 2003, 227). In addition, he believed that contemporary sociology failed to accurately capture the logic of society because it became increasingly ideological, especially in the 1960s and the 1970s (Boudon 1990 [1979], 9–12). He was then curious to understand why false or doubtful ideas can become widely accepted, which led him to write a book on ideology, published in 1986 and translated into English in 1989 (Boudon 1989 [1986]). This book sought to understand what leads actors to adhere to false or doubtful ideas.

This attempt at explaining beliefs would permeate Boudon's work until his death. Most notably, he revisited the topic in his 1990 book on the art of self-persuasion, translated in 1994 into English (Boudon 1994 [1990]). To explain ideologies (and beliefs in general), Boudon applied once again the principles of methodological individualism. He developed typologies of reasons to believe in false or doubtful ideas based on individual positions and dispositions.

It is not because an individual is irrational that he or she ends up believing in false or doubtful ideas. Rather, it is because the social and cognitive contexts in which he or she is located provide him or her with good reasons to believe in their truth. To take an example Boudon frequently borrows from Weber and Durkheim, it is not because individuals from "primitive" times were irrational that they believed in the ability of dancing rituals to make it rain. It is because their social context disposes them to believe in it that they do (Boudon 1989 [1986], 63–65).

To understand such phenomena, sociologists must accomplish a few important tasks. They must first describe the intriguing phenomenon (widespread beliefs in the efficiency of magical rituals), then find out what are the social and cognitive contexts linked to this phenomenon (societies in which the principles of chemistry are not known and in which the unknown is linked with the supernatural), then conceive of ideal-typical actors which are situated within these social and cognitive contexts in order to understand what are their reasons to believe or act in the way they do. This is what can be termed "subjective rationality" (or "ordinary rationality"): even objectively false or doubtful beliefs are held as the result of contextual position, disposition, communication, or epistemological effects that provide the actor with good reasons to believe in them (Boudon 1989; 1992, 39–41). The explanation is hence traceable, once again, to individual actors.

The same logic applies, *mutatis mutandis*, to the understanding of values (Boudon 1995; 1999). Indeed, values are not the result of structural forces imposing themselves on individuals. Rather, they are the result of *thought* processes influenced by an individual's social milieu. For instance, it is understandable that, in democratic societies, values associated with democracy are held as important. The actor's typical context is indeed such that he or she will think of justice and morality *in the same terms* as those linked to democratic values; the latter are held *a priori* in most people's minds and could eventually be put into question only once the actor's social and cognitive contexts drastically change for one reason or another during his or her life course. They hence shape his or her reasoning processes about values. Varying contexts provide varying widely held values. Even in different *types* of democratic societies, one will observe differences in the values most deeply held. This is why, for instance, to take examples given by Boudon, the death penalty or slavery is often perceived as unjust or immoral in the minds of actors whose life course occurred in contemporary Western democratic contexts, whereas most actors in Ancient Greece or Rome, given their very own hierarchized contexts, saw these phenomena as just and moral (Boudon 2001, 49). Simply, the social milieus in which an actor's life course evolves provide the actor with some fundamental *a prioris* which influence his or her reasoning processes.

Given the complexity of individual life courses and the singularity of the path they follow within various social milieus, social scientists *cannot* possibly assert a deterministic causal link between particular milieus and particular values. They nevertheless can reconstruct *typical* adherence to values given the *typical* social milieus of *typical* actors. The only certainty, however, is that values are not just the result of unfathomable passions but are rather the result of socially influenced reasoning processes. Here again, the explanation of collective values resides in the analysis of individual actors conceived as socially positioned.[2]

It is clear now that, if we follow Boudon, the analysis of both beliefs and values requires us to use methodological individualism; it is the only path to find the meaning behind any empirical kind of widely held belief system social scientists may find intriguing.

---

[2] For Boudon's analysis of the discourse according to which values decline in contemporary society, see Boudon (2002). One can note that this does not imply, in Boudon's mind, a blind acceptance of relativism in terms of values. See Boudon (2008).

Classical Sociology, Rationalism, and Apriorism in Boudon's Work

With all these topics of interest having been elucidated in the 1980s and 1990s, it became increasingly important for Boudon to also formalize the epistemological and methodological approach he used to make sense of these. Indeed, one must keep in mind that Boudon's ambitious project was to discover the bases of a general and scientific sociology, thus requiring him to reflect on *how* sociology can provide convincing explanations of social phenomena.

But as is apparent in any of his books, Boudon is not the type of intellectual who attempts to reconstruct everything from scratch. Rather, Boudon considered himself an *heir*, someone who seeks to find what is good and scientific in the work of his eminent predecessors and contemporaries to then build a strong synthetic sociology. Taking from Lazarsfeld the idea that the best way to build a strong and convincing theory is to critically assess the strong and convincing theories of others, Boudon always made sure to root his own analyses on the critical assessment he made of the insightful work of others (Boudon 1980 [1971], 81–82).

It was clear from the very beginning of his career that Boudon found classical sociology provided particularly strong and convincing explanations of social phenomena linked to modernity (Boudon and Leroux 2003, 64–65). In brief, Boudon built his approach by relying quite heavily on Max Weber's typology of social action and on Georg Simmel's formal sociology. He also mobilized multiple examples from Alexis de Tocqueville, Émile Durkheim, Gabriel Tarde, Vilfredo Pareto, and many others. Moreover, he dedicated two volumes to original studies on the contributions of a wide range of classical sociologists (Boudon 1998b; 2000) as well as a full book on the relevance of Tocqueville for contemporary social analyses (Boudon 2006 [2005]).

His reliance on so many classical social theorists may seem odd at first sight. Indeed, many of these key thinkers come from very different theoretical perspectives. How could their respective work possibly be integrated into a common synthesis? The answer to this question is simply that Boudon did not seek to be completely faithful to the authors' original intentions when analyzing their work. Rather, he wanted to take from all these thinkers what he thought was *good* in order to *reinterpret* their work in light of his very own methodologically individualist and rationalist approach.

Boudon's main framework is admittedly neo-Weberian (Boudon 2010, 75–77; Leroux 2019) and contains a strong Simmelian influence in its epistemological foundation (Boudon 1991; Robitaille 2020). Indeed, Boudon's focus on socially positioned individual actors and their reasoning processes is in large part inspired by Weber's typology of social action as delineated in his *Economy and Society* (Weber 2019 [1921], 101–103). If Weber distinguished between instrumentally rational, value rational, traditional, and affective social actions as pure types with different motors guiding the actors in their decision-making processes, Boudon develops a typology of rationality distinguishing between instrumental, axiological, and cognitive reasoning processes. Social action and belief, then, are the result of actors whose position in society provides them with a complex combination of reasons to act or believe in the way they do. As such, empirical social sciences, when confronted with a perplexing or paradoxical social phenomenon, can only hope to find an explanation by focusing on the social and cognitive contexts of the actors involved and by trying to discover how these contexts are likely to affect their thought processes.

This is where Simmel's apriorism can help (Robitaille 2023, 79–88). Indeed, these social and cognitive contexts can be seen as *social forms* that are not put into question by the individuals involved. They hence impact individual reasoning processes as fundamental *a priori* elements on which all thinking is built; they influence the meaning actors find in their own beliefs and actions (Boudon 1992, 22). These elements can lead to beliefs or actions which seem odd from the social scientist's own cognitive and social position. In fact, they can explain why many social scientists have, in Boudon's (2003b, 81–85) mind, been too quick in assuming that irrational forces are causal determinants of actions deemed unfathomable from their own points of view.

Social scientists too have good reasons to resort to such irrationalist explanations, as their very own social context provides them with *a priori* elements on which they themselves reason. Activist social theorists such as Michel Foucault and Judith Butler, to apply Boudon's insights to contemporary examples, given their position in intellectual-activist circles, have difficulty understanding why one would follow the current norms of society out of rational deliberation. Intellectuals often seek to contest traditional hierarchies as they perceive them as oppressive; they fail to see why ordinary people—if they were truly rational thinkers—would not also seek to contest them. They hence resort to constructions such as panopticism or the heterosexual matrix to explain why people are being "irrational"; they are simply conditioned, manipulated, or brainwashed by social forces.

To Boudon (1991), Simmel's apriorism is useful to understand why people other than us hold beliefs other than ours or act differently than we do. If intellectuals such as Foucault and Butler had realized that most people do not share their social position and that, hence, they have *other a priori* frames than their own, they could have made sense of common thoughts or actions much more effectively than by resorting to obscure social forces which would be manipulating individuals to think and act in accordance to some obscure "plans." One could plausibly argue instead that most people find traditional hierarchies *useful* and even *moral* because they allow them to operate in the world with constraints that are relatively clear. Most people certainly do not have the time, desire, or capacity to put everything into question and to recreate a social order from scratch, thus their acceptance of these institutions and traditions. Traditionalism would, in this sense, be *rational* from their point of view.

Combined with Weber's typology of rationality, then, Boudon's use of Simmelian apriorism makes for strong epistemological building blocks to a *general*, *cumulative*, and *scientific* sociology. It is *adaptable* to situational specificities and it makes social scientists attempt to understand why one would act or think in a way that seems counterintuitive from their very own situational specificities.

Now, the manner by which Boudon integrates the other classical key thinkers aforementioned is by using their *examples* as convincing illustrations of this general approach he takes (mostly) from Weber and Simmel. His argument is simple: whenever we encounter a convincing explanation of a social phenomenon, it is because this approach has been by and large used (implicitly or explicitly).

In the case of examples taken from Weber, Simmel, or even Tocqueville, this is not very surprising as their approaches were mostly compatible with one another and hence, trivially, with Boudon's own synthesis. More surprising are instances in which Boudon borrows examples from methodological holists such as Durkheim or from historical materialists such as Marx (e.g., Boudon 1989 [1986], 61–66). Indeed, to take the example of Durkheim, Boudon claimed that, in his most convincing work, Durkheim was in fact *not really* a methodological Durkheimian; his *Suicide* and *Elementary Forms of Religious Life*, in particular, contain, according to Boudon, individualistic explanations of social facts which contrast with the methodological prescriptions delineated in his *Rules of Sociological Method* (Boudon and Leroux 2003, 50; Boudon 2004a; Leroux 2020). He argues that Durkheim *connects* macrosocial data with individual tendencies, thus explaining the former by the influence of the actor's social context on reasoning processes.

Once again, this reinterpretation of the work of Durkheim (and other classical thinkers) is not aimed at providing a faithful account of the author's own intentions, as I have already mentioned above. Rather, it is aimed at showing that successful social analyses can be grounded in the methodological individualist paradigm of social research.

Toward a General Theory of Rationality

So far, we have seen that Boudon's project of discovering the principles of a general manner by which sociology can provide us with cumulative and rigorous knowledge about the social world led him toward methodological individualism. As such, the individual actor's rationality must be put at the forefront of his theoretical approach. Such a focus is quite common in most schools of economic thought, with their paradigm built on the idea of a "homo oeconomicus,"[3] or in some schools of political science. It has also been gaining popularity in sociology with what has been termed "rational choice theory" (RCT), a doctrine according to which social phenomena can be explained by the actors' instrumental choices in their quest to maximize their (expected) utility. This doctrine conceives rationality as utilitarian and instrumental and claims that, therefore, it is sufficient for social scientists to discover what the interests of rational actors were at a given time and place to explain their actions and, by reconstruction, the social phenomena that they contributed to create through their actions. Of course, there exist many variations of RCT, some of which take into account the actor's limited access to information and some of which do not. But they nevertheless conceive of rationality as, to recycle David Hume's famous dictum, being the mere servant of utilitarian passions.

Boudon had a lot to say about RCT and one can capture from his overall assessment that he had mixed feelings toward it (Boudon and Leroux 2003, 76). Indeed, Boudon (2009, 181–182) thought RCT was *good* at explaining phenomena which can indeed be plausibly traced back to the actors' narrow self-interest. For instance, it provides a good explanation for why people look at both sides of the road before crossing it or why the Soviet Union collapsed when it did (Boudon 2003a, 4). But Boudon thought that RCT lacked *generality*. First, it failed to provide a complete explanation of *beliefs*, as many of them are not held *in order to* achieve any utilitarian goal (Boudon 1998a, 818); one does not believe that the Earth is spherical, for instance, *because* of self-interest, but because one thinks this is simply *true*. Second, it failed at explaining *actions* that do not seem motivated by a narrowly defined notion of self-interest (Boudon 2003a, 9); most people do not vote, to borrow one of Boudon's favorite examples, because of any self-interested motive, but because they believe this action to be their duty.

Boudon argues that we can overcome these limitations of RCT by expanding our understanding of rationality. The goal is to avoid the simplistic analyses provided by RCT without falling into the equally simplistic irrationalist

---

[3] See on this Demeulenaere (1996).

approach to social phenomena that prevails in contemporary sociological analyses (Boudon and Fillieule 2018, 4).

Indeed, as discussed above, Boudon (2003b, 49–54) developed a typology of rationality which is directly inspired by Weber. First, rationality can indeed be *instrumental*, as RCT would have it, that is, as a reflection on the appropriate means to attain a given (often, but not always, utilitarian) goal. Second, rationality can be *axiological*, that is, people act or think in particular ways because they believe it to be their duty to do so in order to live a moral, decent, or virtuous life. Third, beliefs can be *cognitively* rational, that is, based on the consistency of a belief with the actor's own *a priori* set of beliefs.

These must be seen as *pure* ideal types. Most empirical actions and beliefs must be explained by a weighted combination of such reasoning processes. For instance, individuals may vote primarily because they believe it to be their duty (axiological reasoning), as Boudon argued. But they must also think that this action will indeed contribute to the goal of following their duty; there must be some form of *justification* connecting the action "voting" with the actor's set of moral principles in the actor's mind (cognitive reasoning). Finally, voting must be conceived as something which is an appropriate *means* in order to pursue one's duty (instrumental reasoning); otherwise, the action would be seen as pointless by the actor and would not be performed. Note here that instrumental rationality takes a different meaning than with most versions of RCT. Reflecting on the appropriateness of a means to reach a goal does not necessarily imply that this goal is rooted in a narrowly defined notion of self-interest. The goal, here, is primarily axiological (one wishes to act according to one's duty). But the reflection on the means to achieve the goal remains "instrumental," that is, there is a reflection about the extent to which the action is an appropriate instrument to reach the axiological goal. Moreover, all of these thought processes are linked to cognitive reasoning on what actors believe to be *true* (such as "it is *true* that voting would contribute to perform my duty"). In fact, as Boudon (2006a, 164–165; Boudon and Leroux 2003, 71) mentioned many times, instrumental and axiological rationality can be conceived as being strongly connected to cognitive rationality. Indeed, if I believe "action X" to be moral, I must also believe that it is *true* that action X is *in fact* in conformity with my views on morality. Likewise, if I believe that "action X" is a good *means* to reach my goal, I must also believe this to be *true*. Reflections on truth permeate reflections on morality and instrumentality. But how much we insist on one or the other as being the main cause of social phenomena will depend on the context in which the action occurred. In our contemporary Western society, for instance, voting can be seen as primarily axiological. We can nevertheless imagine a society in which people would get paid to vote; in such cases, it may be argued that voting can be explained through primarily instrumental-utilitarian reasoning processes.

With this general typology of rationality in mind, the social scientist, Boudon argued, is equipped with the proper tools to make sense of social phenomena. Every intriguing macro-social fact can indeed be decomposed into individual actions and beliefs which can be explained by assessing the extent to which one type of rationality or another had more or less influence in the thought process bringing about these actions and beliefs. To do this, we must analyze the social context of these actors to discover the social forms (the set of beliefs plausibly held as *a priori* by the actors involved) which provided actors with good reasons to act the way they did or believe what they believed. This constitutes a sketch of Boudon's proposal for an approach to sociology which would render it *general*, *cumulative*, and *scientific*, the culmination, as it were, of his ambitious quest.

Final Years: A Refinement of the General Theory of Rationality and Further Applications

In the first decade of the present century up until his death in 2013, Boudon continued to refine his approach to a general and scientific sociology. He systematically presented what he terms the general theory of rationality in various books or collections of essays (Boudon 2003b; 2007).

But in addition to his epistemological and methodological concerns, Boudon became increasingly preoccupied with the elucidation of political and ideological questions. He presented, for instance, a case for a nonrelativistic renewal of Western democracies (Boudon 2006b) based on a defense of common sense which contrasts with the usual views promulgated by sociologists (Boudon 2008). These analyses of politics and morality rest at the intersection of sociology, political science, and philosophy. They illustrate in particular Boudon's increasing confidence in applying his systematic approach to difficult and complex topics such as politics, religion, and morality (Boudon 2012).

For instance, in a book published in 2004, Boudon tried to explain why intellectuals were generally hostile toward classical liberalism. If Boudon agrees to some extent with the thesis put forward by classical liberal and libertarian scholars such as Robert Nozick (Boudon 2004b, 13–14), that is, that intellectuals are driven by resentment directed toward a system in which people they consider to be their inferiors become more successful than themselves—he nevertheless claims that there are more factors at play here. He indicates that intellectuals have indeed *good reasons*, from their own social position, to believe that classical liberalism is a flawed ideology.

Other than instrumental reasons linked to a desire to bypass the market system to obtain privileges and wealth, intellectuals also have cognitive reasons to believe that liberalism brings social problems. Social scientists in particular are studying how society works; they are hence able to find social *issues* quite easily. Given their expertise and position, it is easy for them to believe that they can find *solutions* to these issues. The fact is that state intervention seems like a straightforward mechanism to address any issue. Especially in a world where experts are mostly specialists, they can often *see*, to borrow Frédéric Bastiat's famous expression, how investing state resources would contribute to solve an issue *without seeing* that these resources could therefore not be used for other, perhaps more important, things. Hence, social scientists often try to shape policies in order to bring their preferred solution to their favorite issue (see Boudon's many examples, ibid., 77–118, 189).

Moreover, various social groups often demand an explanation for their situation (e.g., poverty or misery) and intellectuals wish to supply them with answers and solutions (ibid., 138, 189). Liberalism would often simply answer that scarcity or state intervention is the cause of poverty and misery, and that the solution is simply to accumulate capital, allow free markets to operate, support individual autonomy, and so forth until the life of most people improves. Needless to say, the latter solution is often badly perceived, as it seems counterintuitive *not* to provide a collective solution to solve an aggregate problem. Liberalism, to intellectuals (and those who demand explanations for their situation), is simply something that stands on the way of the implementation of a "real," concrete solution; it is, in brief, "easier to understand a 'constructed order' than a 'spontaneous order'" (ibid., 25). This argument, already presented to some extent in Austrian economist Friedrich Hayek's work (Hayek 1944, 55–57; 1955, 52, 83–84), is developed by Boudon (2004b) using the terminology of his own general sociology.

Finally, Boudon claims that, because social scientists task themselves with uncovering what common sense ignores, they actively seek to find out issues to solve at the risk of finding problems where there are none. For instance, they often treat human beings as irrational pawns of social forces; it hence makes sense for intellectuals to argue that notions such as "autonomy" or "free will"— notions that permeate most classical liberal thinking—are tools of oppression and that liberalism should, as such, be fought as the ideology justifying such oppression (Boudon 2004b, 66–69).

Boudon's Social Theory as a General Framework

Boudon's work culminated in the posthumous publication of a book, a few months only after his death in 2013 at the age of 79, in which he reflects on the main threads he addressed throughout his career (Boudon 2013). A clear sense of having contributed significantly to his life goal of developing a *scientific* and *general* sociology permeates the pages of this book. He is not alone in believing so. It has indeed been argued in the recent literature that Boudon himself can be considered as a classical sociologist given the generality of his seminal sociological approach (Morin 2006; Bulle and Morin 2015). Yet, his work remains relatively unknown to the general public and his thought is not taught to undergraduate and postgraduate students to the same extent as the thought of other contemporary key thinkers.

According to a recent article, Raymond Boudon is the 50th sociologist among "scholars who belong to the top 20% of the citation distribution of three national sociologies *and/or* three specialties *and* who were born after 1850" (Korom 2020a, 352). This is well above sociologists such as George Ritzer and Luc Boltanski, whose work nevertheless gathers more attention in contemporary textbooks or in the media. Indeed, Boudon's work is absent from the most widely used sociology textbooks (Korom 2020b, 139) and, in spite of the fact that most of his work has been translated into English, his approach is not well known to anglophone scholars.

After recognizing this, it seems that a book introducing Boudon's complex, yet enlightening and seminal work, to anglophone scholars and students, is well overdue. This is the general goal this book aims to accomplish. It unites scholars from a variety of backgrounds and generations in the quest to make manifest the importance and potentiality of Boudon's work for the understanding of social phenomena. It seeks, in other words, to demonstrate that Boudon has been successful in his endeavor to find the general foundations on which a scientific sociology can rest.

The following chapters all seek to illustrate, refine, develop, or criticize aspects of Boudon's scientific sociology. The order in which they were positioned in this book takes into account the fact that anglophone scholars remain by and large unfamiliar with Boudon's approach. This should not stop more advanced readers from selecting those chapters they find of greater interest for their own purposes. As such, instead of presenting the chapters in chronological order in terms of the themes addressed by Boudon during his career, it was decided that, for the sake of clarity, the first chapters must present discussions linked to the fundamental approach of Boudon's methodological individualism.

The first chapter, written by Massimo Borlandi, explains how Boudon's approach addressed three problems identified in the literature on methodological individualism: (1) one must understand what exactly is meant by individual action *before* seeking in it an explanation of social phenomena, (2) one must clarify the link between individual action and the context in which the actor operates, and (3) one should delineate the causal process by which individual action affects social phenomena. Throughout this discussion, Borlandi presents the scope that methodological individualism takes in Boudon's social scientific thought and explains how Boudon attempts to address these three challenges.

The second chapter, cowritten by Francesco Di Iorio and Enzo Di Nuoscio, while further clarifying Boudon's methodological individualism, also presents Boudon's interpretation of successful applications of its principles in the work of Tocqueville and Durkheim in particular. This discussion is properly permeated by considerations on the insistence Boudon has put in the *cognitive* understanding of social phenomena, something which only methodological individualism allows for. This chapter hence contrasts this approach with attempts to ground sociology in holistic and ideological frameworks.

Once these fundamental concerns are clarified, the reader is then presented with chapters dealing with Boudon's conception of rationality. Indeed, as we have seen above, rationality is of utmost importance in Boudon's methodological individualism; it constitutes the main vector linking individual action and social phenomena of interest. As such, the third chapter, written by Pierre Demeulenaere, provides an account of Boudon's conception of rationality as compared to other conceptions found in the literature (including various forms of RCT). It explains thoroughly, though not uncritically, how Boudon attempted to subsume normative and positive thoughts under the realm of the actor's good reasons to hold these thoughts. The fourth chapter, authored by Emmanuel Picavet, focuses on Boudon's conception of axiological rationality. In particular, it puts forward a discussion of the tension between the quest for generality and the necessity to contextualize in applied axiology, as exemplified in Boudon's own complex attempts at conceiving and ascribing axiological reasoning processes in empirical situations. The fifth chapter, cowritten by Nathalie Bulle and Jean-Michel Morin, explains how Boudon's neo-Kantian apriorism (taken in particular from Simmel) had an impact on his sociology of collective beliefs. It clearly shows how reasoning processes, either based on facts or on values, can be understood by tracing them back to what the actor takes for granted given his or her social context. It also demonstrates, based on these considerations, the fruitfulness of Boudon's epistemology of beliefs in the understanding of complex topics such as religion, morality, and politics.

Finally, this book concludes with applications of Boudon's approach to topics such as social mobility and the prevalence of "critical" approaches in contemporary sociology. The sixth chapter, by Renaud Fillieule, builds on Boudon's work on education and social mobility. It explains, reconstructs, and expands on Boudon's own simulation model developed in 1973 before discussing its relevance in comparison to Bourdieu's cultural approach. It shows the importance of theoretical simulations to make sense of empirical phenomena such as social mobility, as a mere reliance on empirical observations and correlations is misleading without a proper theorization. The seventh chapter, authored by Alexander Riley, explains how Boudon's insights can help in explaining the contemporary prevalence of "critical" sociology as exemplified by the discourse emanating from the American Sociological Association. It also shows how Boudon's theory *contrasts* with the latter. Against the often-held idea that structures of oppression can be proven by the mere empirical observation of their alleged effects, Riley argues that Boudon's approach, which focuses on a socially contextualized individual logic and autonomy, can provide us with an understanding of society in a more effective manner than what currently prevails in the field. Last, my own chapter seeks to demonstrate the general nature of Boudon's research program by explaining how his work has been used to study special topics in the literature since his death in 2013. Topics such as education, relative frustration, gambling, radicalization, and beliefs in conspiracy theories are studied. I also provide readers with suggestions as to possible future studies using Boudon's social theory as a basic framework.

References

Boudon, R. (1965). Réflexions sur la logique des modèles simulés. *Archives européennes de sociologie* 6(1):3–20.

———. (1967). *L'Analyse mathématique des faits sociaux*. Paris: Plon.

———. (1971 [1968]). *The Uses of Structures*. London: Heinemann.

———. (1974 [1973]). *Education, Opportunity, and Social Inequality: Changing Prospects in Western Society*. New York: Wiley.

———. (1980 [1971]). *The Crisis in Sociology: Problems of Sociological Epistemology*. London: The Macmillan Press.

———. (1982 [1977]). *The Unintended Consequences of Social Action*. London: The Macmillan Press.

———. (1986 [1984]). *Theories of Social Change: A Critical Appraisal*. Berkeley and Los Angeles: University of California Press.

———. (1989 [1986]). *The Analysis of Ideology*. Cambridge: Polity Press.

———. (1989). Subjective Rationality and the Theory of Ideology. In: H. Haferkamp (ed.) *Social Structure and Culture*. Berlin and New York: Walter de Gruyter, pp. 269–288.

———. (1990 [1979]). *La logique du social*. Paris: Hachette.

———. (1991). Le 'modèle de Simmel' et le relativisme contemporain. *Revue européenne des sciences sociales* 24 (89): 115–129.

———. (1992). Action. In: R. Boudon (ed.) *Traité de sociologie*. Paris: Puf, pp. 21–55.

———. (1994 [1990]). *The Art of Self-Persuasion: The Social Explanation of False Beliefs*. Cambridge: Polity Press.

———. (1995). *Le juste et le vrai: études sur l'objectivité des valeurs et de la connaissance*. Paris: Fayard.

———. (1998a). Limitations of Rational Choice Theory. *American Journal of Sociology* 104(3):817–828.

———. (1998b). *Études sur les sociologues classiques I*. Paris: Puf.

———. (1999). *Le sens des valeurs*. Paris: Puf.

———. (2000). *Études sur les sociologues classiques II*. Paris: Puf.

———. (2001). *The Origin of Values: Sociology and Philosophy of Beliefs*. New Brunswick and London: Transaction Publishers.

———. (2002). *Déclin de la morale? Déclin des valeurs?* Paris: Puf.

———. (2003a). Beyond Rational Choice Theory. *Annual Review of Sociology* 29: 1–21.

———. (2003b). *Raison, bonnes raisons*. Paris: Puf.

———. (2004a). Durkheim fut-il durkheimien? *Revue européenne des sciences sociales* 42 (129): 39–44.

———. (2004b). *Pourquoi les intellectuels n'aiment pas le libéralisme*. Paris: Odile Jacob.

———. (2006 [2005]). *Tocqueville for Today*. Oxford: Bardwell Press.

———. (2006a). Homo Sociologicus: Neither a Rational nor an Irrational Idiot. *Revista de sociologia* 80:149–169.

———. (2006b). *Renouveler la démocratie: éloge du sens commun*. Paris: Odile Jacob.

———. (2007). *Essais sur la théorie générale de la rationalité*. Paris: Puf.

———. (2008). *Le relativisme*. Paris: Puf.

———. (2009). Rational Choice Theory. In: B. S. Turner (ed.) *The New Blackwell Companion to Social Theory*. Chichester: Blackwell, pp. 179–196.

———. (2010). *La sociologie comme science*. Paris: La découverte.

———. (2012). *Croire et savoir: penser le politique, le moral et le religieux*. Paris: Puf.

———. (2013). *Le Rouet de Montaigne : une théorie du croire*. Paris : Hermann.

Boudon, R. and Bourricaud, F. (1982). *Dictionnaire critique de la sociologie*. Paris: Puf.

Boudon, R. and Leroux, R. (2003). *Y a-t-il encore une sociologie?* Paris: Odile Jacob.

Boudon, R. and Fillieule, R. (2018). *Les méthodes en sociologie*. Paris: Puf.

Bourdieu, P. and Passeron, J.-C. (1990 [1970]). *Reproduction in Education, Society and Culture*. London: Sage.

Bulle, N. and Morin, J.-M. (2015). Raymond Boudon, a Classical Sociologist. *Journal of Classical Sociology* 15(3):286–292.

Davidovitch, A. and Boudon, R. (1964). Les mécanismes sociaux des abandons des poursuites: Analyse expérimentale par simulation. *L'Année sociologique* 15:111–244.

Demeulenaere, P. (1996). *Homo Oeconomicus: Enquête sur la constitution d'un paradigme*. Paris: Puf.

Hayek, F. A. (1944). *The Road to Serfdom*. London: Routledge.

———. (1955). *The Counter-Revolution of Science: Studies on the Abuse of Reason*. London: The Free Press of Glencoe.

Jeřábek, H. (2001). Paul Lazarsfeld—The Founder of Modern Empirical Sociology: A Research Biography. *International Journal of Public Opinion Research* 13(3):229–244.

Leroux, R. (2019). Raymond Boudon, lecteur de Weber. *The Tocqueville Review* 40(1):105–117.

———. (2020). Boudon's Interpretation of Durkheim Sociology. *Durkheimian Studies* 24 (1): 175–184.

———. (2022). *Penser avec Raymond Boudon*. Paris: Puf.

Morin, J.-M. (2006). *Boudon, un sociologue classique*. Paris: L'Harmattan.

Korom, P. (2020a). How Do Academic Elites March through Departments? A Comparison of the Most Eminent Economists and Sociologists' Career Trajectories. *Minerva* 58: 343–365.

———. (2020b). The Prestige Elite in Sociology: Toward a Collective Biography of the Most Cited Scholars (1970–2010). *The Sociological Quarterly* 61(1):128–163.

Robitaille, C. (2020). Simmelian Elements in Raymond Boudon's General Theory of Rationality. *The Tocqueville Review* 41(2):121–135.

———. (2022). Carl Menger on Theory and History. *Cosmos + Taxis: Studies in Emergent Order and Organization* 10(5–6):61–74.

———. (2023). La question de la connaissance *a priori* en sciences sociales: Les points de vue de Simiand, Mises et Simmel. *Revue de philosophie économique* 24(2): 63–92.

Weber. M. (2019 [1921]). *Economy and Society: A New Translation*. Cambridge: Harvard University Press.

Chapter 1

RAYMOND BOUDON'S METHODOLOGICAL INDIVIDUALISM

Massimo Borlandi

Raymond Boudon has linked his name to methodological individualism to such an extent that, mainly in French and French-speaking sociology, whoever talks of Boudon also talks of methodological individualism, and whoever talks of methodological individualism also talks of Boudon. I will first rely on chronology to present two arguments and three major problems of methodological individualism. I will then show how Boudon dealt with these arguments and tried to solve these problems.

A Brief History of Official Methodological Individualism before Raymond Boudon

Methodological individualism is a thesis about the proper explanation of social phenomena. It maintains that a social phenomenon is adequately explained only if we go back to the actions of the individuals involved in it, taken separately. The explanation of social phenomena by the actions of individuals has obviously been practiced since immemorial times. It becomes an official attitude of the social sciences, and of sociology in particular, as soon as it is given a name. There are at least two names here: "methodological individualism," precisely, and "individualistic method," which overlaps perfectly.

"Methodological individualism" was coined by Élie Halévy in a review of Vilfredo Pareto's paper on "L'individuel et le social" at the second International Congress of Philosophy (in Geneva, September 7, 1904). The invention was made easier by the conclusions that Halévy had just reached in his *Radicalisme philosophique*, namely that, alongside an ethical individualism that pleads for the primacy of the individual over the groups to which he belongs, and a political individualism which opposes State intervention in social life, there is indeed an individualism that is "a method for the scientific explanation of social facts" (Halévy 1995 [1904], 238–239). The latter is then best described as "methodological." And he indicates both how this individualism proceeds and what it differs from:

> I can, in sociology, take as initial data the individuals, who are supposed to be absolutely distinct from each other, reflective and egoistic, or even [...] to be endowed with the same mental constitution that I can discover in myself, by simple observation of consciousness. I can then place these individuals in front of each other, guess how they react on each other and thus reconstruct, by way of deduction or construction, all social phenomena [...]. But another method is conceivable, and has been attempted. It has been asserted that, in social phenomena, there is something irreducible to, and inexplicable by, the phenomena of individual psychology, that the society constitutes an overall phenomenon which dominates and overflows individuals [...]. This will be, if you like, sociologism, which will oppose methodological individualism (*Ce sera, si l'on veut, le sociologisme, qui s'opposera à l'individualisme méthodologique*). (Halévy 1904, 1108)

The origins of the expression "methodological individualism" being one of the best hidden secrets of history, it is customary to attribute this neologism to Joseph A. Schumpeter, who used it in a 1908 German work (as *methodologische Individualismus*) and in an English article the following year (Schumpeter 2016 [1908], 90–91, 94–98; 1909, 231). Schumpeter was merely simplifying things: either individualism is political (which includes Halévy's ethical individualism and is then another way of calling liberalism) or it is methodological. Not only does no primacy belong to Schumpeter, but it is highly doubtful that the Moravian economist is involved appropriately. Indeed, Schumpeter restricted the field of validity of methodological individualism to pure economics. Applied to the study of society, this process fails because, he said, we must reject the idea that social phenomena are merely a sum of individual ones (Schumpeter 2016 [1908], 98).

It is already clear in Halévy's work that "methodological individualism" and "individualistic method" are interchangeable expressions. Between 1919 and 1920, in well-known writings, Max Weber wanted sociology to adopt an *individualistische Methode*, consisting precisely in starting from individuals in the explanation, and there was also mention of an *individualistische Methode* in Ludwig von Mises' *Grundprobleme der Nationalökonomie* (1933, 45, 143), who is rightly considered as the most influential promoter of the use of methodological individualism (the thing referred to by this name) in the social sciences. In fact, Mises employed *methodologische Individualismus* only in his *Nationalökonomie*

(1940, 32, 136), which became "methodological individualism" in the American edition of the same book (1998 [1949], 41–44).

Four contributions aiming at becoming key references appeared between 1940 and 1949. These are the following: the first of the three articles Friedrich Hayek put out in *Economica* from 1942 to 1944 (all reprinted in *The Counter-Revolution of Science*, 1952) and *Individualism and Economic Order* (1948), also by Hayek; the third of the three articles Karl Popper published in turn in *Economica* from 1944 to 1945 (later brought together in *The Poverty of Historicism*, 1957), and the 14th chapter of *The Open Society and Its Enemies* (1945), also by Popper. In these texts, "methodological individualism" coexists with "individualist method," "individualistic method," "individualist approach," and even "individualistic analysis."[1]

The success of the word methodological individualism at the expense of its competing synonyms is the consequence of an article and a note by John William N. Watkins (1952a, 1952b[2]) which provoked a decennial controversy about the nature of historical and sociological knowledge.[3] Arthur Danto (1965, Ch. XII), Ian Jarvie (1972, 154–159, 173–178), and Steven Lukes (1973, Ch. 17) set the terms of this debate, the feeling one draws from it being that, by the end of the 1960s, everything had been said about methodological individualism. In the meantime, Mises (1962, 80–83) continued to advocate this method, and in 1954, Schumpeter's *History of Economic Analysis* was published posthumously. He repeated in it his 1908 distinction between political individualism and methodological individualism and maintained his opinion that methodological individualism is not suitable for the study of society, because it is false that social phenomena consist of individual actions only. He suggested to call "sociological individualism" this propensity to reduce social phenomena to combinations of individual actions (Schumpeter 1986 [1954], 854–855).

Two Arguments and Three Problems

Why start from individuals' actions in the explanation of social phenomena? Two arguments stand out. The first is that only individuals exist; the second is that they are the sole masters of their destiny.

---

[1] See Hayek (1948, 6, 23; 1952, 38, 85, 91, 203); Popper (1957, 81, 135, 141, 147–148, 156; 1966 [1945], vol. 2, 87–88, 91, 308).

[2] The two texts are unified in a 1953 edition. It corresponds to Watkins (1973).

[3] Nine authors participated in this debate, for a total of 19 contributions, in three journals in particular: *The British Journal for the Philosophy of Science*, *Philosophy of Science*, and *The British Journal of Sociology*.

The first argument was put forward by Hayek and Mises, who labeled as hypostases the referents of almost the entire vocabulary of the social sciences: classes, nations, religions, and society itself. This argument runs up against the evidence. Actions are governed by norms whose existence is tangible (often readable), and since norms vary according to the groups to which individuals belong, these groups exist in turn. Hayek and Mises' argument was challenged by Popper, for whom any action is subject to the imperatives of the "situation" in which it takes place. It follows that to explain a social phenomenon is to start from both individual actions and their context. Popper's point of view will gradually win out among individualists.

The second argument reflects a sentiment shared by the latter thinkers, most of whom are liberals (political individualists). It is the fear that, in the course of explanation, one will comply with "the assumption that the behaviour of men is directed by some mysterious forces that defy any analysis and description." At the time Mises wrote these words (1962, 82), the list of supra-individual forces supposed to be obscure and to direct human conduct had long included, in addition to the alleged laws of history, still in vogue, the culture, the mentality or the spirit of the people, and the polemical construction of an apparently solid anti-individualist method, set up as a doctrine, has become a *fait accompli*. Popper gave this method a name with a great future, borrowed from evolutionary philosophy: "holism," which, thanks to its steadily increasing indeterminacy, will prevail over some variants, including "methodological collectivism." The taste for symmetries took care of the rest: if to explain in an individualistic way is to deduce social phenomena from the actions of individuals taken separately, the opposite of an individualistic explanation consists in deducing the actions of individuals, taken separately, from constituted social phenomena, that is to say, from the traits of the groups to which the individuals belong or from the positions they occupy in them (Watkins 1973, 149–150; Danto 1965, 267–268).

This opposition is imaginary, as no one is known to have argued that an individual will remain a believer all his life because he comes from a pious family, or that the roles of husband and wife as defined in the Canton of Zurich since Huldrych Zwingli are in themselves responsible for the success or failure of Herr and Frau Müller's marriage. What we know are the two ideas according to which we can (first idea) and even we must (second idea) explain social phenomena without taking into account the individual actions that contribute to the formation of these same phenomena.

We can disregard the actions of individuals in the explanation of social phenomena (first idea) whenever the phenomena to be explained offer themselves to observation through collective properties: this is the case of institutions, organizations, long-lived events, and any fact that recurs on a regular basis, identified by its territorial localization first. When—to go back to the beginnings of this way of explaining—Pierre-Simon de Laplace argued it as plausible that in Paris as in London the number of letters lost due to lack of addresses remained unchanged from one year to the next, he was interested in the characteristics of two sets of individuals and not at all in individual actions, as *wondering how many* is something different than *specifying who*. Since then, increasingly, variables measuring the properties of the phenomena to be explained have been related to variables measuring the properties of other phenomena of the same kind, and statistical regularities that can be understood as cause-and-effect links have been inferred. This process, which is an application to the sociology of the causal analysis stemming from the "path analysis" devised by Sewall Wright in the 1920s, does not deny the individualistic method but is apt to complete it, provided that we find a way to descend from collective properties to the individual ones—which is no small detail, according to a definitive warning from Paul Lazarsfeld and Herbert Menzel (1993 [1961]).

The actions of individuals must be disregarded in sociological explanation (second idea) if we consider that the properties of social phenomena are unique, *sui generis* as Émile Durkheim liked to put it, grounding his point of view in a conception in his time strengthened by their genesis. Because of the way in which social phenomena arise from combined individual actions, their specificity disappears, dissolves if they are brought back to their constituent elements, these very actions; and it is indeed to Durkheim that Halévy alludes in opposing methodological individualism to sociologism—another word, sociologism, of which he seems to be the father.[4] The career of "sociologism" too, promising in the years 1920–1930, will be interrupted by the spread of "holism," except for a few returns.[5]

Apart from the upholders of this second idea (which will soon lend itself to being summarized as follows: the macro is not *per se* reducible to the micro, and it is useless to try to do so), there have not been and there are no resolute opponents of methodological individualism, and it would be advisable to free the remarks of which methodological individualism has been the object since the postwar period (see O'Neill 1973[6]) from the mortgage of the too many "isms" that compete for them. These remarks aim to highlight the difficulties that methodological individualism meets in solving the problems—three, mainly—that it faces.

---

[4] He created it in 1902, in the September supplement (p. 14) of the *Revue de métaphysique et de morale*, during a review of volume V of *L'Année sociologique* precisely to (dis)qualify the theories of its editor.

[5] To which Boudon will bring his input. See below, p. 28.

[6] None of the texts gathered in this anthology is later than 1962.

The first problem is that, in order to be able to explain social phenomena on the basis of individual actions, we must first have these same actions explained. Indeed, actions are not primary causes, but consequences. Behind actions, there are motives, that is, dispositions which are personality traits, and reasons.

Motives are a matter for psychology, both scientific psychology, that of experiments and laboratories, and ordinary, or naive, or "common sense" psychology, which consists of the fact that, inevitably, we attribute causes to the behavior of people with whom we interact, whom we observe acting, or whose actions we describe. Reasons also concern psychology, but in two different ways. On the one hand, a part of scientific psychology (especially psychoanalysis) and a part of ordinary psychology (that involved in the Marxist criticism of ideologies as well as that used by Vilfredo Pareto) do not take them seriously, believing that they are the cover-up of underlying motives or other hidden causes. Reasons are on the other hand regarded as valid explanations of individual actions, on the side of scientific psychology, by cognitive psychology, and, on the side of ordinary psychology, by introspective psychology asserting, with Halévy (1904, 1108), that, as men are all "endowed with the same mental constitution," in order to understand others, it is enough to know oneself.[7]

The border between scientific psychology and ordinary psychology being unclear, Weber proposed a non-empathic understanding of reasons which get away from any psychology. There is only one sure way to avoid resorting to psychology in the explanation of actions if we do not want to explain them by motives, and that is to disregard reasons as well. This is the path taken by Mises (1998 [1949], 11–12, 483–484), whose praxeology studies action as such, and by Popper, followed by Joseph Agassi (1987), who accounts for actions through his "situational logic." So how does methodological individualism explain actions?

The second problem that methodological individualism is called upon to solve is to establish what actions owe to the context in which they take place. It is indeed by taking the context into account that society fits into individualistic sociology, which can thus avoid the blame of atomism. One cannot conflate the two problems. It is one thing to wonder what the individual causes are (motives and/or reasons) of the actions that provoke social phenomena; it is quite another to study the social, supra-individual causes of these same actions.

This second problem arises clearly when we see that several individuals, situated in the same context, behave in the same way. If we share a theory of action focused on motives, the noticed regularities are caused by permanent

---

[7] Introspection is the only form of psychological knowledge accepted by Hayek (1952, 44–52).

features of human nature which manifest themselves in response to conditionings (*stimuli*) emanating from the context. On the contrary, if we rely on a theory of action highlighting reasons, the noticed regularities are due to the fact that the context transmits to individuals their reasons, in full or in part.

The third problem facing methodological individualism is to show how, that is, by what causal processes, actions generate social phenomena. Methodological individualists agree that these processes take place by synthesis or "composition" of the effects of actions, according to a suggestion borrowed by Hayek (1952, 39, 212) from Carl Menger, and also agree that the resulting consequences are mostly unexpected and even unintended. These two things go together and are somewhat self-evident. Indeed, once it has been ruled out that social change happens according to a plan, social order can only be conceived as a spontaneous outcome. This brings back to at least Bernard de Mandeville the beginnings of the individualistic explanation of the origin of social phenomena. According to Hayek and Popper, sociology should just study the unintended consequences of actions. A hiatus thus occurs between the results of actions and the motives and/or reasons that drive individuals to perform them. This gap becomes all the more important when it comes to reasons: individuals set goals for themselves and achieve others. This means that, yes, we start from individual actions in the explanation of social phenomena, but we risk not going far.

Raymond Boudon as Methodological Individualist

It was in *La Logique du social* (foreword dated October 1978) that Boudon embraced methodological individualism (1979a, 61–63, 77, 137).[8] His main source was a 1971 article by Joachim Israel (Boudon 1977, 271; 1979a, 35, 66; 1982, 289). It should be noted that three of Raymond Aron's 1973–1974 lectures at the Collège de France dealt with methodological individualism (Aron 1989, 251–333), that the expression "methodological individualism" itself appeared for the first time in the *Revue française de sociologie* in 1976,[9] and that the controversy over methodological individualism triggered by Watkins was quoted by Paul Ricoeur, only in 1978, in the Second part of the UNESCO report *Tendances principales de la recherche dans les sciences sociales* (Ricoeur 1978, 1283–1286).[10] We might also wonder whether an article by Philippe Perrenoud, also in 1978 (June), which early on called Boudon

---

[8] In *Effets pervers et ordre social* (1977, 248) methodological individualism is mentioned in passing as a typical "paradigm" of political economy.

[9] In a François Chazel review of a 1975 Paul Q. Hirst's book (17-2, p. 366).

[10] Boudon contributed to the First part (Boudon 1970b).

a methodological individualist (Perrenoud 1978), did not influence his decision to adopt this label.

"Methodological individualism" is in any case a term under which Boudon will group the elements of a theoretical scheme in the making. Before *La Logique du social*,[11] the acquired, but not yet linked together, elements of this scheme are the following three, in order of appearance: (1) sociology cannot help questioning the purposes that individuals give to their actions (Boudon 1964; Davidovitch and Boudon 1964); (2) as a quantitative and comparative discipline, sociology relies on causal analysis, that is, as I recalled, on the correlation between variables constructed by translating aspects of social phenomena into indicators (1970a [1967]; 1969); and (3) the composition or aggregation (a word that Boudon would end up preferring) of the effects of individual actions is the only sequence of facts and circumstances that causes social phenomena (1973; 1977).

In *La Logique du social*, then in the *Dictionnaire critique de la sociologie* (Boudon 1982, 4–5, 286–287), and finally in *La Place du désordre* (1984, 62–71), elements 1 and 3 merge in a first definition of methodological individualism (the first of two). It consists in establishing the reasons—at the time Boudon still says the "motivations" (I keep the word "reasons" for the sake of uniformity)—for which individuals perform actions whose effects, by aggregation, make social phenomena. This definition, repeated here and there and which has a variant (to find the logic of the behaviors responsible for the aggregated phenomena),[12] excludes any interest of Boudon in motives. He agrees that actions mean (also) motives. Yet sociology does not consider them. Meanwhile, the three books aforementioned, and the *Dictionnaire* in particular, set four points from which Boudon will never turn away.

(1) In order to establish the reasons for actions, we need to identify ourselves with their authors, the individuals, so as to be able to conclude, at the end of a process of understanding—supposed to be in conformity with the Weberian notion of *Verstehen*—that, in their place, we would have behaved as they did (1979a, 62–63). As soon as we have discerned, and thus understood, its reasons, an action is explained, for "it is probably preferable to treat the notions of explanation and understanding as synonyms in the field of social sciences" (1982, 289). (2) Since individuals are situated, that is, embedded in groups, subject to extensive social and institutional constraints, the action of the context on the actions of individuals must enter into the sociological explanation (ibid., 288; 1984, 40). (3) In the absence of well-established reasons

---

[11] And before the article "Generating models as a research strategy" (1979b).
[12] Cf. Boudon (1986b, 46; 1988a, 230; 1992, 22, 30; 1995, 254–255; 1998b, 367); Boudon and Fillieule (2002, 41).

for actions, the associations between variables that causal analysis brings out remain descriptive. They record the existence of regularities but do not account for them. On the other hand, the understanding of reasons extends and completes the causal analysis (1982, 289). (4) Sometimes, understanding reasons proves difficult or impossible. This is when, because of the many individuals concerned by the phenomena to be explained and the ensuing variability of the logic of action, the sociologist is not able to obtain adequate and manageable data. In such cases, we must make do with causal analysis (ibid., 287–288).

The second definition of methodological individualism, which alternates with the first, crowns Boudon's research on the notion of rationality, which begins with the replacement of the word motivation(s) by the word reason(s) and continues with the rejection of the idea that actions guided by a cost–benefit calculation—those which rational choice theory extends to the characters to most human actions, thanks especially to James Coleman—would be the only rational ones and, therefore, the most understandable (1986a, 24–25, 283–284, 294–295; 1995, Ch. 14; 1998c). Are rational and understandable also actions dictated by beliefs, whether positive beliefs (believing that something is true) or prescriptive (believing that something is right). It all depends on what "rational" means. An action is rational insofar as its author has well-founded reasons—good reasons—to perform it. Indeed, the syntony between reason and rationality goes beyond an agreement of sounds: "this noun [*rationality*] is no more than an abstract word formed from the more elementary notion of *reasons*" (2003b, 158). These developments led Boudon to distinguish between different kinds of rationality (instrumental, cognitive, and axiological) differently brought together into models and theories (1999, Ch. II–III; 2003a; 2007, Ch. 1–2), and it is these developments that he feels he must incorporate in his plan of methodological individualism.

The upshot is a definition based on three postulates, whose first two correspond to the elements of the first definition, in reverse order. These are the following: (1) the postulate of "individualism," ensuring that social phenomena arise from the combined effects of individual actions; (2) the postulate of "understanding," according to which the meanings that actions have for their authors is not obscure; and (3) the postulate of "rationality," requiring us to concede that actions, as well as the beliefs that prepare them, are the product of reasons (2002a, 9–10; 2003b, 19–21; 2012, 236; Boudon and Leroux 2003, 66–69).

Postulate 3, the novelty, is auxiliary. It reinforces postulate 2 and, thus, the first definition of methodological individualism. Indeed, whether actions are rational or not does not change the fact that the process that leads to understanding the reasons for actions is introspective (putting oneself in the place of others) and that the reasons of individuals are the cause of their actions. The proof of the subsidiary character of postulate 3 is that the copresence of the two definitions (the passages from one to the other are regular) does not harm the coherence of the Boudonian reasoning. Incidentally, it should be noted that, by making rationality the distinguishing feature of actions, Boudon joins Mises who asserted from the outset the weakness of the rationality/irrationality opposition. Mises argued that, since human action arises from a state of dissatisfaction that it wants to put an end to (a premise that is difficult to refute), human action is "necessarily always rational" for the individual pursuing it (Mises 1998 [1949], 18).

Boudon's attitude toward his methodological individualism is marked by a constant reworking. For some years, he also calls it "sociology of action," "actionist sociology," "actionist analysis," or "actionism" for short (1992, 21–26; Boudon and Fillieule 2002, 41; Boudon and Leroux 2003, 87). He seems to want to dilute it into a "general rational model," a model finally lifted to the rank of "general theory of rationality" (2002b; 2003b, Ch. 1; 2007), and even to downgrade it at a stage in the construction of analytical sociology, the explanation by mechanisms of which he is, moreover, a pioneer (1998a; 2010, 33; 2012, 235–236). What does not change over the years is the firmness with which Boudon opposes methodological individualism to a rival orientation which, at first, is sociologism—via an article by François Bourricaud who encountered the term "sociologism" in Léon Brunschvicg's *Le Progrès de la conscience dans la philosophie occidentale*, a 1927 book (Bourricaud 1975),[13] but which soon becomes, for him too, holism (1982, 287; 1986b, 53–58; 1988b, 41–41; 2003b, 25–26; Boudon and Leroux 2003, 72).

Boudon criticizes holism for erasing the subjectivity of individuals, reducing them to passive beings, to "soft wax" strained by social or other "forces" that would dictate their behavior and escape from their control. These forces would contribute to the sociological explanation as "black boxes." Examples of these boxes are traditionalism, secularization, conformism, or fashion and culture of course. But what does Boudon describe as holism? An inventory would list the following:

(1) The theories of systems and structures. They express the thought of totality of which Claude Lévi-Strauss is the emblem (Boudon 2012, 218). It should be pointed out that the proponents of these theories are simply not interested in individuals. Individual volitions and feelings are meant to have no appreciable impact on regularities that would occur anyway and

---

[13] Compare §7 of the last chapter of *Effets pervers* ("Deterministic paradigms: from sociology to sociologism") with the preface to the 2nd edition (1983) of *La Logique du social*: "From sociologism to sociology."

evolve slowly. (2) The false consciousness theories, dear to Marxists and depth psychologists (1988a, 222; 1995, 62, 255–256). According to these theories, individuals are unaware of the real causes that drive them to act. Therefore, it is wise to be wary of their reasons. (3) The explanation by norms, advocated by Talcott Parsons and serving as a model for other similar explanations, including that by *habitus* (2003b, 26). A second clarification should be made here: these explanations are aimed at sets, that is, at the results of aggregate effects of actions, and thus do not make us learn anything, nor can they make us learn anything, about these same actions taken singularly. (4) The explanation by correlations between variables, that is, causal analysis, whose presence in the list may be surprising (Boudon and Fillieule 2002, 121). However, we can guess the reason for this. Explanation by norms is based on correlations between variables or, what amounts to the same, can only be tested by this method which is thus devalued by the inadequacy of its results. It brings out macroscopic data that remain cryptic as long as we do not go back to their individual causes.

Once it is agreed that causal analysis comes under holism, an agreement between methodological individualism and that variety of holism, causal analysis, becomes possible:

> Holism and methodological individualism should therefore not be considered as two irreconcilable methods. They are in some cases complementary, when, for example, holism provides facts in the form of a causal analysis which are then explained by the individualistic method. (ibid.)

Being linked by a relationship of complementarity to causal analysis and explanation by norms, methodological individualism enjoys a relationship of otherness with the theories of systems, structures, and false consciousness. The proof of this is that Boudon blames the followers of these theories for not doing precisely what they say should not be done. None of the intellectual postures that Boudon considers holistic enjoys a relationship of contrariety with methodological individualism. The only opposite of methodological individualism remains the thesis according to which the actions of individuals, taken separately, must be explained on the basis of social factors from which they would stem by necessity. Boudon sometimes seems to allude to this thesis in polemical pages. But who really advocated it? It is clear that, in Boudon's work (or in Boudon's work too), methodological individualism does not need the identification of an enemy to be proposed.

We must also attribute to the passions of a lifetime the severe look that Boudon takes at ordinary sociology and its black boxes. Advances in quantification have enabled sociologists to break down into observable and measurable elements even the fuzziest notions they created, such as anomie. Many boxes have been opened or have become less opaque. An avalanche of indicators hit the social sciences in the twentieth century to the benefit of explanations by correlations between variables and, consequently, if we restrict ourselves to the link between causal analysis and interpretive analysis that Boudon points out, to the benefit of the detection of the reasons of individuals.

I will now examine more closely the ways in which Boudon solves the three problems facing methodological individualism, namely: to what individual causes (first problem) and to what social causes (second problem) should the actions that generate social phenomena be attributed? And how do these very phenomena form (third problem)?

Reasons and Motives

Boudon expresses his aversion to any explanation of actions based on motives whenever he states the terms of his method: to grasp the psychology of individuals (why do they do what they do?) by avoiding psychology as much as possible (1979a, 62–63; 1995, 255, 286; 2003b, 63–66; 2013b, 609–610). Boudon sets three restrictions to the use of psychology.

The first is that there can be no question of scientific psychology, which links the actions of individuals to their personality and thus turns their behavioral dispositions into forces that dominate them (1984, 54–55; 1995, 257–258; 2007, 43–46). These are forces other than supra-individual ones definable as inner determinants. To scientific psychology, Boudon prefers ordinary psychology, which he also calls, via Georg Simmel, "psychology of convention" (1998b, 378; 2002a, 22–23; 2010, 18). As I have said, it lies in the fact that we attribute the conduct of others to one or more causes, a mental operation that we make at any time.

However, Boudon—and this is the second restriction—only takes into account the attribution of behavior to purposes and neglects that to the personality of individuals. Thus, yes to clauses such as "he did what he did because he had such and such a goal," but not to clauses such as "he did what he did because he is an anxious, brave, envious man, etc.," which are judgments as frequent as the previous ones in everyday life. Boudon argues that the ordinary psychology interested in intentions has always been used (he cites Aristotle and the moralists of the seventeenth century[14]). The same is true of ordinary psychology captivated by motives, the attention of the great historical narratives, and the fictional stagings of society being often

---

[14] 2004a, 23; 2004b, 13.

given more to the character than to his decisions, whether he is a hero or a secondary character.

Boudon's third restriction to the use of psychology is that it must focus on abstract, ideal-typical individuals, and not attempt to reproduce concrete experiences (1995, 94–95; 2010, 18). A typical abstract individual is, in this sense, the economists' consumer, assumed to be aware of prices and buy on the most advantageous terms.

Boudon's man is a complete man, having his "nature," likings, and emotions. Nevertheless, Boudon assigns these factors a limited explanatory weight. Such a choice is not justified, if we mean by justification the proof of the validity of a statement, for it is a fact that the personality of individuals plays a part in both the beginnings and outcomes of their actions, and for studies on the components of individual motivations (including purchasing motivations) can now be counted in thousands. These studies lead to typologies of behavior that are just as abstract, if we like, but based on elements drawn from a series of observed cases.

Although unjustified, this attitude is allowed by the second founding argument of original methodological individualism, according to which individuals are, on balance, the masters of their own destiny, an argument to which Boudon subscribes. It could be called an *a priori*, that is, an assumption and a prejudice, since Boudon treats as an *a priori* the opposite argument—raised by Mises—that individuals would be moved by forces. The social sciences affected by this *a priori* would see individuals as being heteronomous subjects, when it is more a matter of bringing out their autonomy (2004b, X).

We are at the heart of the long-lasting conflict between determinism and free will, with regard to which Boudon takes a stance since the Introduction to *Effets pervers*: "Sociology and freedom." There is no need to venture down the path of this quarrel, as the following conclusion seems sensible: just as an explanation of actions that ignores the aims of individuals or minimizes their importance is unacceptable, an explanation of actions that does not give the rightful place to the motives of individuals is unsatisfactory.

From Context to Reasons

The attitude to adopt with respect to the constraints of actions, that is, their context, has quickly become unanimous among methodological individualists for whom society and its collectives (groups and institutions) exist, are realities. This attitude consists in saying that the context steers but does not engender. This is indeed Boudon's view, who distinguishes the causes of actions, their reasons, from their parameters (2003b, 89–97; 2004a, 25; 2010, 90).

Parameters are age, gender, status, social belonging, and any other data or circumstances likely to influence actions by delimiting their rooms for success. Clearly, parameters are (or can be reduced to) social phenomena in their own right, assessed under the aspect of their contribution, through the actions of individuals, to the genesis of other social phenomena. The context that Boudon puts at the core of his famous equations—"$M = MmSM'$," "$S = f[a(C, p)]$"—is an arrangement of parameters conceived in this way. They set "the terms of the choice" (1982, 287; Boudon and Fillieule 2002, 75); the reasons are parameterized.

Among the components of the context on which Boudon dwells, because the sociologist cannot take them all into account (2013a, 3), communication between individuals comes first, that is, their interaction, insofar as it leads, at variable times, to the constitution of shared or "transsubjective" reasons. These corroborate everyone's good reasons, which consequently become "strong reasons." In other words, the individual is supported in his choices by the fact that his neighbors, colleagues, and coreligionists do as he does (1995, 67–79; 1999, 130, 135; 2010, 92).

Thus, Boudon too comes to note that, many times, in the same context, individuals perform the same actions, which means that they allege the same reasons. This fact, all the more expected as the parameters are rigid and reduce the range of choices, proves to be revealing if the shared reasons come from afar and are related to deep-rooted values, since a community of reasons cannot be improvised.

The usual explanation of the uniformities of behavior in social groups is an effective socialization of individuals who repeat what they have been taught, the ways of acting they have "interiorized." The action of the context on the individuals' actions is direct and it is precisely in this sense that it determines them. The individualistic explanation, I recall, departs from this one in that it demands that we recognize that between the action of the context on the individuals' actions and the beginning of these same actions, there is a space, even minimal, where takes place the individuals' reflection on the goals they are pursuing, their awareness of the reasons they have for doing what they are going to do.

However, if everyone behaves in the same way, driven by the same reasons, in any situation where two individuals can say to each other: "my reasons are like yours and they are the same as our fathers," the deduction to be drawn seems to only be this one: individuals adhere to reasons they find already made. The first element of the first definition of methodological individualism, or postulate 2 of the second definition (the postulate of understanding), is safe, provided that the point where the context influences the individuals' actions is moved: the context does not cause the actions, it causes the reasons that cause them. Which is to say that it causes them indirectly.

All this results from the paradigm of sociological explanation set out in chapter 2 of *La Place du désordre* and is assured by Boudon, explicitly, in a passage of his interview with Robert Leroux, a passage that is an involuntary reprise of the statements of *Les Règles de la méthode sociologique* on the phenomenon of constraint:

> I do not support in any way the idea of a primacy of the individual. Each individual is placed in a context of which he is not the author. There is therefore a primacy of the context. But, on the other hand, the context is the product of past actions. The language we speak, the state of science we work with, the roads we travel on, these all are for us data that impose themselves on us and thus characterize the context in which we move. But these data have been forged by social actors. There is therefore a primacy of the individual: a new version of the chicken and egg problem. (Boudon and Leroux 2003, 133[15])

We can rely on this passage to come to the solution that, following the example of Hayek (reader of Menger) and the anti-constructivist tradition to which the latter belongs, Boudon gives to the third problem of methodological individualism: social phenomena arise from the aggregate effects of individual actions.[16]

From Reasons to Social Phenomena?

The aggregation of the effects of individual actions will complete a circular movement (chicken–egg–chicken, according to the aforementioned metaphor) that can be summarized as follows: context (social phenomena) → reasons → actions → effects of these same actions → aggregations of these same effects → social phenomena (context). The way in which the context transmits to individuals their motives being self-evident, there are two kinds of aggregation: that of effects of actions performed independently of each other, outside of any explicit or implied agreement or obligation between individuals (a situation Boudon describes as a "state of nature"); and the aggregation of effects of interdependent actions, where individuals modulate their behavior according to that of others. This occurs, in particular, when individuals comply with

---

[15] See also Boudon (1995, 253–254).

[16] This formulation, which I have used up to now, is to be preferred, because of its transparency, to Boudon's shortened one, which has since become quite common, assuring that social phenomena arise from the aggregate actions of individuals. Actions generate anything only through the effects they achieve, each one its own. It is therefore these effects that mutually aggregate.

commitments related to their roles (a situation that Boudon symmetrically describes as a "state of contract") (1977, 196–199). In the first case, the resulting phenomena take the form of a sum. In the second case, Boudon lists 13–14 composite forms: phenomena of amplification, reinforcement, reversal, stabilization, neutralization, divergence, segregation, innovation, paralysis, chain reaction, etc. (1979a, Ch. IV; 1981; 1984, 66–70; 1992, 44–50).

What unifies the two kinds of aggregation is the nature, first called "perverse," then, repeatedly, "emergent," of the social phenomena thus generated, "emergent" meaning here that the properties of these phenomena are not involved in the effects of the actions which compose them. These properties spring up once the effects of the actions separate, free themselves from the intentions of the individuals and, each at the end of its journey, come together: "[...] it is as if the consequences of their actions slipped out them" (1979a, 131).

In short, even for Boudon, social phenomena are usually unexpected and/or unintended.[17] This means that for him too—especially for him, given the quantity of emergent phenomena that he manages to enumerate—, there is no continuity between the explanation of actions and that of social phenomena. Actions are explained by the reasons that lead individuals to perform them; social phenomena are explained by combinations of the effects of these same actions, but these combinations owe little to the reasons of the actions. Let us suppose that actions are caused by motives and not by reasons. Their effects would not, however, aggregate differently. The reasons of individuals do not enter into the explanation of social phenomena. There is no needed link between the two elements of the first definition of methodological individualism, that is, between postulates 2 (of understanding) and 1 (of individualism) of the second one. The methodological individualism defended by Boudon consists of two distinct programs.

Comparisons and Limits

It is Lars Udeh who has compared Boudon's methodological individualism to other versions of the same method. He does this in two stages. First, he places Boudon, along with Coleman, among the representatives of the strong variant

---

[17] In *Effets pervers* (1977, 7–9) Boudon adds the Robert K. Merton of "The unanticipated consequences of purposive social action"— 1936—to the later theorists of the unintended consequences of actions, Hayek and Popper. See then Boudon, 1981. *Effets pervers* is translated in 1982 as *The Unintended Consequences of Social Action*. Boudon points out in the *Traité* that "unexpected" does not necessarily equate to "undesirable" and that "unintended" does not mean "unpredictable" (1992, 45–46).

of what he calls the weak version of methodological individualism (Udehn 2001, 306–309; 2002, 495–496).[18] Whereas, according to the strong version of methodological individualism, social phenomena must be explained solely by individuals (their actions and interactions), according to the weak version, they must be explained by both individuals and extra-individual factors. In the weak variant of this version, or the Popperian variant, these factors are the institutions. In the strong variant, these factors bring out the social structure that Coleman conceives as an interweaving of relationships between preexisting positions of the individuals occupying them—which is why this variant is called by Udehn "structural individualism." Udehn takes advantage of the translatability of Boudon's explanatory paradigm into Coleman's macro–micro–macro scheme (Coleman's boat). This analogy is not contested by Boudon and will be perpetuated under the name assigned to it by Mario Bunge (1996, 148–149): "the Boudon-Coleman diagram."[19]

In a second moment, Udehn (2009) separates Boudon from Coleman, without however changing his categorization, duly noting his overcoming of the theory of rational choice.[20] Udehn's assessment of Boudon's methodological individualism is likely to displease the supporters of strong methodological individualism as much as the opponents of any methodological individualism: "What makes Boudon's methodological individualism fruitful is the fact that it treats human individuals as cultural beings, who act in a context of social institutions and social structures" (ibid., 361).

We find in Boudon's work the statement that methodological individualism has limits, but also that it does not have any. This is made possible by the duality of Boudonian methodological individualism, which is bivalent depending on whether we consider one or the other of the disjointed terms of its definitions. The limits of methodological individualism are imposed by the size of the phenomena to be explained and are important. Boudon repeats it, almost in the same words, since the *Dictionnaire critique* (see above, p. 27). Here is how he does it in the *Traité*:

> It often happens [...] that the principle of methodological individualism cannot be applied in research situations where it is nevertheless relevant. This occurs when the individual causes of the aggregate phenomenon we wish to explain are too numerous and too heterogeneous to be identified and described. (1992, 51[21])

---

[18] Udehn (2001, 297) dates Coleman's embrace of methodological individualism to 1986.
[19] See Jepperson and Mayer (2011, 58–59).
[20] Boudon (1989) formalized this overcoming in Coleman's own journal.
[21] See also Boudon (1986b, 56; 1988b, 40–41); Boudon and Fillieule (2002, 53).

The individual causes remain the reasons and the recalled principle is the postulate of understanding. Boudon deems it inapplicable to the study of statistical regularities covering complex systems of actions (Boudon and Fillieule 2002, 53)—consider what myriad of events are packed into a demographic rate—and not adequate if the analysis concerns widespread and long-lasting facts. The family customs in the *Ancien Régime* and the evolution of religions investigated by Philippe Ariès and Robert Bellah, respectively, are two examples cited. For this kind of phenomenon, whose micro-foundations we would like to detect, we must simply "ask descriptive rather than explanatory questions" (1992, 52). It follows from all this that methodological individualism (postulate 2) is not suitable for the study of at least half of the themes covered in any sociology textbook.

Methodological individualism has no limits according to *La Place du désordre* (1987, 56) and its appendices. It is what is best suited to account for social changes, even long-term ones. This is methodological individualism defined by its postulate 1: the aggregation of the effects of individual actions. No social change having spanned the centuries is really explained by Boudon. He deduces the superiority of the individualistic method from the failure (according to him) of three ordinary modes of explanation: nomological, structuralist, and ontological (the quest for the primum mobile). Once the rubble of these modes has been removed, what remains is the aggregation of the effects of the actions, to be studied on a case-by-case basis.

Still, Boudon's predilection goes to bounded phenomena, enclosed in precise sets of data, such as "partial and local, dated and situated" social processes whose elucidation is entrusted to medium-range theories (1984, 207–208, 219–220). Boudon's work relies entirely on the exemplary value of enigmas of this kind, suggested by him or borrowed from the most various sources. He presents them by preceding them with a punctual "why?," which sums up his abstract formula of sociological explanation: "Why M?" (ibid., 52).[22] Why does the democratization of school systems not automatically increase social mobility? Why do birth control policies fail? Why does social segregation occur independently of (and sometimes against) individuals' will to exclude? Etc. As sociologists continue to be fascinated, rightly or wrongly, by broader questions (the nature of social bonds, kinship systems, the origins—or fall—of modernity, etc.), it is easy to understand that Boudon's methodological individualism does not warm many hearts.

---

[22] How to "explain a fact M in the sense of positive science" is the subject of an excursus of François Simiand's Introduction to his *Le Salaire, l'évolution sociale et la monnaie* (1932, vol. 1, 15–25). Cf. then this text in Boudon and Lazarsfeld (1966, 28–36).

References

Agassi, J. (1987). Methodological Individualism and Institutional Individualism. In: J. Agassi and I. C. Jarvie (eds.), *Rationality: The Critical View*. Dordrecht: Martinus Nijhoff Publishers, 119–150.

Aron, R. (1989). *Leçons sur l'histoire. Cours du Collège de France*. Paris: De Fallois.

Boudon, R. (1964). La 'statistique psychologique' de Tarde. *Annales internationales de criminologie* 3(2): 342–357.

———. (1969). *Les Méthodes en sociologie*. Paris: Presses universitaires de France.

———. (1970a [1967]). *L'Analyse mathématique des faits sociaux*. Paris: Plon.

———. (1970b). Modèles et méthodes mathématiques. In: S. Friedman (ed.), *Tendances principales de la recherche dans les sciences sociales et humaines. Première partie: Sciences sociales*. Paris–La Haye: Mouton/Unesco, 629–685.

———. (1973). *L'Inégalité des chances. La mobilité sociale dans les sociétés industrielles*. Paris: Armand Colin.

———. (1977). *Effets pervers et ordre social*. Paris: Presses universitaires de France.

———. (1979a). *La Logique du social*. Paris: Hachette.

———. (1979b). Generating Models as a Research Strategy. In: R. K. Merton, J. S. Coleman and P. H. Rossi (eds.), *Qualitative and Quantitative Social Research. Papers in Honor of Paul F. Lazarsfeld*. New York: Free Press, 51–64.

———. (1981). Undesired Consequences and Types of Structures of Systems of Interdependence. In: P. M. Blau and R. K. Merton (eds.), *Continuities in Structural Inquiry*. London: Sage, 255–284.

———. (1982). Action and Individualisme. In: R. Boudon and F. Bourricaud (eds.), *Dictionnaire critique de la sociologie*. Paris: Presses universitaires de France, 1–8, 281–289.

———. (1984). *La Place du désordre*. Paris: Presses universitaires de France.

———. (1986a). *L'Idéologie, ou l'origine des idées reçues*. Paris: Fayard.

———. (1986b). Individualisme et holisme dans les sciences sociales. In: P. Birnbaum and J. Leca (eds.), *Sur l'individualisme*. Paris: Presses de la Fondation nationale des sciences politiques, 45–59.

———. (1987). The Individualistic Tradition in Sociology. In: J. C. Alexander, B. Giesen, R. Münch and N. J. Smelser (eds.), *The Micro-Macro Link*. Berkeley—London: University of California Press, 45–70.

———. (1988a). L'acteur social est-il si irrationnel (et si conformiste) qu'on le dit. In: C. Audard, J.-P. Dupuy and R. Sève (eds.), *Individu et justice sociale. Autour de John Rawls*. Paris: Éditions du Seuil, 219–244.

———. (1988b). Individualisme et holisme: un débat méthodologique fondamental. In: H. Mendras and M. Verret (eds.), *Les Champs de la sociologie française*. Paris: Armand Colin, 31–45.

———. (1989). Subjective Rationality and the Explanation of Social Behavior. *Rationality and Society* 1(2): 173–196.

———. (1992). Action. In: R. Boudon (ed.), *Traité de sociologie*. Paris: Presses universitaires de France, 21–55.

———. (1995). *Le Juste et le Vrai. Études sur l'objectivité des valeurs et de la connaissance*. Paris: Fayard.

———. (1998a). Social Mechanisms without Black Boxes. In: P. Hedström and R. Swedberg (eds.), *Social Mechanisms. An Analytical Approach to Social Theory*. Cambridge—New York: Cambridge University Press, 172–203.

———. (1998b). L'‘analyse empirique de l'action' de Lazarsfeld et la tradition de la sociologie compréhensive. In: J. Lautman and B.-P. Lécuyer (eds.), *Paul Lazarsfeld (1901–1976). La sociologie de Vienne à New York.* Paris: L'Harmattan, 363–382.

———. (1998c). Limitations of Rational Choice Theory. *American Journal of Sociology* 104(3): 817–828.

———. (1999). *Le Sens des valeurs.* Paris: Presses universitaires de France.

———. (2002a). Théorie du choix rationnel ou individualisme méthodologique? *Sociologie et sociétés* 34(1): 9–34.

———. (2002b). Utilité ou rationalité? Rationalité restreinte ou générale? *Revue d'économie politique* 112(5): 755–772.

———. (2003a). Beyond Rational Choice Theory. *Annual Review of Sociology* 29: 1–21.

———. (2003b). *Raison, bonnes raisons.* Paris: Presses universitaires de France.

———. (2004a). *Quelle théorie du comportement pour les sciences sociales?* Nanterre: Société d'ethnologie.

———. (2004b). Préface inédite à la 7e édition. In R. Boudon and F. Bourricaud (eds.), *Dictionnaire critique de la sociologie.* Paris: Presses universitaires de France, V–XV.

———. (2007). *Essais sur la théorie générale de la rationalité. Action sociale et sens commun.* Paris: Presses universitaires de France.

———. (2010). *La Sociologie comme science.* Paris: La Découverte.

———. (2011). Ordinary Rationality: The Core of Analytical Sociology. In: P. Demeulenaere (ed.), *Analytical Sociology and Social Mechanisms.* Cambridge–New York: Cambridge University Press, 33–49.

———. (2012). *Croire et savoir. Penser le politique, le moral et le religieux.* Paris: Presses universitaires de France.

———. (2013a). Qu'appelle-t-on un contexte? *Le Libellio d'AEGIS* 9(1): 3–25.

———. (2013b). Ma traversée dans le monde scientifique. *Commentaire*, n. 142, 343–349; n. 143, 603–612.

Boudon, R. and Lazarsfeld, P. (eds.) (1966). *L'Analyse empirique de la causalité.* Paris—La Haye: Mouton.

Boudon, R. and Fillieule, R. (2002). *Les Méthodes en sociologie.* Paris: Presses universitaires de France.

Boudon, R. and Leroux, R. (2003). *Y a-t-il encore une sociologie?* Paris: Odile Jacob.

Bourricaud, F. (1975). Contre le sociologisme: une critique et des propositions. *Revue française de sociologie* 16(sup.): 583–603.

Bunge, M. (1996). *Finding Philosophy in Social Science.* New Haven–London: Yale University Press.

Danto, A. C. (1965). *Analytical Philosophy of History.* Cambridge: Cambridge University Press.

Davidovitch, A. and Boudon, R. (1964). Les mécanismes sociaux des abandons de poursuite. Analyse expérimentale par simulation. *L'Année sociologique*, 3rd s., 15: 111–244.

Halévy, É. (1904). Compte rendu de la 4e séance générale du Congrès international de philosophie, 2e session. *Revue de métaphysique et de morale* 12(6): 1103–1113.

———. (1995 [1904]). *La Formation du radicalisme philosophique*, III. *Le Radicalisme philosophique.* Paris: Presses universitaires de France.

Hayek, F. A. (1948). *Individualism and Economic Order.* Chicago: University of Chicago Press.

———. (1952). *The Counter-Revolution of Science. Studies on the Abuse of Reason.* Glencoe (IL): Free Press.

Jarvie, I. C. (1972). *Concepts and Society.* London: Routledge & Kegan Paul.

Jepperson, R. and Meyer, J. W. (2011). Multiple Levels of Analysis and the Limitations of Methodological Individualisms. *Sociological Theory* 29(1): 54–73.

Lazarsfeld, P. F. and Menzel, H. (1993 [1961]). On the Relationship between Individual and Collective Properties. In: P. F. Lazarsfeld (ed.), *On Social Research and Its Language*. Chicago (IL): University of Chicago Press, 172–189.

Lukes, S. (1973). *Individualism*. Oxford: Blackwell.

Mises, L. (1933). *Grundprobleme der Nationalökonomie: Untersuchungen über Verfahren, Aufgaben und Inhalt der Wirtschafts- und Gesellschaftslehre*. Jena: Gustav Fischer.

———. (1940). *Nationalökonomie. Theorie Des Handelns Und Wirtschaftens*. Genève: Éditions Union.

———. (1962). *The Ultimate Foundation of Economic Science: An Essay on Method*. Princeton (NJ): D. Van Nostrand Co.

———. (1998 [1949]). *Human Action. A Treatise on Economics*. Auburn (AL): Mises Institute.

O'Neill, J. (ed.) (1973). *Modes of Individualism and Collectivism*. London: Heinemann.

Perrenoud, P. (1978). Les limites de l'individualisme méthodologique. À propos des Effets pervers et ordre social de R. Boudon. *Revue française de sociologie* 19(3): 442–454.

Popper, K. R. (1957). *The Poverty of Historicism*. London: Routledge & Kegan Paul.

———. (1966 [1945]). *The Open Society and Its Enemies*. London: Routledge & Kegan Paul, 2 vol.

Ricoeur, P. (1978). La philosophie. In: J. Havet (ed.), *Tendances principales de la recherche dans les sciences sociales et humaines. Deuxième partie / Tome second: Science juridique. Philosophie*. Paris—La Haye—New York: Mouton/Unesco, 1125–1622.

Schumpeter, J. A. (1909). On the Concept of Social Value. *Quarterly Journal of Economics* 23(2): 213–232.

———. (1986 [1954]). *History of Economic Analysis*. London: Routledge.

———. (2016 [1908]). *Das Wesen und der Hauptinhalt der theoretischen Nationalökonomie*. Berlin: Duncker und Humblot.

Simiand, F. (1932). *Le Salaire, l'évolution sociale et la monnaie*. Paris: Alcan, 3 vol.

Udehn, L. (2001). *Methodological Individualism. Background, History and Meaning*. London: Routledge.

———. (2002). The Changing Face of Methodological Individualism. *Annual Review of Sociology* 28: 479–507.

———. (2009). Raymond Boudon as a Methodological Individualist. In: M. Cherkaoui and P. Hamilton (eds.), *Raymond Boudon, a Life in Sociology. Essays in Honour of Raymond Boudon*. Oxford: The Bardwell Press, vol. 4, 361–377.

Watkins, J. W. N. (1952a). Ideal Types and Historical Explanation. *The British Journal for the Philosophy of Science* 3(9): 22–43.

———. (1952b). The Principle of Methodological Individualism. *The British Journal for the Philosophy of Science* 3(10): 186–189.

———. (1973). Ideal Types and Historical Explanation. In: J. O'Neill 1973, 143–165.

Chapter 2

METHODOLOGICAL INDIVIDUALISM AS AN EXPLANATORY PRACTICE: RAYMOND BOUDON AND THE IMPLICIT METHODOLOGY OF TOCQUEVILLE'S AND DURKHEIM'S EMPIRICAL SOCIOLOGY

Francesco Di Iorio and Enzo Di Nuoscio

Raymond Boudon posits that methodological individualism (hereafter, MI) is an explanatory framework characterized by two integral components: a micro-level analysis centered around rationality (where rationality does not mean necessarily that action must be explained in utilitarian terms) and a macro-level analysis focused on unintended aggregation effects. According to Boudon, this explanatory model aligns with the research practices employed by major social scientists who made substantial scientific contributions. This study unfolds in two parts. The initial segment (the first four sections) delves into a more comprehensive understanding of Boudon's MI by examining its relationship with key themes in social methodology. These themes include the demarcation between scientific and ideologically oriented explanations, the ontology of collective concepts, various forms of rationality, essential aspects of a comprehensive sociological approach, and the discourse surrounding explanations, deductive-nomological models, and mechanisms.

The analysis in the first part of this study serves as a foundation for comprehending its second part. The latter, encompassing the last two sections, delves into Boudon's quest to validate the explanatory prowess of MI. Boudon scrutinizes the history of sociology, seeking evidence of implicit applications of MI with paradigmatic significance due to their prominence.

According to Boudon, the historical trajectory of sociology attests to MI's capacity to elucidate a diverse range of crucial social phenomena, including social change, ideology, false beliefs, and moral sentiments—issues often traditionally explained through holism or methodological collectivism. Boudon contends that MI found application as an explanatory tool even among classical authors who either failed to articulate the theoretical and methodological underpinnings of their empirical accounts of the social realm or overtly embraced holism without practical implementation.

This study zeroes in on Boudon's analysis of the implicit methodology employed by Tocqueville, whom he regards as one of the pioneering individualist sociologists. Additionally, the study examines Durkheim, highlighting the paradox between his methodological claims and the actual provision of an individualist account of magic and other social phenomena.

Boudon and the Cognitive Function of the Social Sciences

To grasp Boundon's conception of MI, it is essential to delve into his perspective on the nature and objectives of scientific social research. According to Boudon (1993, 4), social sciences have historically served three primary functions.

(i) There is a *cognitive function* akin to the natural sciences, where they unravel puzzles to explain seemingly inexplicable phenomena, contributing to the expansion of scientific knowledge. Examples include Weber's analysis of the origins of capitalism in Northern Europe and Durkheim's exploration of magical thinking and suicide; (ii) Boudon identifies a *performative function*, signifying the social sciences' influence on political and social realms. They propose knowledge and viewpoints that shape institutional decision-making and public opinion. An illustration of this is the Labeling Theory, asserting that human behavior is significantly influenced by societal labels. Social movements advocating for improved conditions for ex-convicts have drawn on this theory; (iii) Boudon points out a *descriptive function* wherein the social sciences articulate new and intricate phenomena, making them accessible to a broader audience. Refined quantitative methods contribute to this function, offering scientific information to both insiders and the public. While these functions are challenging to isolate in their purest forms due to their inherent cognitive and explanatory aspects, this tripartition undeniably holds significance in the annals of social sciences (ibid., 4–5).

According to Boudon, among the three functions of social sciences, the most crucial is the cognitive function—specifically, the causal explanation of the multifaceted social world. By emphasizing this, he distances himself from a prevalent trend in the 1970s and 1980s, wherein social research was assigned a salvific and political role. This role envisioned social research as the revealer of hidden truths to the masses, guiding them toward liberation from various forms of domination and oppression ingrained in Western capitalist society.

Boudon contends (Id.) that the primary mission of social sciences should be the pursuit of empirical evidence. He argues that only descriptive knowledge founded on rigorous logical and empirical scrutiny can be socially beneficial. Conversely, he posits that ideological and political interpretations of social phenomena weaken a society's capacity to solve problems.

This perspective elucidates Boudon's dedication to MI. In his view, MI is imperative for elevating the scientific rigor of social research, liberating it from ideological biases and political agendas, and disassociating it from the collectivistic approach that often underlies these biases and goals. Boudon (2001, 56) contends that "the progress of knowledge"; "generally consists in a shift from the holistic paradigm to the individualistic paradigm" (Boudon 1991). Examining the history of sociology, Boudon asserts that sociological analyses demonstrating resilience over time, such as those of Tocqueville, Merton, or Marx, and even less evidently in Durkheim's case, have all subscribed to the principle of methodological individualism (Boudon 2001, 38; see also Allardt 1972, 54–68).

Boudon subscribes to an epistemic and research-oriented interpretation of MI, a perspective that has remained relatively obscure beyond the realm of empirical sociology. This viewpoint contrasts sharply with the abstract and critical stance developed in analytic philosophy from the 1950s and 1960s, a perspective divorced from the history and practices of the social sciences. This philosophical interpretation is closely tied to the philosophy of language and the logical-empiricist tradition (see Lukes 2006; Lukes, Bulle, and Di Iorio 2023) and has overshadowed MI in the broader post-Mengerian and post-Weberian debate initiated by the essays of Hayek, Schutz, and Popper in the first half of the 1940s, notably in *Economica*.

As Lukes (1977 [1968], 178) clarifies, this philosophical interpretation of MI prevalent in the Anglo-American world posits that individualist explanation is fundamentally a linguistic issue related to a specific type of factual knowledge. It asserts that facts about society and social phenomena should be explained solely in terms of facts about individuals. Consequently, explanations under MI should solely consist of "predicates" about "individuals" and their properties, excluding predicates about social and institutional factors and their properties (ibid., 180). According to this interpretation, MI proponents are constrained to discuss the tribesman but not the tribe, the bank-teller but not the bank (ibid., 184). In essence, it contends that the vocabulary of the social sciences should be entirely restricted to individual properties.

Critics argue that this reading portrays MI as an exclusivist, prescriptive doctrine about the form explanations should take, centered on a "futile linguistic purism" (Lukes 1977 [1968], 184) that prohibits the use of social and systemic concepts. Consequently, they deem it both useless and implausible.

Boudon never took the uninformed and caricatural interpretation of MI seriously. As evident in his works on the history of the social sciences, this understanding of MI lacks merit. Scholars such as Menger, Weber, and Simmel, as elucidated by Boudon, did not define their methodology with the linguistic exclusivism mentioned above. Instead, they extensively employed social predicates and conceived of social phenomena as systems of interaction capable of imposing varying degrees of constraints on individuals. Additionally, these scholars viewed individuals as theoretical constructs, asserting that beliefs and actions could only be defined based on historically situated social and cultural concepts essential for understanding the social conditioning of individuals (see Lukes, Bulle, and Di Iorio 2023; Lukes 1977, 80).

In his work, *Uses of Structuralism*, and other writings, Boudon (1971:1–4) emphasizes that analyzing social phenomena in terms of systemic or structural properties, which are semantically irreducible to individual ones, is an inevitable and indispensable characteristic of any sociological research (see also Boudon and Bourricaud 2004, 387–388; Di Iorio 2015, 75–120; Di Iorio 2023).

What Are Collective Concepts?

Boudon gives the following research-oriented definition of MI: "The principle of methodological individualism enunciates that, in order to explain any social phenomenon—which concerns demography, political science, sociology or any other particular social science—it is indispensable to reconstruct the reasons of the individuals and regard the phenomenon under investigation as the result of the aggregation of the actions dictated by these reasons" (Boudon 1989a, 644).

Methodological individualism posits that social phenomena, even the most intricate, result from intentional or unintentional manifestations of rational human behavior. This perspective implicitly entails an ontological stance. Within the framework of MI, collective concepts denoting various social phenomena like society, state, and capitalism (viz., Weber's *Kollectivbegriffe*) are not to be reified or hypostatized; instead, they are to be traced back to individual actions. This viewpoint aligns with ontological individualism, a term often used to describe this perspective (see Antiseri 2023).

While Boudon doesn't explicitly use this philosophical term to describe his approach, his stance seems closely aligned with the principles it represents. According to Boudon (1986, 39), assigning primacy to collective concepts over individuals leads to a "sociocentric illusion." This illusion, as Boudon argues, is typical of observers who, lacking detailed information about social phenomena, attribute these phenomena to generic and impersonal social causes. Boudon's viewpoint resonates with Weber's perspective. Weber, as articulated in a notable letter to a marginalist economist in 1920, asserted that sociology must refrain from explanations rooted in collective concepts and should instead "adopt strictly 'individualistic methods.'" This implies treating individuals as the ultimate causes of the phenomena that sociology seeks to scientifically elucidate (Boudon and Bourricaud 2004, 11).

According to Boudon, human action should not be seen as a mere deterministic outcome of social structures in a collectivist sense. This stance rests on two fundamental reasons. First, there are no social structures that exist independently of the individuals comprising them. Instead, the social environment, encompassing its rules, roles, constraints, and systemic properties, emerges from the intentional or unintentional aggregation of purposeful actions by individuals. Second, the impact of this environment on the individual is not a direct or mechanical process; rather, it is mediated by the interpretative skills of the individual.

While Boudon rejects collectivism, he does not endorse an atomistic standpoint. His MI regards the agent as intentional but endowed with bounded rationality and conditioned by the institutional and situational context in which he/she is embedded. In his view, interpretative sociology must reconstruct and understand the individual decision-making process through a complex and refined theory of subjective rationality that can make sense of mistaken ideas and ethical beliefs in terms of good reasons. As opposed to collectivism, which was still quite popular in the 1970s and the 1980s, his approach is thus incompatible with what D. Wrong (1961) has called the "hyper-socialized conception of man," according to which the agent is remote-controlled by social structures since his/her behavior is the effect of the socialization process rather than of his/her intentionality. Referring to Weber, Boudon argues that individual actions should not be considered as mere behaviors mechanically produced by a structural determinism ("merely reactive" acts, to use Weber's words) but as dictated by rationality. Boudon's MI is thus neither atomistic nor naively reductionist in the sense of analytic philosophers but rather opposed to sociologism, that is, the doctrine whereby "the intentions and actions of the social agent should always be considered as effects and never as causes" (Boudon 2005, 22).

Boudon's MI as a Wide-Ranging Explanatory Model

Boudon's MI is rooted in Weber's perspective that the fundamental focus of sociology is social action. Understanding social action is crucial to making sense of social phenomena, whether they result from the intended or unintended consequences of individuals' imperfect and socially conditioned rationality. In line with Weber's (1968, 4) assertion that "action is 'social'" when its subjective meaning considers the behavior of others (Id.), Boudon extends Weber's methodology to develop a nuanced theory of subjective rationality.

Unlike traditional views that solely concentrate on the rationality of action, Boudon's theory encompasses the rationality of beliefs. Moreover, it does not presume that rationality is exclusively utilitarian and instrumental. Boudon recognizes positive beliefs (descriptions of the world and its mechanisms) and normative beliefs that, while not explained in utilitarian terms, are still grounded in *good reasons* (i.e., sensible interpretation and evaluation). These *good reasons* arise from a fallible, argumentative, non-utilitarian, non-instrumental, non-Cartesian, and partly tacit rationality, termed "cognitive" or "ordinary" by Boudon.[1]

While sharing the foundational belief with other proponents of MI that individual actions have ultimate causal power in the social world, Boudon's MI has a broader application compared to other popular variants of this approach. Specifically, it extends beyond the scope of (i) the rational choice model, (ii) the paradigm of spontaneous order, and (iii) the micro-level interactionist perspective.

In contrast to the strictly utilitarian and instrumental theory of rationality in the rational choice model (e.g., Coleman, Becker, and Elster), Boudon's MI accommodates explanations of individual good reasons through cognitive or ordinary rationality. Consequently, his MI framework can elucidate a wide range of economic actions and positive and normative collective beliefs. Traditionally interpreted in collectivistic terms, these beliefs don't solely originate from utilitarian and instrumental reasoning.

While the paradigm of spontaneous order (exemplified by figures like Smith, Menger, and Hayek) places the explanation of unintended consequences at the forefront of the social sciences, Boudon's MI does not overlook the dimension of human action. Instead, it asserts that comprehending the situated rationality of individuals is equally vital alongside the study of invisible-hand mechanisms. Boudon's MI also equips scholars with refined hermeneutical tools to make sense of micro-level social phenomena. It facilitates a meticulous understanding of the foundational aspects of invisible hand mechanisms—specifically, the intentional acceptance of common social rules from which these mechanisms arise. Moreover, compared to the interactionist perspective, which concentrates solely on the meanings individuals attach to micro-level human interaction (e.g., Mead, Blumer), Boudon's methodology possesses a wider explanatory scope. It can be applied to examine the subtle micro-dynamics of small groups and complex unintended macro-phenomena.

---

[1] For more details on this theory of rationality, see Di Iorio and Di Nuoscio (2014); Di Iorio (2015, 121 ff.); and Morin (2023).

Distinct from approaches relying on less sophisticated theories of rationality or those focused solely on macro or micro-analysis, Boudon's brand of MI can unravel any relationship between the agent and the system of interaction. This holds true regardless of the degree of autonomy the agent possesses within the system, or the typology of structural constraints imposed on the agent and their freedom. This is because, Boudon's methodology is rooted in a highly articulated form of situated rationality, which can elucidate any micro–macro link.

MI, Causal Explanation and Social Mechanisms

Boudon rejects Dilthey's famous dichotomy between causal explanation, typical of the natural sciences, and hermeneutic understanding, typical of the interpretive human sciences. In his opinion, the logic of individualist explanation consists in reconstructing the causal chain of *reasons–actions–social phenomena*. This causal chain refers to two cause–effect connections: the first traces the action back to the reasons of which it is the effect; the second traces the social phenomenon under investigation back to the actions of which, intentionally or unintentionally, it is the consequence. As Boudon (1992; 2006) clarifies in some of his works, the reconstruction of these two cause–effect connections requires nondeterministic sociological laws. Therefore, his perspective on the nature of explanation matches the deductive-nomological model (hereafter DN model) as understood by Hempel and Popper. However, Boudon has never discussed in detail the relationship between his individualist sociology and the logical structure of this model.

To further clarify the nature of Boudon's MI, the following part of this section analyzes this relationship. The DN model, which is often misunderstood, is indispensable for reconstructing the two abovementioned cause–effect connections studied by MI (see Di Nuoscio 2004, 163–191; Di Iorio and Di Nuoscio 2022; Opp 2013a; 2013b).

Boudon (2005, 29) accounts for the first connection in the following terms: "The causes of action, beliefs, attitudes of social actors must be sought in the meaning they have for them, or more precisely in the reasons why they have adopted them."[2] From the standpoint of the DN model, this means that to explain the action, sociologists must consider the reasons as the *explanans* and the action as the *explanandum*. They, therefore, must reconstruct the *initial*

---

[2] According to Hempel and Oppenheim (1948, 143), "Motivations and determining beliefs must be classified among the preceding conditions of a motivational explanation, and in this respect, there is no difference between a motivational and a causal explanation."

conditions represented by the agent's knowledge, beliefs, goals, resources, anticipation of the consequences, and perception of the situation, without which the agent, *ceteris paribus*, would not have acted. Moreover, the sociologist needs to consider another initial condition, which is particularly relevant from the standpoint of causality, that is, the reconstruction of the "rational calculation" that leads the agent to choose a certain goal and a certain line of action.[3] As pointed out by Weber (2005 [1903–6], 11), who, especially in *Roscher and Knies and the Logical Problems of Political Economy*, develops a theory of explanation that matches Hempel's and Popper's, this "goal is the representation of an effect which becomes the cause of the action." In Weber's opinion, "there is a causal relationship without teleology but there can be no teleological concepts without causal rules," that is, without empirical covering laws in the broad sense attached to this term by Hempel and Popper (Weber 2005 [1903–6], 11). According to the DN model, empirical laws are not necessarily acquired through scientific research but partly belong to common sense. Commonsense laws about human action and other natural and social phenomena were learned by our ancestors in everyday life through trial and error. The DN model assumes that empirical laws are not necessarily deterministic but can also be probabilistic. This model considers most of the laws used by the social sciences to be of the latter kind (for more details on this point, see Di Iorio and Di Nuoscio 2022).

Using covering laws as understood above is necessary not only to reconstruct the link between action and reasons but also to account for the intentional and especially unintentional emergence of macro-social phenomena. According to the DN model, the actions and their either planned or unplanned results must be regarded as the initial conditions of this emergence's explanation (i.e., they must be regarded as part of the *explanans*), while the systemic effects, no matter if they are simple or complex, as the *explananda*.

Let's consider an example of individualistic explanation, viz. Weber's analysis of the genesis of capitalism (Weber 2010 [1904–5], 101 ff). To make sense of the genesis of capitalism, Weber answers what Boudon considers to be the three key questions of any explanation in terms of MI: (i) Who

---

[3] It should be noted that, as Hempel (1965, 202) points out in his response to William Dray, explaining action means reconstructing a causal link between reason and action without introducing any value judgment. For Dray (1957, 89), who opposed his "action principle" to the DN model, explaining action in terms of good reasons means providing "an element of evaluation of what has been done," in order to understand "in what sense the action is appropriate."

caused the phenomenon under investigation? The Calvinist entrepreneurs did not aim at accumulating profits but reinvesting them; (ii) Why did they act this way? Because based on a religious belief, they regarded professional success as a sign of salvation, etcetera …; (iii) How is it possible to move from the micro level of the individual actions to the macro social level? The simple aggregation of a very large number of typical actions carried out by the Calvinist entrepreneurs who behaved in this way gave rise unintentionally to a capitalist economic system.

The causal explanation of the fact that the Calvinist entrepreneurs reinvested their profits because they believed that professional success was a sign of salvation presupposes the following implicit commonsense law that links these actions to the reasons behind them: "When one wants to expand his/her economic activities one tends to reinvest his/her profits." The causal explanation of the fact that the actions of the Calvinist entrepreneurs produced a capitalist system presupposes another trivial commonsense law that links these actions to their outcome: "The large-scale diffusion of entrepreneurial economic activities gives rise to the system of economic relations called capitalism."

As it is well-known, the DN model is often criticized by analytical sociologists and interpretative sociologists more generally (see, e.g., Hedström and Ylikoski 2010), many of whom maintain that their approach is based on explanations in terms of social mechanisms rather than on the DN model. As is argued (see Di Iorio and Di Nuoscio 2022), this aversion to the DN model stems from a misunderstanding of its assumptions (see also Opp 2013a; 2013b). According to its critics, this model must be rejected because it is a deterministic account of explanation and allows neither accurate and precise explanations nor explanations that give individuals and their actions a privileged role. This view neglects three relevant facts about the DN model as understood by Hempel, Popper, and their precursors like Weber.

First, as already pointed out, this model does not necessarily require deterministic laws for causal imputation. The above example shows that the laws employed in sociological explanation are usually probabilistic. They are "law-like sentences" (Hempel 1965, 458), "less-than-universal-laws" (Scriven 1959, 464), that is, statements that are like general laws but are not exceptionless. These probabilistic laws have also been called "common sense maxims" (Nagel 1961, 389) and "judgment of possibilities" (Boudon 1984, 239). They explain what individuals do tendentially when they are in a typical situation (Di Nuoscio 2018, 43–48). In *Roscher and Knies and the Logical Problems of Political Economy*, Weber (1903–6, 15) argued that the laws employed in the historical and social sciences are "rules of experience" related to how "men are accustomed to react to certain situations," that is, statements "describing the concrete causal links" between typical actions and typical situations.[4]

Second, the DN model allows for accurate explanations and gives individuals a privileged role because it attaches crucial importance to what Popper (1957, 149; 1966, 205) calls situational analysis. Hempel (1965) clarified that the explanations based on probabilistic laws are more problematic. This is because they do not allow the sociologist to deduce for sure the *explanans* from the *explanandum*. Using probabilistic laws means having either different *explananda* compatible with the same initial conditions or different explanations compatible with the same *explanandum* (see also Di Nuoscio 2018, 35 ff.). Situational analysis allows us to overcome this problem and provide accurate explanations. This analysis is a careful historical reconstruction of the combination of typical initial conditions that generated the *explanandum*, a fundamental aspect of empirical research. Such a historical reconstruction allows the sociologist to select the appropriate commonsense probabilistic law to explain the different potentially appropriate commonsense probabilistic laws (see Di Iorio and Di Nuoscio 2023, 60–62).

Third, contrary to what is often believed, the DN model and social mechanisms are compatible conceptual tools. This is because, as clarified by Hedström (2007, 73–76), it is possible to make sense of these mechanisms in terms of Weber's ideal–typical categories. Like the latter, mechanisms are abstract schemes referring to either typical pure actions or typical pure social processes (e.g., rational imitation, wishful thinking, self-fulfilling prophecy). Understood in this way, social mechanisms can be regarded as functional for the development of empirical hypotheses that, without covering generalizations, lack explanatory power (see Di Iorio and Di Nuoscio 2023, 62–66). For example, the account of a concrete historical case of self-fulfilling prophecy will presuppose a careful situational analysis and the use of empirical laws in the sense of the DN model to reconstruct the concatenation of circumstances that produced this actual case.

---

[4] Note that the laws of social science should not be confused with historical *trends* (e.g., the progressive increase in the number of workers in England in the second half of the nineteenth century) or *accidental generalizations* (e.g., all my students are for democracy), which are mere descriptions of facts, mere accounts of experience, describing finite sequences of facts that they have been empirically proved. Since both historical trends and empirical generalizations are about a finite number of singular predicates, they cannot be projected beyond the cases they describe and therefore have no explanatory or predictive power. They are rather *explananda*, i.e., descriptions of effects that must be explained by laws (Di Nuoscio 2004, 227–231).

Analyzing the relationship between interpretative sociology and the DN model is a technical and complex topic that deserves in-depth treatment. However, this subject remains beyond the scope of the current study.[5]

Tocqueville as a Methodologist of the Social Sciences

Having clarified the fundamental aspects of Boudon's MI, the following two sections review his analysis of the implicit methodology of two classic authors, Tocqueville and Durkheim.

It was not until the publication of Raymond Aron's *Main Currents of Sociological Thought* that Tocqueville became definitively recognized as one of the originators of sociology (see Aron 1998, [1965]). It was from this influential book, in fact, that the conviction began to take hold among social scientists that Tocqueville's major works are masterpieces of historiography and the history of political thought and sharp sociological investigations in which the genesis and development of important social institutions are analyzed in the context of the time's newly emerging socially shared ideas.

While in *Les étapes* Aron places Tocqueville among the greatest sociologists (namely Montesquieu, Comte, Durkheim, Weber, and Pareto), in *Tocqueville for Today*, Boudon (2006) places Tocqueville among the greatest methodologists of the social sciences along with Weber, Durkheim, Popper, and Hayek. At first glance, this is surprising, given that Tocqueville left us no methodological writings. However, Boudon's view is also well founded and innovative. Boudon's approach, though effective, is little practiced by historians of the social sciences: reconstructing the implicit methodology of scientific explanations.

Boudon dissects Tocqueville's theories in detail, showing that if *The Democracy in America* and *The Ancien Régime and the Revolution* have remained relevant, with their arguments presenting valid scientific contributions, it is due primarily to the methodological rules that these two books implement. In Boudon's opinion, Tocqueville's explanations prove his implicit commitment to epistemological fallibilism, MI, nondeterministic social evolutionism, and the DN model. This is why the empirical testability of his explanations is particularly good.

According to Tocqueville (2002, 298; 367), the fallibility of human knowledge is the epistemological justification of tolerance and freedom and a useful assumption of sociological research. This is because the development of the shared ideas that lay at the bottom of the social order must be interpreted as a response to the limits of individual knowledge. These ideas stem from trying to work out crucial navigational charts, given that the social actors need

---

[5] For a more thorough investigation of its nature, see Di Iorio and Di Nuoscio (2022).

principles and landmarks to orient themselves in a complex and partly opaque present and toward an unknown and indeterminate future.

Tocqueville's firm awareness of the limits of human knowledge, which is for Boudon (2006, 107) a direct anticipation of K. Popper and F. Hayek's methodological approach, is part and parcel of Tocqueville's avowed attempt to outline a "new political science" aiming at explaining major historical and social phenomena avoiding the mistakes of both historicism and radical positivism.

In Boudon's opinion, Tocqueville succeeded in his aim of developing a new political science, which is a form of "historical sociology," essentially because he used an individualistic and nomological approach (Boudon 2006, 104). This approach is characterized by the following assumptions:

i.   *Ontological individualism.* Tocqueville (1896, 80) criticizes the great philosophies of history that he calls "absolute systems" because, in his view, they end up eliminating men from the "history of humankind." Moreover, he argues that social institutions are nothing more than collections of individuals and shared behaviors repeated over time.

ii. *MI.* According to Tocqueville, social phenomena are either the intentional or the unintentional result of human actions. He explains the collapse of the Ancien Regime largely as an unintended consequence produced by the attempt of the monarchy and other traditional institutions to defend themselves by centralizing the power. In Tocqueville's view, the revolt against strong centralized power turned, beyond the intentions of the insurgents, into a subversion of the existing order: the fall of Paris marked the end of the entire Ancient Regime (see Boudon 2006, 89).

iii. *The rationality of human action.* Unlike the Hegelian, Comtian, and Marxian traditions, Tocqueville does not develop explanations in terms of "depth psychology," which interprets human action as a derivative of more or less hidden forces of which individuals are unaware. Instead, he explains social phenomena in terms of what Boudon (2006, 91) calls an "ordinary psychology" that conceives action as an attempt to solve problems in light of individuals' intentions and knowledge. If the main French landowners of the eighteenth century abandoned their businesses to move to the city, this happened because they had "good reasons" for doing so: they wanted to more easily escape the taxman and find greater career satisfaction in public administration. For Boudon (2006, 119), the development of this logic of explanation in terms of rational action represents a decisive step in the history of the social sciences because the terrain of interpretation is abandoned in favor of that of empirically testable conjectures.

iv. *Science as a value-free process.* Developing sociological and historiographical analyses, Tocqueville explains the selection mechanism that led to the establishment of certain great ideas, such as equality, while refraining from making value judgments. He condemns without appeal the tendency of certain authors to alternate factual and value judgments, which prevents an objective and rigorous explanation of social events. This tendency, which aims more at interpreting and judging than at explaining (and thrived even in the twentieth century—think of the Frankfurt School's critical sociology) often ends up subordinating the reasons of science to those of philosophy and ideology (see Boudon 2006, 124).

v. *The DN model.* Tocqueville explains innumerable social phenomena by tracing them back to their causes through empirically testable laws. In a famous passage of *The Democracy in America*, he argues that the large-scale establishment of the feeling of equality is a major cause of the rise of the critical attitude and the development of science. This is an example of sociological law. In a social environment in which each individual does not feel inferior to others, since there are no longer authorities holding truths recognized as superior, everyone feels entitled to dissent from the ideas of others. This is precisely why modernity is characterized, according to Tocqueville, by a general erosion of "dogmatic beliefs," that is, by the phenomenon that Weber (2010 [1904–1905]) would later call the disenchantment of the world. Boudon (2006) lists up a valuable catalog of sociological laws through which Tocqueville causally links very relevant social phenomena.

vi. *Ideal-typical concepts.* Tocqueville elaborates and makes extensive use of ideal-typical categories: think, for example, of the distinction between "aristocratic society" and "democratic society." These are categories through which he does not provide a description of actually existing events, but rather offers patterns of interpretation, which, by identifying abstract typical elements and relationships that connote families of social phenomena, guide empirical research and provide sociologists with valuable information for the formulation of testable hypotheses.

vii. *Individualist social evolutionism.* According to Tocqueville (2002 [1835], 389) institutions, and, more generally, the kind of relationships that become established in a society, are the product of a rational selection of ideas with respect to their ability to adapt to the social context. Social evolution can be explained, as a combination of "universal" and "singular," of general ideas and particular social institutions: social institutions will tend to assert themselves only if they are in line with the broad shared ideas that dominate in a society. Thus, in a democratic society, characterized by the "general and dominant passion" of equality, universal suffrage will tend to assert itself, since this innovation satisfies the demand for equality (Tocqueville (2002 [1835], 601). This is an individualistic evolutionism, which interprets social evolution as a spontaneous order: an order that evolves through the spontaneous interactions of individuals, moved by ideas, which, for Tocqueville, are not to be regarded as deterministic derivatives of the cultural environment (see Boudon 2006, 99).

After unveiling the implicit methodology underpinning Tocqueville's theories, Boudon concludes that they represent valid examples of scientific explanation. In his opinion, "a more precise statement of a 'good theory' as it emerges from Tocqueville's analysis is that it makes social phenomenon a product of attitudes, beliefs, and understandable human actions in the light of ordinary psychology, that can be successfully tested by observational data" (Boudon 2006, 109). Precisely because they are based on good methodological rules, many of Tocqueville's theories are examples of foresight in the social sciences, as they anticipated some fundamental phenomena that have occurred in the last hundred to fifty years. Such phenomena include the persistence of the American religious exception, the steady increase in the weight of the French state, the difficulty of reforming it, the secularization of modern societies, the splitting, privatization, and tendency to immanentize religions, the failure of attempts to implant any secular religion, the weakening of traditional sources of authority, the reign of opinion, the competition between "social power" and political power, the appearance of superficial cultural production, the success of these abstract and general ideas we call ideologies, the development of relativism and skepticism, the softening of customs, the "humanization" of "social control" procedures, the cult of human rights, the development of individualism or the deployment of a vast middle class, among others, and the list, Boudon contends, remains open (see Boudon 2006, 111).

Thanks to Boudon's *Tocqueville for Today*, the "history of influence" to use Gadamer words, generated by Tocqueville's work is significantly enriched. From the standpoint of empirical sociology, this history has been limitedly relevant; from the standpoint of methodology, it has been inexistent before the publication of Boudon's innovative writings on Tocqueville. The detached style of this French aristocrat, who always preferred to be nuanced and well considered in his historiographical and sociological investigations, has exerted a limited appeal in the social sciences of the nineteenth and twentieth centuries, which were often dominated by collectivistic large-range theoretical systems, incompatible with Tocqueville's MI; so much so that, even an individualist intellectual like Aron (Aron R. (1998 [1965], 19) himself, surprisingly admitted to "having more interest in the mysteries of Capital, than in the limpid and grim prose of Democracy in America." This shows that perhaps Tocqueville (2002 [1835], 132) was right when he stated that "a false but clear and precise idea always has more power in the world than one which is true but complex."

Durkheim on Suicide and Magical Thinking

Like other scholars (e.g., M. Hirschhorn and J. Coenen-Huther 1994), Boudon argued that some of Durkheim's work are implicitly based on an individualist approach (see Leroux 2020). In his opinion, a distinction must be made between the methodology Durkheim recommends in *The Rules of Sociological Method*, which is collectivistic and positivistic, and the one he actually implements in *The Elementary Forms of Religious Life* and *Suicide: A Study in Sociology*, which is broadly speaking individualist. "Durkheim rejects 'psychology' in his doctrinal texts," writes Boudon, "but it is omnipresent in his analyses. Not only does he not do away with Simmel-Weber's 'abstract psychology' in practice, but behind many of Durkheim's analyses, not only in The Formes but also in The Suicide, one finds an application of the methodology of understanding" (Boudon 1994, 112–113). While it is true, for example, that in studying the phenomenon of suicide, Durkheim focuses on relationships between macro-variables, it must be considered, for Boudon, that the choice of such variables is based on the "psychology" of individuals. The famous correlation between economic cycles and suicides is reformulated by Boudon in the following terms:

> Suicide is more probable when disillusionment is more frequent; disillusionment results from the need of the actor and especially of the economic actor to foresee the future; the method of extrapolation from the present is the easiest way to reduce the uncertainty of the future; disillusionment is due to the fact that the actor has good reason to be exaggeratedly optimistic in the best phase of the cycle: this is why the best situation is accompanied by particularly high suicide rates (…). If this reconstruction is correct, it means that Durkheim proposes us to analyse the correlation between economic cycles and suicide cycles as the outcome of anticipations based on good reasons. In its simplicity, this theory contains some genius. In any case, behind the analysis of correlations, and beyond the holistic language used by Durkheim ('suicidal currents'), one discovers without too much difficulty a comprehensive analysis of behavior. (Boudon 1994, 113–114)

Particularly interesting is Durkheim's explanation of magical thinking. The interpretation of this phenomenon has generally represented a classic case of explanation in terms of irrationality: magic rituals and beliefs have often been regarded not as resulting from individual reasons, but from subconscious social or psychological determinants. In other words, these rituals and beliefs have often been considered to be the product of impersonal forces that are beyond the individuals' control (Boudon 1997, 25 ff.). Lucien Lévy-Bruhl (1923 [1922]), one of Durkheim's followers, was surely the scholar who developed the most authoritative and influential anti-individualist theory of magical thinking. For him, magical beliefs stem from the fact that primitive people are characterized by logical and psychological mechanisms that differ from ours. For example, this is shown by the fact that they tend to confuse a *post hoc* relationship with a *propter hoc* relationship, viz. a chronological relationship with a causality relationship. According to Lévy-Bruhl (1923 [1922], 19 ff.), these people are characterized by a primitive or "pre-logical" mentality, which, following Comte's historicist evolutionism, must be regarded as an earlier stage in the intellectual evolution of humankind than the logical mentality.

Mentality is considered by Lévy-Bruhl (Id.) to be a dependent variable of the social and cultural characteristics of a certain society: magic is ultimately the result of impersonal social causes. For Lévy-Bruhl (1923 [1922], 107), since there are multiple systems of thought, historically and socially contextualized, it is necessary to "give up ascribing mental operations to a single type, regardless of the societies considered, and to explain all collective representations by a psychological mechanism that is always the same."

Ten years before Lévy-Bruhl's *Primitive Mentality*, Durkheim (2008 [1912]), in *The Elementary Forms of Religious Life*, developed what Boudon (Boudon 1989b, 42) considers one of the best individualistic explanations of magic. Interestingly, this explanation matches quite well with Weber's interpretation of this phenomenon in *Economy and Society* (see Weber 2019 [1922], 105).[6]

Like Weber, Durkheim believes that the notion of magic only exists in the eyes of the Western observer, who considers primitive people's behaviors without considering their different cultural backgrounds. Rather than being an attribute of their behaviors, magic is a concept resulting from a particular kind of relationship between the observed people and the observer. Instead, one must consider (Boudon 1989b, 42) contends that "if the act of rubbing

---

[6] According to Weber (2019 [1922], 400), "religiously or magically motivated behavior is relatively rational behavior, especially in its earliest manifestations. It follows rules of experience, though it is not necessarily action in accordance with a means-end schema. Rubbing will elicit sparks from pieces of wood, and in like fashion, the mimetical actions of a magician will evoke rain from the heavens. The sparks resulting from twirling the wooden sticks are as much a 'magical' effect as the rain evoked by the manipulations of the rainmaker. Thus, religious or magical behavior or thinking must not be set apart from the range of everyday purposive conduct, particularly since even the ends of the religious and magical actions are predominantly economic."

the piece of wood to produce fire appears to us to be different from the act of the rainman, it is because we have read Hume, it is because we have learnt to manipulate the notions of cause and effect, it is because we spontaneously apply Mill's rules of induction; it is, in short, because we have a more or less precise idea of the rules of controlled experimentation. But we had to wait until Bacon, Hume, or Mill for these rules to become natural to us. Is it then not unreasonable to suppose that principles which it took Western thought centuries to codify are present in the mind of the primitive?"

The opposition between the rationality of the fire expert and the irrationality of the rain expert is artificially created by the observer through the meta-conscious application of *a priori* principles, such as the causality principle, that the primitive people do not possess because they did not learn the same knowledge as the observer, that is, the kind of knowledge that is typical of the Western tradition. Both the fire and the rain experts interpret the world in terms of supernatural forces. The fire expert does not understand how he/she can start a fire, assuming that the kinetic energy can be transformed into heat energy or that the relationship between rubbing and sparking can be described in causal terms. Fire and rain are both caused by magical powers. Consequently, there is no opposition between the assumptions of the fire expert and those of the rain expert who performs the rain dance to propitiate the rain gods. If we give up projecting our cultural categories onto primitive peoples, it becomes apparent that both experts are rational, considering the difference between the primitive peoples' knowledge and ours:

> Activities as complex as fishing or agriculture imply of course not just mastery of technique, but, beyond that, the use of more general theories such as the origin and growth of plants, interaction between plants and soil, or the influence of humankind on agricultural production. People in the West tend to borrow these general theories, at least in part, from the corpus of knowledge which for them has a monopoly of legitimacy—science." Primitive people' borrow them from theories which, equally, give them a general interpretation of the world and are for this reason invested with legitimacy, that is, the theories of religion obtaining in their society. Magical beliefs should therefore, according to Durkheim, be regarded as 'applied' theories drawn by traditional societies from religious doctrines recognized as true, just as in modern societies techniques used by engineers are drawn from the corpus of science. (Boudon 1997, 13)

Moreover, it must be noted that to get rid of a belief, one needs to consider another belief to be better. However, in a traditional society, where worldviews change slowly, "the market of theories is not very active" (Boudon 1994, 106; 1992, 508 ff.).

Durkheim's account of magical thinking is, like Weber's, a striking example of situational analysis: magical rituals should be regarded as rational because they are appropriate to the situation as perceived by the actors. To use Boudon's words, for Durkheim, primitive people have good reasons for endorsing their magical beliefs that are neither objectively correct nor arbitrary. Moreover, these people also have good reasons for continuing to believe in the efficacy of magical rituals despite there are counterexamples showing their lack of efficacy. If we consider the case of rain dance, we can see that this happens for different reasons. First, this ritual is performed when rain is necessary for crops, that is, at times of the year when it is most likely to rain, which creates the illusion that the ritual is often working (Boudon 1997, 14). Second, as shown by Lakatos, it is rational to stick to a theory despite its empirical falsifications because of the Duhem-Quine problem. This is true both in science and common sense. Falsifications do not necessarily entail the rejection of a theory because understanding if a falsification really depends on the falsity of the theory or just on the falsity of some background assumptions is problematic (Boudon 1994, 105–106). Third, it must be added that primitive people, like any other people, use ad hoc assumptions to save their theories from falsification. For example, they believe the ritual fails if not performed correctly or the gods are in a bad mood (Id., 104 ff.). Fourth, primitive people are not familiar with statistics and, therefore, cannot build time series data that allow them to estimate in percentage the confirmations and falsifications of their theory (ibid.).

This interpretation of magic in terms of good reasons turns out to be heuristically more powerful than Lévy-Bruhl's since it allows us to explain from a sociological standpoint: (i) the variation in time and space of magical beliefs; (ii) why they spread, in the sixteenth and seventeenth centuries, to the more advanced parts of the European continent; and (iii) why, even today, albeit marginally, they still exist in Western societies. From an epistemological viewpoint, Lévy-Bruhl's theory is, according to Boudon (1997, 17), ad hoc because the existence of primitive mentality is inferred solely based on the effects (magical beliefs) it is supposed to explain. Moreover, Lévy-Bruhl's theory is also tautological because it explains, "They explain why primitive people confuse verbal associations and causal relationships by saying they have a tendency to confuse the two, a tendency shown to be true by the fact that they do in reality confuse them" (Boudon 1997, 17). On the other hand, the individualistic explanation of magic is not ad hoc because it asserts explaining adherence to magical beliefs has validity independently of the effects of such adherence and, therefore, can be tested empirically. Moreover, this explanation is not tautological either because it is not "a mere translation into another language of the phenomenon to be explained" (Boudon 1997, 16).

The account of magical beliefs in terms of cognitive rationality represents a significant example of the application of MI to the analysis of phenomena that have traditionally been explained in holistic terms. It shows that replacing holistic-irrational with individualistic-rational explanations makes sociological theory heuristically more robust and defensible.

References

Allardt, E. (1972). Structural, Institutional and Cultural Explanations. *Acta Sociologica* 1(15): 54–68.

Antiseri, D. (2023). Viennese Methodological Individualism. In: N. Bulle and F. Di Iorio (eds.), *The Palgrave Handbook of Methodological Individualism: Volume I*. London: Palgrave MacMillan.

Aron, R. (1998 [1965]). *Main Currents in Sociological Thought: Montesquieu, Comte, Marx, Tocqueville and the Sociologists and the Revolution of 1848, Volume One*. London and New York: Routledge.

Boudon, R. (1971). *Uses of Structuralism*. London: Heinemann.

————. (1984). *La place du désordre*. Paris: Presses Universitaires de France.

————. (1986). *Theories of Social Change: A Critical Appraisal*. Berkeley: University of California Press.

————. (1989a). *The Analysis of Ideology*. New York: Polity Press.

————. (1989b). Razionalità soggettiva e disposizioni. In: L. Sciolla and L. Ricolfi (eds.), *Il soggetto dell'azione*. Milano: Franco Angeli.

————. (1991). Individualisme et holisme dans les sciences sociales. In: P. Birnbaum and J. Leca (eds.), *Sur l'individualisme*. Paris: Presses de la Fondation National de Science Politique.

————. (1992). Connaissance. In: R. Boudon (ed.), *Traité de sociologie*. Paris: Puf.

————. (1993). La sociologie est-elle une science rigoureuse? In: M. Juffé (ed.), *Aux frontières du savoir—Compte-rendus des conférences*. Paris: Ecole des Ponts et Chaussées.

————. (1994). Durkheim et Weber: convergences de méthode. In: M. Hirschhorn and J. Coenen-Huther (eds.), *Durkheim, Weber vers la fin des malentendus*. Paris: L'Harmattan.

————. (1997). *The Art of Self-Persuasion: The Social Explanation of False Beliefs*. New York: Polity Press.

————. (2001). *The Origins of Value*. Piscataway, NJ: London: Transaction Publishers.

————. (2005). Teoria della scelta razionale e individualismo metodologico: sono la stessa cosa? In: M. Borlandi and L. Sciolla (eds.), *La spiegazione sociologica*. Bologna: il Mulino.

————. (2006). *Tocqueville for Today*. Oxford: The Bardwell Press.

Boudon, R. and Bourricaud F. (2004). *A Critical Dictionary of Sociology*. London and New York: Routledge.

Di Iorio, F. and Di Nuoscio E. (2014). Rethinking Boudon's Cognitive Rationality in the Light of Mises' Apriorism and Gadamer's Hermeneutics. *Journal des Économistes et des Études Humaines*, ISSN (Online) 2153-1552, ISSN (Print) 2194-5799, DOI: 10.1515/jeeh-2014-0010, December 2014, pp. 1–14.

Di Iorio, F. and Di Nuoscio, E. (2022). On Situational Analysis and the Explanatory Power of Mechanisms: Analytical Sociology and the Deductive-Nomological Model. *Social Science Information*, First Published February 25, 2022, https://doi.org/10.1177/05390184221078737.

Di Iorio, F. (2015). *Cognitive Autonomy and Methodological Individualism*. Chaim: Springer.

———. (2023). Methodological Individualism and Reductionism. In: N. Bulle and F. Di Iorio (eds.), *The Palgrave Handbook of Methodological Individualism: Volume II*. London: Palgrave MacMillan.

Di Nuoscio, E. (2004). *Tucidide come Einstein: La spiegazione scientifica in storiografia*. Soveria Mannelli: Rubbettino.

———. (2018). *The Logic of Explanation in the Social Sciences*. Oxford: The Bardwell Press.

Dray, W. H. (1957). *Laws and Explanations in History*. Oxford: Oxford University Press.

Durkheim, E. (2008 [1912]). *The Elementary Forms of Religious Life*. Oxford: Oxford University Press.

Hedström, P. (2007). Explaining Social Change: An Analytical Approach. *Revista de Sociologia* 80: 73–95.

Hedström, P. and Ylikoski P. (2010). Causal Mechanisms in the Social Sciences. *Annual Review of Sociology* 36: 49–67.

Hempel, C. G. and Oppenheim, P. (1948). Studies in the Logic of Explanation. *Philosophy of Science* 15(2) (Apr., 1948): 135–175.

Hempel, C. G. (1965). *Aspects of Scientific Explanation and Other Essays in the Philosophy of Science*. New York: Free Press.

Hirschhorn, M. and Coenen-Huther, J. (eds.) (1994). *Durkheim, Weber vers la fin des malentendus*. Paris: L'Harmattan.

Leroux, R. (2020). Boudon's Interpretation of Durkheim Sociology. *Durkheimian Studies / Etudes Durkheimiennes* 24(1) 2020: 175–184.

Lévy-Bruhl, L. (1923 [1922]). *Primitive Mentality*. Kansas City: Beacon Hill Press.

Lukes, S. (1977 [1968]). Methodological Individualism Reconsidered. In: S. Lukes (ed.), *Essays in Social Theory*. London: MacMillan.

———. (2006 [1973]). *Individualism*. Lanham, USA: Harper & ECPR Press.

Lukes, S., Bulle, N. and Di Iorio, F. (2023). Methodological Individualism and Social Facts: A Discussion with Steven Lukes. In: N. Bulle and F. Di Iorio (eds.), *The Palgrave Handbook of Methodological Individualism: Volume II*. London: Palgrave MacMillan.

Morin, J-M. (2023). Ordinary Rationality Theory (ORT) According to Raymond Boudon. In: Bulle N. and Di Iorio F. (eds.), *The Palgrave Handbook of Methodological Individualism: Volume I*. London: Palgrave MacMillan.

Nagel, E. (1961). *The Structure of Science*. New York: Harcourt Brace & World.

Opp, K. R. (2013a). Rational Choice Theory, the Logic of Explanation, Middle-range Theories and Analytical Sociology: A Reply to Gianluca Manzo and Petri Ylikoski. *Social Science Information* 52(3): 394–408.

———. (2013b). What is Analytical Sociology? Strengths and Weaknesses of a New Sociologicalresearch Program. *Social Science Information* 52(3): 329–260.

Popper, K. R. (1957). *The Poverty of Historicism*. Boston, MA: Beacon Press.

———. (1966). *The Open Society and Its Enemies, Vol. 1: The Spell of Plato*. Princeton, NJ: Princeton University Press.

Scriven, M. (1959). Truism as the Ground for Historical Explanation. In: Gardiner, P. (ed.) *Theories of History*. Glencoe: Free Press, pp. 443–475.

Tocqueville, A. (1896). *The Recollections of Alexis de Tocqueville*. New York: The Macmillan Co.

———. (2002). *Democracy in America*. Chicago: University of Chicago Press.

Weber, M. (1968 [1922]). *Economy and Society: An Outline of Interpretive Sociology*. New York: Bedminster Press, 1968.

———. (2005 [1903–6]). *Roscher and Knies and the Logical Problems of Political Economy*. New York: Free Press.

———. (2010 [1904–1905]). *The Protestant Ethic and the Spirit of Capitalism*. Oxford: Oxford University Press.

———. (2019). *Economy and Society*. Cambridge, MA: Harvard University Press.

Wrong, D. H. (1961). The Oversocialized Conception of Man in Modern Sociology. *American Sociological Review* 26(2):183–193 (Apr. 1961).

Chapter 3

THE IDEA OF RATIONALITY IN RAYMOND BOUDON'S THEORY: A DISCUSSION

Pierre Demeulenaere

It can be said that the development of a theory of rationality is at the core of Raymond Boudon's general conceptualization of social life based on individual human behaviors. His attempt at reframing the commonly accepted so-called rational choice theory (RCT) is very important and has indeed a very ambitious scope: interpreting most of the human and social behaviors on the basis of rational attitudes. His aim is thus to restore a more comprehensive sense of rationality than the one that currently prevails in the framework of the RCT, in order specially to include the normative dimension of preferences and values. In his perspective, this implies going beyond a restriction of the idea of rationality to its "instrumental" dimension, that is the means/end relationship, and including in its jurisdiction the "ends" themselves that are predominantly left outside the domain of rationality by the conventional economic approach.

In this respect, it is clear that Boudon follows Weber in two directions: first, he is interested in interpreting peoples' behaviors in terms of motives, those motives being equated to "reasons," the latter concept implying then for him a direct link with the idea of rationality; second, this idea of "reasons," further associated with "good reasons" implies a sense of "relevance," or of correctness, that can be found in people's behaviors, and that includes, through "axiological" rationality, the normative preferences involving a sense of duty. I will argue in this chapter that, although Boudon considers himself as a follower of Weber in this emphasis on the so-called axiological rationality, he develops nevertheless a theory that goes beyond, in a significant way, Weber's classical position, in particular, regarding the issue of the relativity of values. When he extends the scope of correctness to the domain of values, his move can be seen as partly opposed to Weber's commonly understood legacy.

More generally, his insistence on the rationality of choices implies that people are responsible for their choices and the values they endorse, and therefore cannot be said to be only radically "socialized." Boudon defends on the one hand a notion of rationality that highlights the possibilities of interpretation of actions as irreducible to two "causal" deterministic frameworks: one that refers to "psychological" prerational or irrational properties and the other that would refer norms and values to various cultural or social variations alien to any dimension of rationality. But, on the other hand, he develops the idea that rationality should not be equated with "utilitarian" rationality, equated with instrumental rationality, of the type commonly understood in contemporary social sciences.

Boudon's theory has been mainly developed in French through various books and papers I will refer to in this chapter. Useful summaries of his position in English are also available (1989; 2011).

Going Beyond "Rational Choice Theory"

Boudon's main aim is to reaffirm the importance of the idea of rationality against a causal approach to behaviors that would explain them either on the basis of unconscious psychological determinants, or, conversely, of a socialization foreign to any deliberation. However, in doing so, he distances his theory of rationality from the one that currently prevails in the social sciences which is considered to be only a subset of a more comprehensive approach.

Principles of explanation in the social sciences

Boudon reconsiders the idea of what a rational choice is and modifies its basic characteristics that prevail in the contemporary social sciences literature. His aim is to depart from a so-called utilitarian instrumental rationality and to introduce, in complement to it, the notion of axiological rationality.

He outlines three basic general assumptions that must be retained in order to interpret social behaviors, and three others that are not necessary (although important in some explanation procedures that are however limited, not general). The three basic propositions are (Boudon 2009, 29–31):

  P1: the individualism postulate. It implies that all social phenomena should be explained on the basis of individual actions.

  P2: the "understanding" postulate, which implies the importance of finding out the "meaning" actions have for actors.

  P3: the rationality principle, which is that people have "reasons" to do what they do.

Those three principles are considered to be indispensable to any explanatory device in social sciences. They lead, however, to the issue of determining what it is exactly to "understand" an action, and to which extent it can be labeled as "rational."

In addition to these three principles, he declares as being *always* valid, Boudon associates RCT with three other postulates he asserts as only *sometimes* valid; his strategy is to accept them for specific local analyses, but to insert them in a broader framework that goes beyond their intrinsic limitation:

P4: "consequentialism," which is that the meaning of an action is related to its consequences for the actor.

P5: "selfishness," which is that the only consequences that interest an actor are the ones that affect him directly.

P6: the "cost/benefit" analysis, which stipulates that an actor always tries to maximize his "advantages" or equivalently to minimize his "costs."

Those three latter principles are altogether labeled as "instrumental," and therefore linked to the concept of "instrumental rationality," which is also associated with the idea of "utilitarianism." Utilitarianism is related to a series of authors including Bentham, Pareto, and the preeminent contemporary leaders of the rational choice movement (Gary Becker and James Coleman in particular).

Ordinary rationality

Consequently, in opposition to such a "narrow" definition of rationality set up by those three latter principles, Boudon seeks to introduce a sense of "ordinary" rationality (he had previously named it "subjective" rationality), which is thus not necessarily instrumental, nor necessarily utilitarian, but can also include all the dimensions of an action, in particular, the preferences and the values, notoriously left outside the realm of rationality by the economic approach since Pareto. He stresses that decisions typically function in the same way for the normative issues as for the descriptive ones, that is that they both rest on "reasons" that are found satisfactory by actors given their position. This is the central proposition of ordinary rationality.

This idea of "ordinary" rationality displays thus four basic features:

First, it corresponds to the fact that it is not dependent on cultural attitudes: It is consubstantial to human nature, and people are ordinarily rational, anteriorly to the variation of cultures. In particular, Boudon insists that we should not introduce some kind of pre-logic attitude in order to interpret a "primitive" mentality, the way Levy-Bruhl has conceptualized it.

However, Boudon has not developed a theory of the emergence of rationality in the human species, the way, for instance, Sperber and Mercier attempt to do so (Mercier and Sperber 2017). He takes this human feature as something that is given and he does not engage in explaining either its formation or its origin. He only insists on those ordinary competences of rationality and opposes them to either a naturalistic approach based on preconscious causal determinations or a radically "socialized" version of behavior. Both of them are said to be irrelevant approaches because they do not take into account the reasons people have to act in a certain way in a given situation with all its constraints.

The second main dimension of ordinary rationality is that it is not in any sense a "perfect" rationality, since it is strongly limited by the available information and the given resources in a specific context and a particular position. It adapts to various contexts. Boudon retains in this perspective Herbert Simon's legacy highlighting the limitation of rationality, but endeavors to go beyond Simon who is said to remain in the classical framework of "utilitarian" rationality. However, defining a limited rationality rests on the perspective of a more complete rationality. Boudon's theory describes on the one hand attitudes that are called rational in a complete sense and on the other hand beliefs or actions that can, although erroneous or incomplete from the standpoint of a more complete sense of rationality, be nevertheless considered as rational from the point of view of the situation of the actor. Error is thus not to be opposed to rationality. An example of that is magic which seems irrational to contemporary observers, but stops being so when we think that it occurs in a world where the notion of natural law has not yet been precisely formulated.

The third dimension is that ordinary rationality occurs in most aspects of decisions in social life, they are not limited to the choice of means given ends, that would for their part remain outside the domain of rationality. People have beliefs regarding their preferences and their values, they do not restrict them only to the means that lead to them. They also tend to consider that their preferences and their values are valid and legitimate, and they often tend to make them prevail because they have reasons to adopt them, and they assume that those reasons can be shared by others. Rationality is something that is shared by people.

The fourth dimension is that, although Boudon does not endorse the development of contemporary psychology (the one that follows Kahneman and Tversky in highlighting the importance of unconscious biases in decision-making), he nevertheless stresses the importance of a common "psychology," the one that is necessary to interpret ordinary behaviors. It is also related to an idea of "common sense." Boudon refers to Georg Simmel who had highlighted the necessity of such a standard psychology for the interpretation of historical events. There is, however, no attempt at defining the roots of this psychology, nor at linking it to the current cognitive psychology or to the cultural variation that is linked to psychology (Henrich 2020). It is a necessary tool for any interpretation, but it is irreducible either to cognitive biases or to cultural norms. Both do not allow for finding the "reasons" that are at play for the actors. Although Boudon knows that Simmel insists on the fundamental unpredictability of human psychology that can lead, in the face of similar events, to opposite actions and outcomes, he does not take into account the effects of this major uncertainty in his reference to Simmelian psychology, assessing it instead to a proof of the fact that people are not definitely socialized since they can always act in opposed ways.

Rational choice theory in perspective: the two different localizations of rationality and their conflation

It must be noted that Boudon's critique of RCT does not focus on its internal conceptual ambiguities, but on its external consequences: the basic difficulty he points at is that it cannot allow for an understanding of the sense of values that is so important for actors in their ordinary social life. This is why he constantly refers to Weber and to Durkheim who had both similarly stressed the role of values and the sense of duty in social life, which are absent from RCT. He does not either address directly the important epistemological reasons why such a deliberate restriction of the possible scope of rationality had been initially developed by philosophers and social scientists, except when he refers to the necessity of a "self-sufficient" theory: referring to the interests seems to constitute a self-sufficient explanation. I will briefly evoke those two aspects (the internal difficulties and the issue of the justification of the attribution of rationality) in order to characterize Boudon's contribution to the debate.

Boudon, when he describes the "utilitarian," "consequentialist," and "instrumental" theory of rationality, often refers to Bentham as the father of such a utilitarian tradition leading to RCT. However, it can be said that this RCT tradition is not fundamentally Benthamian, but Paretian in substance, because it departs from the substantive notion of utility initially displayed by Bentham. Vilfredo Pareto's theorization depends more on Hume than on Bentham (Demeulenaere 1996). Pareto has had a very important role in the framing of the issues leading to RCT, and his theory involves the difficulties linked to a "positivistic" approach and to a "utilitarian" one, as well as to a strict restriction of the idea of rationality to the choice of means. He can be seen as one of the major inspirers of RCT and of the three propositions linked by Boudon to the "instrumental" version of rationality.

In Pareto's theory, there are two major positions that lead to one major uncertainty regarding the ultimate meaning of RCT and the localization of rationality in the so-called utilitarian and instrumental framing of rationality.

The first idea that underlies his approach is the Humean contrast (although Pareto never quotes Hume) between the description of a fact and the motives (or the values) that trigger an action. Any action rests on motives that can be triggered by various desires, sentiments, or residues, in his terminology, but those desires cannot technically correspond to the positive description of an external fact. Desiring an option is not describing it. Therefore, there is a contrast between the "logical" dimension of action (which is based on the possible description of the means, depending on external evidence), and the a-logical dimension (the motives). It is important to note that Pareto introduces the idea of a "judge" for controversies in order to define what a "logical" stance is: empirical evidence is the judge that can conclude any controversy regarding what a fact is (and this includes what the correct means are in order to achieve an end), but it cannot reconcile opposite contentions about values. This is the problem Boudon will precisely try to solve.

However, in addition to that, Pareto considers that economic actions (and technical ones) are logical because people in economic life tend to follow their interests. Where should then be located the idea of rationality in this respect? There is an ambiguity in Pareto's theory (and consequently in the RCT that is dependent on his legacy) of preferences. They involve personal preferences, like a preference for tea or coffee, as well as "moral" preferences, like preferences for justice or altruism. In this respect, Pareto claims two opposite things:

1. On the one hand, he insists on the fact that preferences are intrinsically different from one person to another, and this is why he replaces the notion of "utility" by the notion of "ophelimity" that reflects this inevitable tendency to divergence, based on natural differences among persons. Therefore, the notion of utility is not a substantial one, since it reflects essentially variable preferences (for instance, for tea or coffee). It is not a substantial notion, and therefore its Benthamian roots must be abandoned. In consequence, the theory cannot be called "utilitarian" in a Benthamian sense. This leads to the canonical problem of the interpersonal comparison of utility that has been set up by Pareto: if people's preferences are different, how can we compare them in terms of a common measure of utility? This leads him to the theorization of an *optimum* that does not rely on any specification of the preferences involved. And preferences are clearly outside the domain of a "logical" characterization.

2. However, on the other hand, Pareto states that people are mostly selfish, and that they often tend to follow their interests, whatever they are, although they sometimes have also altruistic attitudes. He also characterizes economic actions as logical, and he introduces the idea that people tend to act logically when their motives are selfish (in particular, when they pursue wealth and power). But it should be straightforwardly noted that this cannot involve the same sense of rationality as before.

There are here two competing different "localizations" of rationality that are at stake: one locates it in the choice of the means leading to some ends (whatever they are) and rests on empirical evidence; the other identifies a rational attitude with the selection of "selfish" economic ends, that is the choice of a certain type of preferences opposed to any kind of values that would prevent from such a "utilitarian" selfish attitude. Those are clearly two *different* constitutive elements of the current idea of "rational choice," which includes at the same time those two irreducible dimensions of rationality that are however often conflated: on one side the relevant choice of means regarding an end, that is the instrumental dimension, and on the other side the selection of specific (self-interested, or "utilitarian") preferences, set against values that would limit them, that is the "utilitarian" dimension.

But the attribution and the vindication of a "rationality" norm cannot be the same in the two cases. The first one refers to the empirical evidence of a fact (which is the empirical knowledge of what are the relevant means to achieve an end); the second one identifies rationality with the choice of certain specific ends, related to "utility" (whatever is the exact content of this notion), and to a "cost–benefit" analysis, as opposed to the submission to "values." This second dimension implies as has been said two issues: the difference of preferences and the possibility of its relatedness to a shared idea of utility; the interpretation of this choice of utility in terms of rationality, which can no longer rely on the idea of the evidence of an empirical fact.

Boudon's conception of what rational choice theory is

Where does Boudon stand regarding all those issues and what is his strategy? He does not make explicitly the distinction between those two localizations of rationality in the framework developed by Pareto (rationality of the choice of means whatever are the ends versus rationality of the choice of certain ends, that is so-called utilitarian ends). He criticizes a standard theory of rational choice which is itself relatively ambiguous and vague regarding the effective localization of the idea of rationality (again, either choice of means or choice of specific ends linked to "selfish interests"). He is not directly focused on discussing the norms that should allow a legitimate attribution of a "rationality" label, the way Pareto had introduced the idea of a "judge" incarnated by empirical evidence to resolve disputes. He instead equates being rational with "having reasons" to act in a certain way and elucidating these reasons that go beyond empirical evidence. These reasons can be, in his vocabulary, either utilitarian or non-utilitarian. He sometimes refers to a "utilitarian" notion of preferences, but at times acknowledges that utility does depend on various preferences that cannot be linked to a substantial definition of utility in a simple way. He does not engage in a reflection on what justifies the attribution of rational properties and the legitimation of those properties in terms of rationality. His direct aim is to oppose (following Kant as well as Durkheim or Weber) the idea that people are constantly selfish, in order to introduce a sense of "duty" and commitment to values; and to interpret this sense of duty and values in terms of rationality, and therefore to characterize a notion of rationality that fits those objectives. In this perspective, having reasons to act can include either utilitarian or non-utilitarian motives. The problem becomes then to understand the way people make their decisions when they can act either on the basis of selfish utilitarian motives or on the basis of values that are opposed to them, if both attitudes can be said rational because they equally stem from reasons. Boudon will in this case develop a sort of predominance of axiological rationality over instrumental rationality.

It can be argued, however, that the common endorsement of the "instrumental rationality" label for characterizing the idea of rationality involved in the RCT is inaccurate for three reasons corresponding to the three dimensions Boudon selects.

- First, a moral reasoning or a dedication to values can indeed also be consequentialist, as Weber notes himself: consequentialism is canonically opposed to "deontology," but this is something that can intervene *within* the realm of moral reasoning when it takes into account opposed attitudes toward moral principles. It is not necessarily a conflict between selfish amoral or immoral consequentialism on one side and a moral deontological behavior on the other: for instance, in the so-called trolley problem, should I kill some people if this allows me avoiding a more important killing, or should I exclude any kind of such endeavor out of respect of a definitive non-killing imperative—leading however to more deaths (Greene 2013)? Consequentialism is a moral debate that often does involve moral principles, it is not necessarily something that should be seen as opposed to any sense of morality and to the prevalence of utilitarian motives. This is a point that had been developed by Weber himself in his famous essay about the politician's calling: he has the choice between either sticking to his moral principles or assessing the consequences of his action regarding those principles, and then making a compromise with them, but in order to make those principles *more successful* at the end of the day by taking into account the foreseen consequences of his action. Clearly, in both cases, he is interested in moral principles. Therefore, the importance of values does not necessarily imply a departure from consequentialism, since consequentialism can be a feature of moral reasoning. In addition to that, Weber, when he introduces the sense of duty in order to characterize axiological rationality, insists himself on the fact that there is no clear gap between the two dimensions, since individual interests can involve value dimensions.

- Second, selfishness is a complex issue, since, in Pareto's thinking, it can be said to be formal or substantial: substantially, being selfish corresponds to the fact that one typically prefers her own interests to the others' when the same interests are at stake, in particular, in the pursuit of wealth, or power, in typical zero-sum games situations. But since Pareto notes as well that the notion of wealth itself is not unequivocal, because people may have different preferences, this leads to a more formal notion of interests, whatever their content is, which can be conflicting on the basis of moral values as well (when, for example, different religions oppose each other). Therefore, in instrumental action, the well-being of others can be present and taken into account.

- Finally, and this is a consequence of all that has been said previously, the very notion of cost and benefit analysis is not a straightforward one: since, in Pareto's analysis, costs and benefits ultimately depend on various preferences that can be sometimes opposed.

It can be noted that Coleman's theory somehow reproduces itself this ambivalence: on one side, he evokes instrumental rationality and the fact that preferences are arbitrary, but on the other side, he builds up a model of preferences based on narrow selfish "interests." And in fact, he also refers to, the way Boudon does, "reasons," and to an ordinary understanding of human behaviors (Demeulenaere 2022).

Axiological Rationality

In order to go beyond the restrictions of "instrumental rationality," Boudon introduces the ideas of "cognitive" rationality and "axiological" rationality, both of them integrated into the more general and inclusive category of "ordinary" rationality. The exact attribution of rationality properties in Boudon's theory does not rely on a discussion and exploration of the possibilities and limits of what ultimately vindicates the attribution to these properties of a "rationality" qualification. He is more interested in modeling behaviors, and in "extending" a model of rationality in order to allow introducing normative dimensions within its domain (Manzo 2012). He is not satisfied with the fact that, despite people having "good reasons" for defending their normative choices, RCT cannot make sense of that. People can have utilitarian reasons, but they typically also have non-utilitarian reasons that depend on cognitive or axiological rationality.

Boudon's theory of ordinary rationality regarding the issue of normative rationality has two main dimensions: one that links the idea of rationality, in a rather classical way, to the "reasons" one has to act in a certain way, which is a classical approach in the interpretation of historical events (Collingwood 1946; Dray 1964), following Simmel and Weber. I will argue here that this traditional path does not necessarily lead to the satisfaction of Boudon's claim regarding normative issues, which is to go beyond a relativistic interpretation of them and to set up a consensual normative common framework. Reasons can indeed only refer to various social situations and social norms people endorse in such situations that do not necessarily correspond to a unified set of values stemming from a convergent axiological rationality in a stronger sense.

Therefore, second, he introduces, in addition to this general approach, more substantial elements in order to explain and justify, in a foundational perspective, the roots of those normative behaviors, beyond the relativity of the various norms linked to various reasons or permitting various reasons. Those fundamental principles allow at the same time giving a sound basis to normative claims and explaining their variety and divergence. This leads him to a theory of changes of values and to an effort to articulate the idea of "objective" values and their tendency to change.

Reasons and good reasons: the foundational motives of axiological attitudes

Boudon takes many examples from the classical authors of social sciences in order to highlight the fact that, even in normative affairs, people have "good reasons" to do what they do. One of his favorite examples is taken from Weber's analysis of religious attitudes. He contrasts the fact that peasants were reluctant to adopt Mithraism in the Roman Empire with the beliefs of the bureaucrats who were inclined to do so. How to explain that? The peasants are interested in the various natural forces that can have an effect on their crops, and therefore they feel motivated by a polytheist religion that gives importance to those plural elements; on the opposite, the Roman bureaucrats have a strong sense of hierarchy and of the unicity of power, and this leads them to be attracted by a religion—Mithraism—that reflects such an integrative source of power. The "reasons" here introduced by Boudon, following Weber, correspond to an *affinity* between one's social situation and one's religious beliefs. He does not, however, explore here the involvement of what a more demanding rationality would require beyond this intrinsic diversity of religious preferences associated with various social situations. The preferences are here clearly "understood," they correspond to motives, and therefore to "reasons," but it is less obvious that they can be genuinely called "rational" in any stronger sense—the sense Boudon advocates and wants to push forward in order to combat relativism. In the domain of religious beliefs, he asserts at the same time that religions correspond to efforts at solving problems (and he gives some examples of that, like the emergence of the notion of soul); but he adds that, at the end of the day, there is no real possibility of solving them in a conclusive manner.

Boudon introduces regarding this notion of reasons two different levels: one is reasons and the other is "good" reasons. Although he does not conceptualize a very sharp characterization of the distinction between those two orientations, it can be related to the idea that people obey a *system* of reasons and that they will tend to adopt the "best" one available to them. The issue is then to see what characterizes the fact that one system of reasons is "better" than another, and whether people do have access to other reasons or not. It is likely that in this religious example of Mithraism people do have access to other beliefs and to other reasons that could lead them in other directions. It is not the same case as in the situation of the "primitive" people where no one has the idea of a natural law, and where therefore magic cannot be contrasted with a science based on such natural laws that have not yet been theorized.

In order to resolve this issue of defining "good" reasons, Boudon introduces three substantial dimensions for the foundation of normative attitudes; he adds to them, moreover, a general principle of selection governing their evolution.

The first one is the idea of an "ordinary" psychology we have already described. Boudon refers to common typical attitudes that are the bedrock of rationality, and that are anterior to and more fundamental than the cultural variety of norms and the different social situations. He does not formalize or enumerate the constitutive elements of this common psychology, which is illustrated through various examples. Religious beliefs are thus submitted to such an ordinary psychology underlying attitudes (for instance, the one that relates a given social situation as an influence for encouraging a set of beliefs). However, Boudon does not equate this ordinary psychology with cognitive psychology that highlights the role of various *unconscious* biases. He rejects indeed this path for two reasons: one is that it is considered to be an *ad hoc* interpretation of behaviors, and therefore it is not explanatory, because it does not take into account the actual reasons people have to behave in a certain sense. On the contrary, ordinary psychology is not *ad hoc* because it is common and general; and second because people can be conscious of their reasoning leading to their choices, it is not reducible to causes the actor is not aware of. It can be said nevertheless that there is also a causal dimension in this ordinary psychology he refers to, since people do not choose to be submitted to its requirements. Boudon does not explore this path since he is not engaged in elucidating and tracing the origins of this ordinary psychology. It can be added that Boudon, however, refers himself at times implicitly to what may resort to unconscious biases in the explanation of people's attitudes: for instance, he mentions the fact that people will tend to adopt erroneous ideas because they are "simple" devices easy to remember or to understand (this echoes Kahneman's theory (Kahneman 2011) of *fast thinking*). For example, in trying to explain why intellectuals reject liberalism, Boudon highlights the role of simple ideas that seem explanatory and easy to understand (Boudon 2004). He adds, following in this Pareto, that people will often adopt ideas because they find them *useful*, not because they are true, which means that there is a causal role of *desire* that leads to the adoption of a belief beyond the sole appreciation of its veracity: clearly, this cannot be said to depend on strictly conscious reflexive attitudes.

The second foundational dimension of normative attitudes is the central idea of human "dignity." This is something he refers to constantly, as the ultimate basis of all moral reasoning; he does not, however, develop why it is so, but considers that it relies on an *indemonstrable* principle (available among others). He says two somehow different things about this importance of human dignity in social life: on one side, it is not a historical value, it is congenial to human life. He equates it to "individualism" in the sense of an interest in individual values (that is the protection of individual persons). This interest appears everywhere (this affirmation is based on quotations from Durkheim or Simmel). However, on the other side, Boudon does locate a development of the notion of human dignity in history and considers that some periods are more favorable to its full realization than others. He describes notably a contemporary "irreversible" acceptance of democracy in an assumed evolutionary fashion. He does not explain why in certain times and circumstances people do not respect at all this human dignity principle (e.g., in the case of slavery) despite its effective availability. An alternative analysis would be to follow the appearance and disappearance of democracy in other ways than an evolutionary irreversible trend (Baechler 1985; Stasavage 2020).

The third foundational normative principle is the idea of an impartial spectator, taken from Adam Smith and that is likened to Rousseau's theory of *volonté générale*. The initial idea is that, in a social dilemma, people have at the same time an interest in adopting a rule that is beneficial to everyone, but also an interest in not respecting this rule. This major classical problem leads Boudon to introducing the specific notion of *axiological rationality* which is that people will tend to adopt a norm that is in the interest of everyone, although it can be in the interest of the person not to respect the norm. It is the case in the paradox of voting. The common idea of morality, as opposed to one's interest, is here equated with the notion of axiological rationality. There is here a rational justification of a moral behavior that cannot be interpreted on the basis of strictly individual interests (and therefore by RCT). This theory involves however two different things: first, the definition of a norm that should be beneficial to all participants (and that includes therefore some kind of "utilitarian" motive); second, the fact that people will tend to respect the norm. Those are in fact two different issues that are however subsumed in the same notion of axiological rationality.

This is (although he does not really develop the argument in depth) an important vindication for "liberalism" he refers to, that is an institutional framework that fundamentally respects the dignity of everyone and the management of their interests. Boudon does not address the details and the difficulties of the emergence of such a normative framework, nor does he explain all the limitations of such an emergence. He does not either make an explicit link between the issue of "interests" that lead, in a social dilemma, to the demand of norms, and the overall issue of human dignity, although both dimensions are convocated in order to build up the legitimacy of liberalism.

Consequently, the values have basically two dimensions regarding those major foundational principles of human dignity and of the impartial spectator: the ones that derive directly from them, and the ones that do not. Although Boudon does not present things in such a direct deductive way, many values he stresses as being "objective" and important in the contemporary societies stem in fact from political liberalism: in particular, the importance of the separation of institutional powers, the rejection of slavery, the ban on excision, the acceptance of homosexual rights, etc. Regarding those, and in particular the right of homosexual couples to adopt children, we have a good example of Boudon's way of illustrating what axiological rationality is and its relation to instrumental rationality (Boudon 2007: 327). He says that we have no information regarding the psychological situation of children adopted by homosexual couples. Despite that, there is a clear normative vindication of the right of homosexual couples to adopt children, based on the idea of equality of rights. It is therefore referred to as an axiological rationality that should prevail over instrumental (consequentialist) rationality, since, on the basis of the latter, it cannot clearly be said what the *consequences* are for children. However, it should be noted that, in this example, the issue of consequences clearly involves itself an axiological dimension, which is that children, in principle, should not be harmed. This is a very important normative principle in contemporary societies, and this demonstrates here that the instrumental consequential rationality depends in fact ultimately on a reference to accepted values, if we consider that children should not be harmed. Therefore, it cannot be straightforwardly opposed to axiological rationality. If there was some kind of evidence that children adopted by homosexual couples were harmed, it is clear that there would be here a normative conflicting issue (the right of children not to be harmed, and the rights of homosexual couples), and this would not be a conflict between instrumental rationality and axiological rationality. Here clearly the issue is that there is a convergence of norms, and this convergence stops if they are seen to be conflicting, and that would not be a case of opposition between instrumental rationality and axiological rationality, but a case of opposition between different values.

Boudon refers also to many values that cannot easily derive directly from this principle of equal human dignity in a democratic society. A very important issue is that of inequality. Are there norms related to inequality that can be vindicated on a rational basis and especially in a society that claims the equality of rights? Boudon has here three basic propositions. The first one is the affirmation of basic equal rights, which corresponds to political liberalism, depending itself on the affirmation of equal human dignity. He does not discuss extensively the link, similarity or difference, between political and economic liberalism. He evokes very rapidly the importance of property rights, that are said to be linked to liberalism in general, but there is no theory of the status of those rights. A second position regarding inequality is the importance of equality of opportunity. Boudon has in fact strongly contributed to the explanation of the social factors that inhibit the possibility of an effective equality of opportunity. However, he reaffirms the importance of this value and favors the practical policies that can reinforce it, and conversely criticizes the ones that impede it. It must be added here that if there is fundamentally a possibility for equality of opportunity, it is precisely because people are rational, that is not subordinated to a socialization that would definitively inhibit their aspiration to higher positions. Finally, in addition to the importance of equality of rights and equality of opportunities, Boudon accepts the idea that there are legitimate inequalities: he says two things regarding this. One is that there are some that are "functional," and therefore acceptable because of this functionality, and he makes therefore a difference between inequalities that are acceptable because they correspond to various competences, and the ones that are not acceptable because they rest on "privileges" (which would go beyond what is acceptable for an impartial spectator). He does not however describe exactly what a privilege is in a contemporary society, and whether inequalities can directly favor privileges. He adds to this idea of functionality the principle of proportionality between contribution and retribution, that is sometimes possible to measure, sometimes not. He consequently stresses the importance of taxes: they are set up in order to help "the poor," and therefore are imposed on the middle class, because it is the most numerous. The consequence of this is that the burden should be shared as well by the richest so that the middle class does not have the feeling of being in a disadvantaged position. This leads to an introduction of progressive taxation based on progressive income. Boudon does not discuss however the issue of the importance of inequalities on the level of taxes, and whether it is strictly functional, and corresponds genuinely or not to a meritocratic principle. The issue of inheritance is briefly associated with the idea of merit. He does not address either the issue of externalities. He often emphasizes the principle that a legitimate order is one where one should do whatever he wants provided he does not harm others: the existence of externalities clearly violates this principle, but Boudon does not address this difficulty.

In this example of taxation, he introduces again a contrast between axiological rationality and instrumental rationality. If taxes are too high, they will favor tax evasion, which is associated to "instrumental rationality," as opposed to the "axiological rationality" that leads to accepting paying moderately progressive taxes. But this division can be contested, because if one person accepts paying taxes on the basis of normative requirements and stops doing so because the taxes are perceived as too high, it can be said that it is equally on the basis of normative principles (if the person finds the taxes too high). Conversely, if the idea of the refusal of paying higher taxes is due to the consequences (for oneself, or for the general economy), then it should be admitted that the acceptance of a lower level of taxes is itself linked to the perception of acceptable consequences for oneself or for the economy.

Thus the opposition between interests and values is not necessarily linked to a contrast between two types of rationality (Demeulenaere 2014; Gravel and Picavet 2000). And it is difficult to understand why people, when they have the choice between an interested behavior and a normative behavior opposed to the interested one, will select one or another.

Rationalization and selection of values

Boudon has stated the possibility of going beyond the arbitrariness of values, naming them "objective" as opposed to "relativism." An obvious difficulty for that claim is that values tend to vary, which is the main argument in favor of relativism. Boudon addresses this difficulty with a triple strategy:

- First, he stresses the existence of stable values, that are not essentially variable, but that depend for their full development (however, never achieved) on various given historical circumstances. Of that kind (and in fact the central one) is human dignity, which is related to "individualism" (because it values every individual person).
- Second, he proposes an evolutionary selection mechanism whereby new ideas appear and are thereafter selected on the basis of human dignity (2008: 81). This is not opposed to the previous one, since those new ideas that are selected are not incompatible with the main stable one, or can stem from it, but Boudon suggests here that there are new institutional arrangements that appear, which are consequently selected. The two main examples here are democracy and, within democracy, the separation of institutional powers. The move toward democracy and the separation of powers is seen as "irreversible."
- Third, this selection is interpreted in terms of "rationalization," a notion borrowed from Weber. Weber's rationalization notion encompasses two main dimensions: one is systematization, such as when a set of beliefs or norms becomes more systematic if it is unified by a limited number of principles; it is the case, for instance, of the principles of natural law from which many given particular rights can be deduced. The second main dimension of rationalization in Weber's theory is the growing importance of factual, causal, and scientific knowledge, which leads to a departure from magical attitudes and religious beliefs, religion becoming ultimately the "irrational" force, because it is not based on factual or scientific knowledge. In this perspective, values themselves cannot derive from scientific knowledge. Boudon contends—controversially—that Weber's theory should be moreover interpreted as a selection mechanism that leads to the prevalence of norms that can be justified on a rational basis, that is, fundamentally, liberal democracy, derived from the principles of human dignity. I am not sure that Weber's writings can support straightforwardly such an interpretation. But whatever is the case, the more fundamental issue is whether this is an acceptable theory, independently of what Weber really meant. I will shortly discuss this point.

Boudon has engaged extensively in a comparative approach to social phenomena that is characteristic of classical sociology. This allows him to explain various attitudes on the basis of common behavioral patterns confronted to different circumstances. For instance, he refers to an analysis developed by Tocqueville who explains the contrast between England and France regarding aristocracy. In France, the aristocracy was interested in gaining advantages from the court and the very strong royal power, whereas in England, as a class of landowners represented in the Parliament, it had a more direct interest in trying to take care of the local situation in order to be elected. This explains in consequence the very different attitudes toward the aristocracy in the two countries: a more favorable one in England, and the rejection of its privileges in France (2010: 64). But those motives, depending on a "common psychology" (which corresponds here to what Boudon names "utilitarian" motives), applied to different circumstances, does not allow the idea that one institutional system is as such more *rational* that the other, or that the values related to the two situations are objective in one case and not in the other, or that there is a selection mechanism that ultimately favors one at the expense of the other: there are *reasons* in both cases. In order to go beyond this difficulty, Boudon defends the intrinsic validity of certain values, which is the basis of their selection. In order to do so, he refers to an idea of wide *acceptance*. But he does not explain why, precisely, they are frequently not accepted, except when referring to "historical circumstances." In the Darwinian model of selection, there is a clear criterion for the spread of certain mutations, which is the fact that they are adaptive in a given environment, and this consequently favors their selection. There is no problem understanding the anterior situation of a species before new mutations have intervened. Here, in the domain of values, especially since there are stable values like human dignity, of which people are in principle aware, in any circumstance, we should understand why in some situations it is respected and why it is not in others. There are some examples of adaptation, for instance, the aristocracies' attitudes and the attitudes toward aristocracies in France and England, based on previous different historical events. But, more generally, there is no clear criterion for understanding why, for example, when the notion of human dignity is already available, it is rejected, and why there is slavery in certain situations, or why there is a sense of inherited hierarchy that goes beyond the principle of a relationship between contribution and retribution. Boudon equates Weber's rationalization theory with a principle of moral *progress*: but here again, the idea implies the *general acceptance* of the new values and poses the problem of all the controversies regarding their actual adoption and the variety of their possible interpretation. Boudon refers to "historical forces" that stop them, but he offers no general theory for explaining why there is no unanimous support for the values that are named objective.

The limits of rationalization

Boudon does not say however that everything can be perfectly rationalized and homogenized on this basis. He sees three major limits to that. The first one is that there are always different possible arrangements of the basic institutions and norms, even when they are clearly expressing a concern for human dignity.

Therefore, there is room for some social and historical diversity that is not reducible to a unique rational option. Esthetic values have been included by him to this possibility of rational judgment that selects the "objective" values in art, but he has not developed an analysis of all the "preferences" that are constitutive of economic life and are clearly related in various ways to the social fabric (in a certainly more complex way than a reference to a homogenous notion of utility criticized by Pareto the way we have seen), and that are constitutive of the rational choice model that necessarily includes such various preferences.

Second, he insists on the importance of social customs that are different from one society to another. This excludes social norms that can be rationalized (for instance, excision or death penalty), but this gives room to different ways of organizing social life, the expression of politeness, for example. In this sense, there is thus a possibility of various social norms foreign to the constraint of rationality. He has not displayed a precise analysis of what a social custom is as opposed to a moral issue subjected to rational judgment. Boudon has not addressed either the issue of the various conflicts that occur on the basis of the separation of groups linked to various cultural norms (subjected or not to a norm of rationality).

Finally, there is the case of religion: Boudon says two different things regarding it. On one side, he describes religion as a set of beliefs addressed at resolving problems, and thus subjected to cognitive rationality. In this sense, religion is rational. However, he also says that since religious matters cannot be ultimately decided on an empirical basis, different types of beliefs are possible, and there is no possible rational convergence to unity in this respect.

Fact and value, cognitive and axiological rationality

Boudon maintains the distinction between fact and value that had been theorized by David Hume. We have an illustration of this stance in the following quotation:

> The correct statement of Hume's theorem is as follows: one cannot draw a conclusion in the imperative from premises that are all in the indicative. Or: a prescriptive conclusion can result from a system of reasons in the indicative, provided that at least one of them is in the imperative. It suffices that, in a system of reasons, a single reason be in the imperative for one to be able to draw a conclusion in the imperative. Reasoning as simple as "red lights are a *good* thing and worth installing, because traffic would be even worse without them" suffices to confirm that normative or appreciative judgments are commonly derived from both factual reasons and normative or appreciative reasons. (Boudon 2008, 15–16)

This distinction between fact and value does not lead to any kind of relativism, for two reasons.

First, any knowledge rests on *indemonstrable* principles, but this is also the case in scientific knowledge which aims at objectivity, therefore the normative field is not distinct from the positive one in this respect. Second, a normative assessment can include at the same time positive affirmations and normative ones. Therefore, the normative engagement can be founded on a mixed combination that includes normative affirmations. This can be derived easily from Weber's general principles. He admits that knowledge is based on indemonstrable principles, and he says that from normative principles, when they are accepted, can derive normative injunctions. Boudon at the same time maintains a separation between the descriptive and the normative (which is commonly the basis of the distinction of the "objective" and the "subjective," although nonobjective does not necessarily mean something that is arbitrary, since there can be common "subjective" reactions to an event), and considers that the normative is however "objective." How does he reconcile those two contentions? As has been outlined previously, the idea is that there are "reasons" in both the descriptive and the normative judgments, despite their status distinction. Those reasons are susceptible to triggering consensus, either in the scientific and factual knowledge or in the normative one, and therefore the difference among them is limited. I believe this is why Boudon mentions the idea of an "objectivity" of values. By this appellation, it is likely that he refers more to something that should be uncontested than to a true objectivity of the type of factual evidence, since he does maintain the contrast between positive knowledge and normative knowledge.

We can analyze the example of the role of the very simple normative assessment he gives in the previous quotation, about traffic lights, and see how it articulates the positive dimension and the type of consensus it requires. It can be seen as an example of simple instrumental rationality: it is empirically proven that traffic lights are useful to make traffic easier; consequently, *if* we want traffic to be easier, then we *can* adopt traffic lights. This implies:

- One positive consensus derived from factual evidence (when appropriately perceived):
  1. that traffic lights make traffic easier, and
- Two normative consensuses:
  1. people want to make the traffic easier and
  2. people are ready to adopt traffic lights in order to achieve that end.

Thus, there are three different moments in the collective decision if it is made. However, it is clear that there is a contrast between the first proposition (which can be easily characterized as "objective," even if the setting of traffic lights is not the only available means to control the traffic) and the two following ones which require a normative consensus. It is not obvious that everyone wants to make the traffic easier (for instance, some cities want to suppress the traffic or make it slower), and in order to manage the traffic, there are different possible options (like roundabouts and priority signs at a roundabout, or toll systems). Moreover, if traffic lights are set up, one driver can find it in her interest not to respect them, and this will trigger the issue of the role of sanctions and the legitimate importance of those sanctions (in a social dilemma): is it acceptable to have very important sanctions (based, for instance, on cameras), or should this be banned in order to respect a certain sense of freedom? So from the simple fact that traffic lights help regulate traffic, it seems hard to derive directly a normative imperative that people should adopt traffic lights similar to the evidence that traffic lights help regulate the traffic. It happens frequently that people agree on that, because they have reasons to do so, but it can happen also that they do not agree (because they have other reasons linked to different conceptions of how the traffic should be managed), and therefore there is no simple "objectivity" here. The problem of the contrast between factual and normative knowledge stems from situations where precisely there is no necessary common *agreement* on the various normative principles (from which derive separately various practical consequences that are seen as obligations if the principles are seen as mandatory). For instance, should traffic be banned from the center of a city? Should speed be severely limited by traffic lights, or on the contrary authorized in a city, and so on? The fact that there are indemonstrable principles does not preclude from the possibility of a conflict between them, or of the fact that there is no consensus in adopting the consequences of the same principles. The difficult thing is to understand why people achieve common agreements, or not.

It is the case also for the notion of "cognitive" rationality introduced by Boudon along instrumental and axiological types. It rests ultimately on principles that are not demonstrable. Boudon here makes two cases: first, cognitive rationality is opposed to instrumental and axiological rationality; second, it obeys, similarly, to reasons that evolve in different contexts, and therefore is by no way opposed to objectivity. However, it should be stressed that any notion of instrumental rationality implies a sense of cognition that allows people to recognize the proper means leading to given ends. This implies a sense of objectivity that relies on the evidence (if it is available) of a fact that depends on a cognitive approach. When Boudon opposes it to instrumental rationality, he has in mind the interests motivating an action, that are constrained by a cognitive dimension: but it is inevitably present in the classical notion of instrumental rationality and should not be seen as different from it.

Finally, I would like to make a general comment on the very use of the notion of reasons. In French and in English, a verbal link can be made between the word "reasons" (in the sense of having reasons to act) and the word "Reason" (as the general ability to be rational); therefore a linguistic link exists between the notion of rationality and the notion of reasons. This is clearly not the case in German, and that reduces the intrinsic conceptual link between the two notions. It is interesting to note that Weber, since he writes in German, does not equate "motives" with "reasons" in a rational sense of what would be justified by a rational approach. He makes the distinction between the two. This is of major importance regarding any theory of rationality. Boudon has attempted to reconcile normative and positive beliefs dimension through this notion of reasons, linking them to indemonstrable principles in both cases. The issue is, however, to see whether those principles can be genuinely reconciliatory of whether they still allow room for major dissensions.

References

Baechler, J. (1985). *Démocraties*. Paris: Calmann-Lévy.

Boudon, R. (1989). Subjective Rationality and the Explanation of Social Behavior. *Rationality and Society* 1(2): 173–196.

———. (2004). *Pourquoi les intellectuels n'aiment pas le libéralisme?* Paris: Odile Jacob.

———. (2007). *Essais sur la théorie générale de la rationalité*. Paris: Presses Universitaires de France.

———. (2008). *Le relativisme*. Paris: Presses Universitaires de France.

———. (2009). *La rationalité*. Paris: Presses Universitaires de France.

———. (2010). *La sociologie comme science*. Paris: La découverte.

———. (2011). Ordinary Rationality: The Core of Analytical Sociology. In: P. Demeulenaere (ed.), *Analytical Sociology and Social Mechanisms*. Cambridge: Cambridge University Press, 33–49.

Collingwood, R. G. ([1946] revised edition 1993). *The Idea of History*. Oxford: Oxford University Press.

Demeulenaere, P. (1996). *Homo oeconomicus, Enquête sur la constitution d'un paradigme*. Paris: P.U.F. Réédition « Quadrige », 2003.

———. (2014). Are There Many Types of Rationality? *Papers, Revista de sociologia* 99(4): 515–528.

———. (2022). Rationalité, intérêts et normes dans la théorie du choix rationnel de James S. Coleman. In: F. Blanchot and P. Maclouf (eds.), *Conduite et fondements de l'action organisée. Une mise en perspective pluridisciplinaire autour de James S. Coleman*. Paris: Editions EMS, 161–177.

Dray, W. H. (1993 [1964]). *Philosophy of History*. Upper Saddle River, NJ: Prentice Hall.

Gravel, N. and Picavet, E. (2000). Une théorie cognitiviste de la rationalité axiologique. *L'Année sociologique* 50(1): 85–118.

Greene, J. (2013). *Moral Tribes. Emotion, Reason, and the Gap between Us and Them*. New York: Penguin Books.

Henrich, J. (2020). *The Weirdest People in the World. How The West Became Psychologically Peculiar and Particularly Prosperous*. Allen Lane: Penguin Books.

Kahneman, D. (2011). *Thinking Fast and Slow*. New York: Farar, Straus and Giroux.

Manzo, G. (2012). Reason-Based Explanations and Analytical Sociology. *Revue Européenne de sciences sociales* 50–2: 35–65.

Mercier, H. and Sperber, D. (2017). *The Enigma of Reason. A New Theory of Human Understanding*. Allen Lane: Penguin Books.

Stasavage, D. (2020). *The Decline and Rise of Democracy. A Global History from Antiquity to Today*. Princeton: Princeton University Press.

Chapter 4

RAYMOND BOUDON AND MORAL VALUE JUDGMENTS: INTERACTION AND SUBSTANCE

Emmanuel Picavet[1]

Introduction

Raymond Boudon (1934–2013) developed a theory of values and normative beliefs that makes his sociological work a substantial contribution to debates—both theoretical and applied—on axiology. Raymond Boudon's *Le Juste et le vrai* and closely related writings, under focus here, have offered a comprehensive theory in the field. The author's axiology is rooted in the Weberian legacy of a general contrast between value-based rationality and goal-oriented rationality. The way in which this legacy has borne fruit in Boudon's work reflects a wide-ranging investigation of the scope and limits of so-called instrumental rationality and consequence-based explanation, as well as in-depth reflections about ethical inquiry as an object for social sciences. In contrast with the methodological choices in important sectors of individualistic social science (including the vast majority of contributions to so-called orthodox economics), rationality and morality appear to be closely associated in Boudon's thought and a basic reason for this is their affinity with the structure of deliberation and action.

As a result, it seems appropriate to handle Boudon's axiology and his views about human action together. Rationality and morality, in Boudon's approach, are connected with each other for reasons which are directly relevant to the scientific, explanatory approach to individual and social behavior. This thematic, which has gradually come to the forefront in Boudon's writings,

---

[1] The author thanks Pierre Demeulenaere and Jean-Michel Morin for very helpful remarks on an earlier version of this chapter.

has allowed him to articulate science and values in a very interesting way, which offers resources for ongoing debates about value-neutrality, the value of science, and the importance of human values in human endeavors (including social science and philosophy).

The theory of action and the theory of values actually come into contact with each other in the Boudonian corpus, and the resulting theoretical richness calls for methodological attention. To be sure, the way this conjunction proves fruitful in Boudon's research exhibits a degree of complexity. In particular, how do the reasons for action testify to our commitment to values and how do they relate, consequently, to the explanation of value-based action? The sociologist's appeal to substantial moral values is ubiquitous, especially in the systematic theory which is put forward in Boudon's great book, *Le Juste et le vrai*, and this suggests a solidarity of reasoning, commitment, and explanation. Simultaneously, his reliance on general and rather formal social mechanisms for explanatory purposes has been strong. This prompts questions about the comparative roles, in explanation, of formal aspects of social interaction on the one hand, and individual commitment on the other hand.

On the face of it, explaining individual action out of general good reasons—moral or other—might seem awkward because individual action is rooted in personal perceptions and singular circumstances. In the tradition of methodological individualism, this has provided reasons to doubt all-too-mechanical social laws and hypothesized causality links.

Referring to a number of problems faced by methodological individualism when dealing with action and consequences proves helpful for the understanding of Boudon's notable and distinctive methodological choices, and for assessing their contribution to the development of a constructive attitude in the face of a number of important challenges. Boudon's "actionism" amounts to agent-centered interactionism and this helps understand his attitude toward the justification–explanation connection (as illustrated by his treatment of contractualism (sec.2). Paying attention to contexts is inevitable, following this approach, for the purposes of applied work at least. Raymond Boudon, however, put much emphasis on general reasons which are potentially similar across contexts and individual perceptions, even though his synthetic theory of ordinary rationality acknowledges the role of contexts in a significant way. How may this harmonize with sociological explanations which give much importance to specific contexts, especially in the individualistic contributions within social science? (sec.3). Arguably, the apparent tension provides insights into some remarkable aspects of Boudon's distinctive methodological doctrine.

Values, Contexts, and Actions in Agent-Centered Interactionism

Values, explanation, and social life

Although Boudon is rightly acclaimed as one of the key authors in the tradition of "methodological individualism" in the social sciences, his "actionism" has developed in such a way that it has caused a deliberate estrangement from the conventional rational choice models of human behavior which have been associated with the reception of methodological individualism in France and elsewhere. "Narrow" methodological individualism was clearly not Boudon's last word on methodological matters. A noteworthy fact is that the author made it apparent that his conception of methodological individualism and social explanation, while rooted in the tradition of sociology (surveyed in Boudon 1998a), was also part of the larger picture of action, knowledge, and society. In the systematic exposition we find in *Le Juste et le vrai* (Boudon 1995), the reconstruction of the analysis of moral judgments (especially in Chapter 5 and the sequel) can be viewed as a contribution to the humanities in a broad sense.

It is indeed arguable that his scientific methodology is a way to address the constraints which structure the space of problems associated with the pillars of social understanding—action, knowledge, society—and their mutual relationships. In this framework, a concentration of narrow self-interest and its "maximization" (the art and science of making it as fulfilled as possible) is bound to be extremely restrictive and lead to a distorted view of human motivation and human action. Overlooking the role of institutions and social expectations might also be misleading. In short, an impoverished conception of methodological individualism is likely to be a scientific disaster.

In Boudon's comprehensive brand of methodological individualism, the diversity of factors and motivations to be contemplated is akin to the variety of human reasons as they are expressed in human action. Human values therefore find a useful role in social explanation and they need not be dissolved into other, presumably deeper, explanatory factors, such as neuronal processes, unconscious operations of the mind or a sophisticated direct or indirect calculus based on self-interest. This widened picture has enabled the Boudonian adoption and the consistent defense of "methodological individualism" to provide impetus to the quest after systematic explanations of individual judgments and action—hence also of the resulting social phenomena—down to his mature elaboration of a "theory of ordinary rationality" which states that the reasons in an individual's mind are the causes of his or her statements, decisions, and preferences, as well as normative and positive beliefs (*convictions*) (Boudon 2013, 87).

There is no denying that individual values—for example, moral values (which will be under focus here)—have a potential role to play in this respect. Should they be treated as independent psychological or social "objects," however? In the sociologist's eyes, of course, predominant or influential values, as they are expressed, for example, in the statutes and functionings of collective entities (such as government institutions or firms), could be held eligible for such a treatment. However, values have a rooting in subjective attitudes and personal knowledge. After all, it is a familiar experience, in social life, to realize that "values" are treated as "subjective," because their endorsement seems to reflect personal attitudes, a particular cultural heritage, and the individual's singular worldview. In the universe of scientific explanations all the same, general human values are often dismissed as "too subjective" (and possibly transient or idiosyncratic) to provide a bedrock of scientific explanation. This possible weakness can be converted, from an individualistic point of view, into an explanatory advantage: subjectively endorsed values do provide reasons for action, as Boudon emphasized.

Indeed, it is quite natural, or "common-sensical" in Boudon's final choice of words, to consider that the endorsement of values should come into contact with individual reasons, provided that individuals prove "rational" to some degree, that is to say, provided they prove able to understand reasons and to compare their relative strengths with some insight. Boudon launched an all-out attack on contemporary relativism (the terms of the debate are explained in Boudon and Clavelin 1994) but even an anti-relativist should come to terms with the fact that individual attitudes and behavior which exemplify a commitment to values—for example, moral values—also reflect individual reasons, with their important variability. The question then arises as to the possible explanations of such reasons and this comes under the jurisdiction of methodological individualism. From a "cognitivist" point of view, R. Boudon had the ambition of providing guidelines for such explanations, placing maximal weight on individual "good reasons," thus prompting intensive and lively debates about the connections between cognition within the limits of social science methodology and the study of human cognition generally speaking (as exemplified in Boudon et al. 1997).

Individual reasons and explanation

Individual "good reasons" as Boudon thought of them are partly idiosyncratic and the explanatory framework of which they are a cornerstone should be flexible enough to accommodate particular circumstances and individual viewpoints, in line with contemporary conceptions of "subjective rationality," which go beyond the all-too-narrow economic or sociological analyses which center on a restricted list of standardized motivations (such as money, power and social prestige, or domination). Individual reasons have to be true "reasons" first of all, which can be causal factors in action and social phenomena, because of their role in individual motivation. From the point of view of mainstream methodological individualism and in the eyes of Boudon, this very status of "reasons" is supposed to warrant a content to be shared with partners in social life and tacitly with the researcher. Among the reasons which have a particular interest for systematic research, we find the good reasons which follow from the social actor's understanding of the role of his or her own action in social interaction. Following time-honored precepts of methodological individualism in the social sciences, the scientific treatment of such individual reasons must acknowledge objective constraints which are the result of "what is to be understood" (by the social actor and the scientist on a par), given the nature and details of the situation and the kind of social interaction which takes place.

Following this methodological path, the analysis of individual reasons is, of necessity, both subjective and objective. On the one hand, it must incorporate objective facts, which play a role in individual representations and reasonings, and as humans, we have a direct access to the latter. On the other hand, taking such personal reasons into account for the purposes of scientific explanation makes sense only if agents are considered capable of reflection, starting from the available data and their own values, knowledge, and beliefs. This is at root a reflective kind of methodology: the scientist tries to understand the structure of individual reasons, and this provides sufficient ground for the explanation of social phenomena. Hence "understanding" is not deemed foreign to full-fledged scientific explanation and Boudon rejected the "positivist" ban on "understanding" as a scientific ideal.

A remark may be useful here. Raymond Boudon was a very important sociologist, and his intellectual profile is also connected to philosophy as a discipline. He had in-depth training in philosophy, and he played a major role for many years in the doctoral school of old-time "Paris-Sorbonne" University, combining sociology and philosophy in an original and fruitful way. R. Boudon has made an essential contribution to the philosophy of the social sciences, particularly in the fields of the structure of causal explanation and the methodology of methodological individualism and the connection to complexity, but also in the analysis of the structure of beliefs and reasons, especially in the field of ethics. To his mind, the language of values was a common ground for philosophy and sociology and both intellectual pursuits were indebted to universal rationality ideals. Collective volumes in honor of Boudon reflect the interdisciplinary nature of his contributions and heritage (Baechler et al. 2000, Cherkaoui and Hamilton 2009), even though he clearly took his rank among classical sociologists (Morin 2006).

There is, in fact, a marked solidarity between classical philosophical ambitions with respect to the theory of values and the ambitions of a sociologist who saw himself as (and actually was) heir to the tradition of methodological individualism in social science and the humanities. A basic reason for this is that the analysis of the structure of beliefs (be they well-grounded or misguided ones) which play a role in normative judgment is an asset for understanding social phenomena or mechanisms, which ultimately depend on individual reasons.

Moreover, R. Boudon's treatment of values is very closely linked to the assessment of actions and the preparation of action in deliberation, the moment of comparison between the reasons which can help address a particular situation. Concerning morally significant examples, the general explanations that are offered focus on typical configurations of individual actions and give credentials to the idea that some forms of individual action are in themselves good, admirable, or simply appropriate, while others are inappropriate or even disgusting. This *a priori* surprising continuity between the explanation, reconstruction, and indeed first-person enunciation of value judgments about actions reflects the sheer fact that our actions are the objects of value judgments, for scientists and social agents alike. Boudon saw a very special relationship between ethical evaluation and action. Quite simply, social scientists and other researchers in the humanities are concerned with human action.

Values and consequences: the example of contract-based explanations of moral judgments

A clarification of the legacy of R. Boudon's thinking on axiology is to be expected from the close coupling of the companion questions of rationality in action and the contract-based model of justification. Favoring a procedural approach and based on assumptions of equal rationality, the question of contract-based justification and its limits was quite important in Boudon's reflections on moral values, moral sentiments, and justification. Boudon's discussions reveal the impact, in his theory of values and norms, of his critique of the most traditional assumptions of "rational choice theory." They bring the relationship between forms of social interaction and moral beliefs into play.

Classical contractarian theories, as well as the "moral contractualism" developed today (following Rawls 1971), offer a notable methodological landmark for the explanation of normative judgments and it is used in applied work aiming at explaining individual judgments about social justice in an empirical perspective (Forsé and Parodi 2010). Through the representation of normative, institutional, and social arrangements as the object of agreement between human agents which are capable of formulating aspirations, the agreement thus characterized is shown to involve reasons, beliefs, and values that are those of the agents themselves. This brings normative analysis into the vicinity of "methodological individualism" as we think of it in the descriptive, explanatory, comprehensive, and/or predictive social sciences, provided it is accepted that human behavior is usually governed by reasons, which pertain to beliefs and values (Picavet 2015).

Moreover, contractualism relies on general considerations about the typical forms of social interaction and the conditions under which it takes shape. Such considerations (e.g., the Rawlsian "circumstances of justice") are supposed to be accessible to the reflective agents who are envisaged with a theoretical purpose. The type of justification or critique we are interested in, following this path, is thus based on representations of action and interaction that enable individual action to be situated within collective interaction and, ultimately, within social life itself. The considered value judgments thus stem from an understanding of interaction, even when they superficially seem to concern only the action of a subject and his or her own values.

Human agents, as they are represented in contractualist analytical frameworks, examine generic problems and a rationalist and rigorous author such as Rawls was congratulated by Boudon (2012, 213) because his effort to articulate the rational elaboration of political judgment ran contrary to the relativistic slippery slope. It must be noted, however, that Boudon's earlier comments on Rawls were quite critical (Boudon 1977, Ch. 6), as they borrowed part of their substance from a general, skeptical reading of possibly "utopian" contributions to the study of social justice. In Boudon (1995, Ch. 9–10), the Rawlsian model of social justice was again discussed in a rather critical manner, with a view to the empirical assessments of the comparative importance of various views of justice. To be sure, the very exercise of putting normative theories to empirical test is controversial. However, trying to identify and explain various degrees of proximity between elaborate theories of justice and ordinary reflections or feelings about justice is far from incongruous in the work of a post-Weberian sociologist who believed in some kind of basic homogeneity between the ways theoreticians and situated agents, respectively, sort out the good reasons they discern.

In the moral and political domains of contractual thinking, we usually encounter a high level of generality on the one hand, and the need to resort to models of action and interaction on the other hand. If we set forth to explain the judgments and actions of social agents as "rational" ones, we must pay attention to the reasoning of actors in the face of the problems they encounter. This is an occasion to rely on the threefold foundation of Boudonian social science: individualism, understanding, and rationality (Coenen-Huther 2019). The moral attitudes of individuals, to be considered as motivated answers to existing problems, are inevitably rooted in "cognitive rationality" and they are to be understood as such—that is to say, through the "R3" layer of rationality (Boudon 1998). "Axiological rationality," if it is a variety of rationality at all, must have an essential connection to cognitive rationality.

This suggests that "axiological rationality" is by no means an insulated kind of rationality. Indeed, Boudon proposed to look at it as a "kind of cognitive rationality" (Boudon 2003, 127), even though he consistently favored the use of two distinct phrases, further stating that axiological rationality "differentiates itself from" cognitive rationality because "the systems of reasons it begets lead to evaluative conclusions" (Boudon 2003, 123); in *Le Juste et le vrai*, the readers were invited to consider "axiological rationality" *and also* "cognitive rationality" (Boudon 1995, 273). All in all, axiological judgments and cognition are involved in normative argument and their respective domains are quite difficult to identify. This is because axiology provides space for reasoning, and indeed for the use of models or theories.

Sociological work on argumentative strategies raises various questions about the possible specificities of "ordinary" reasoning (Bouvier 1997) and the best theoretical way to address them but at least the very presence of reasoning about moral matters is hardly questionable. Boudon's interpretation (or new use) of the classical *Zweckrationalität/Wertrationalität* distinction (Weber 1922) is *de facto* an explicitly cognitive one (Boudon 1998, sec.8). It portrays axiological (or value-based) rationality as the way cognitive rationality shows itself in the ethical-practical domain (Boudon 1998, 29). This kind of rationality explores systems of reasons and the relative strength of reasons, with the stronger reasons having a determinant role in the elaboration of judgments. This is the foundation for a theory of ethical evaluations (not a foundational theory for moral values themselves). This rather modest camp doesn't impair the relevance of Boudon's theory to the explanation of moral reasoning. It can be allowed, however, that it helps differentiate the sociologist's viewpoint from a kind of inquiry which retains its full significance in moral theory proper.

Boudon's examination of the relationship between values and actions has given a certain importance to the figure of interest-based contractualism, in a limited and, as it were, "regional" form (for certain categories of practical problems only). Within these limits, and despite the fact that they might seem restrictive to advocates of a "moral contractualism" with more encompassing ambitions, it is interesting to note that R. Boudon was willing to consider certain contractualist explanations as fully convincing in their own sphere of rationality. Thus, in *Le Juste et le vrai*, following an illuminating analysis of the famous stag hunt example in Rousseau' second *Discourse* (on inequality) and the discussion of a model of cold war deterrence, Boudon stated that the "utilitarian" analysis of normative phenomena was both crucially important and irrevocably insufficient.

A "regional" variety of actionism is indeed at work in interest-based contractarian models, and it provides access to definitive forms of understanding. However, this is only a synthesis of limited arguments, which prove insufficient to characterize the full rationality of axiological statements (Boudon 1998c). The problem–solution pair turns out to be decisive because the contractarian approach adequately amalgamates certain data which are relevant to a well-formulated problem; thus, it appears convincing. It is a matter of effective "cognitive rationality," illuminating some of our value judgments (but not all of them).

A number of features of interest-based contractarian models and more general contractualist analysis, in particular, the explicitness of certain background conditions of interaction and of certain typical patterns of motivation, require the theorist's attention. They can certainly help us to tackle some of the problems associated with the elaboration of value judgments, especially moral judgments. Because of the contextual conditions of action plans and interaction structures, it is always questionable whether the commitment to translating attachment to values (or a certain perception of the configuration of relevant correct value judgments) into practical categories and reasons is easily identifiable in social life. However, even though contractualism has been criticized for its tendency to favor abstractness (as criticisms of John Rawls' *Theory of Justice* frequently attest), it also proves capable of accommodating the individual agents' expectations about variability in the conditions of social life or interaction. This variability is considered only within the limits of its relevance to the problems under study—for example, the problems of authority and its justification, or the delineation of the scope of rights and the properly conceived domain of social justice.

The correlation between the degree of contextual variability that is taken into account in the explanation of value judgments and the kind of looked-for explanation is therefore crucial. Ensuring this correlation in a reasoned manner certainly contributes to making explanations adequate and solid. R. Boudon saw this clearly in the case of interest-based contractualism, whose field of relevance was determined by him in a very restrictive way, as limited to problems that could be dealt with on the basis of the interests involved alone, and on a consequentialist basis. Boudon's "regional" approval of contractualism draws attention to the importance of the correlation between explanation and variability, in a way that may serve to defend the author's confidence in perfectly general explanations based on moral arguments (in the format of "axiological rationality"), regardless of the actual variability of contexts.

We can draw attention to the fact that contractualist approaches that deal with issues other than the good consequences of social interaction (e.g., Rawls's justification of principles of justice expressing concerns for freedom and respect for persons) mobilize actors' "good reasons" in a very general format (even though Boudon stated that Rawls's concentration on justice as fairness gave a limited picture of the involved complexity, reasons, and concerns, see Boudon 1995, Ch. 10). Generality does not make irrelevant those generic variations of the circumstances of social life which have an impact on value judgments, but it makes it possible to move ahead of narrowly context-dependent explanations which verge on hardly instructive, purely *ad hoc* explanations.

Sharing reasons is both a lived reality in social life and what is foreseen by the rationalist philosophy of values, once agreement between reasonable people on the proper approach to certain questions seems clear. If I say that my action is supported by reasons, if I explain it in this way, I am referring to reasons that cannot apply only to this person (me) at this precise moment in this unique situation. If a real explanation is at hand, the reasons mentioned must apply to this person and this situation by virtue of characteristics that are deemed relevant and that are present in this situation. They are also present for every person and situation possessing the relevant characteristics, and therefore similar to each other in this respect.

It can certainly be argued that this follows from what we mean by "explanation" in a general way. After all, we wouldn't be talking about explanation if the mentioned reasons weren't capable of being mobilized in other contexts similar in terms of the relevant characteristics. Therefore, if an action alpha is considered adequate, rational, or acceptable for certain reasons for individual i in situation s, then the same should apply to "the same action" (i.e., in reality, an action considered similar and, for this reason, treated as identical) in a pair (i', s') similar to (i, s) in all relevant aspects.

Suppose that I judge the situations of the other agents in the interaction that brings us together at a given moment to be similar to mine in all relevant aspects. If this is the case, I can only consider as good reasons for my choice those reasons that I must at the same time hold as good reasons for corresponding (similar) choices to be made by other people. For example, in a Prisoner's dilemma with "identical" agents, I can consider that a good reason to act is the argument that supports the choice of the dominant strategy. This is convincing if I consider the choice of action from a strictly causal perspective: I ask myself how my action can cause the best result and successively examining the possible cases leads to the conclusion (making use of "instrumental" rationality if my system of motivations can be encapsulated in a "goal").

On the other hand, there is another way of looking at action, in terms of reasons (even if these are instrumental in nature as in Gravel and Picavet 2000). I may consider that my reasons, provided they are the best reasons, are also the best reasons for anyone else who would be placed in a similar position, having characteristics similar to mine. Then there's a massive problem with the individual adoption (by everyone) of the dominant-strategy kind of "best reasons": the mediocrity of the result. This can lead to a kind of reasoning that is both consequence-based and located beyond the matching of means to ends in particular circumstances; a legitimate interest pertains to the sharable reasons which lead to the best results, provided agents are supposed capable of a reflection on the appropriate norms. In some cases at least, it is perhaps not paradoxical, after all, to associate axiological rationality with consequentialist benchmark models of the agreement between individuals.

Similarly, in the context of studies on social justice or civic ties whose foundations have to do with the respect for persons, it may be pointed out that the reasons for respecting people in social or political organization may take the form of collective efforts to promote this or that goal (or purpose) for each individual, or collective or institutional commitments in this direction, without this leading us to believe that this goal is what each individual should take as his or her goal. At this institutional level, axiological reasoning about appropriate focal values and collective norms can, and certainly should, encompass the active care for positive consequences. It is perfectly true that Boudon's search of the objectivity of moral judgments and his well-considered elaborations about the foundations of this objectivity are an essential part of his intellectual legacy and a very effective contribution of sociology to the understanding of the central character of dignity in social life and institutions (Mesure 2020). Boudon's arguments against the "reduction" of axiological rationality to instrumental rationality (Boudon 1995, Boudon 1998) can be considered decisive and they have enabled the author to enrich the picture of methodological individualism and the companion action theories (in itself a complex framework, see Valade 1996, Goldthorpe 1998, Bulle 2020, Di Iorio 2020), through the building of a rich and instructive general sociological theory (see Boudon 2007, 2008) and a general examination of normative judgment (Boudon 1995) and rationality (Boudon 2009). However, the occasional but insistent association of the renewed, post-Weberian "axiological rationality" thematic with a rejection of consequentialist benchmark models of action and social interaction is questionable upon examination.

Contexts of Interaction and Context-Independent Values

Contexts and methodological choices

A specific attention to the complexity of human agency and justification is illustrated by Boudon's resistance to a systematic "consequentialist" approach in both ethics and moral sociology. Consequentialism, here, is to be understood in a broad sense in the study of value judgments, as pertaining to any treatment of value judgments which postulates that these judgments derive from a treatment of the results of action, of interaction, or of the enforcement of rules. Boudon has given momentum to a study of normative judgments that finds its roots in the characteristics of actions as such, not just their results. At the same time, he has consistently resisted the relativistic consequences of an over-emphasized contextualism, and resistance to consequentialism plays a decisive role in this respect.

Indeed, the consequences of actions are always and quite deeply context-dependent. Should we rely on context-independent consequences only, we should acknowledge that the value judgments we may grasp are deeply idiosyncratic, with little room for general scientific explanations. Boudon (1979) made a distinction between the contexts of functional relations, interdependence contexts, and the contexts of changes. What we may frame as a distinctive Boudonian dual characteristic—the quest for explanations with a high degree of generality, and the companion criticism of hopes in the general explanatory power of consequentialism with respect to value judgments—understandably leads to giving a central role to the structure of human action, in the development of a genuine "actionism." Here, the richness of "contexts" and their diversity play an important role. Indeed, this paves the way toward an appropriate answer to the (seemingly paradoxical) simultaneous "injunctions" of generality in explanation—as part of a scientific ideal—and respect for social complexity (Boudon 1984) and individual agency, the latter being an essential dimension of social complexity. Individual reasons and circumstances are always "particular" alright, but some elements in the structure of human action and interaction are fairly general in character, sometimes amenable to quite abstract formulations, and they jointly provide an *explanans* for many real-world *explananda*. In Boudon's final epistemological reflections (Boudon 2013, III), a critical examination of "good" and "bad" abstraction was conducted and it appeared that the distance from the natural world and the close connection to rationality (especially "rational psychology") were very important to his mind, in the efforts to choose an appropriate kind of "abstraction" for explanatory purposes.

Relying on the characteristics of the action undertaken (or simply envisaged) by an agent should not lead to overlook the insertion of this action in social life, which can be understood as the *locus* of interactions. In this respect, Boudon's "individualism" is by no means a reductionist approach; on the contrary, it is adjusted to the complexity of the social world, described and analyzed with relevance in Boudon's work. The judgments made about my action (including by myself as an individual) usually depend on a certain understanding of the complementarity between my action and the initiatives taken by other agents. The understanding of such judgments can therefore be based with some relevance on simplified models that capture typical or recurrent aspects of the conjunction of actions, as well as important features of the relationship between this conjunction and other features of the states of society and the world. The central question, then, is the choice of models, in particular with respect to their ability to reflect, in a relevant way, key dimensions of the practical problems which are concretely encountered by social agents.

Human action is not only rooted in will and values; it is also rooted in contexts, it is shaped by natural, technological, cultural, and institutional circumstances, and by the habits of life in given surroundings, with inherited features which can be equated with historical legacies. These "deep" contextual elements are likely to have a significant influence on our understanding of what is at stake in action, and in particular on what is at stake in the individual connection to values, especially moral values. This reflective dimension, again, is not alien to the sociologist's scientific outlook, if only because words and descriptions, as well as personal judgments about their adequacy, are part of the agents' awareness of circumstances, hence also of the conditions and relevance of their own choices and judgments.

From this perspective, an important problem, inherited from R. Boudon's approach, is that of the conjunction between general concerns on the one hand and motivations that depend on contexts or circumstances which are specific to the agent's role in social life on the other hand. How can we combine these two aspects? R. Boudon has placed emphasis on the scientist's responsibility to elaborate general explanations; has this been detrimental to in-depth attention to contexts? It is arguable that Boudon's work has contributed to illuminate the challenges associated with such methodological choices.

Doubts about the adequate attention to contexts may arise about Boudonian methodology because the elaboration of value judgments and the consequences in decision-making processes take shape in specific contexts. The characteristics of the contexts have an impact on deep-seated interpretations of acts that express value judgments (think of the qualification of given actions as "courageous"), even though it is perfectly right (as explained by Demeulenaere 2003, 93 sq.) that a relevant and meaningful examination of "reasons" should leave room for the notion that reasons are somehow independent of particular social norms, and indeed have a role in their justification or criticism.

The expression of values in action seems to rely on several operations: "implementation" (of projects, plans, or intentions in line with the best value judgments), "following" (a judgment, a rule, or a resolution), checking of "compliance" (with value-related criteria or norms), and so on. These steps are likely to witness the significant influence of important contextual elements, far beyond the details of transient situations, even when widely shared moral values are at stake. A justified treatment of the relevant "invariant" features of normative or value-based judgments thus appears essential.

Weak context-dependence and identification problems in inductions about values

In Boudon's extensive writings on the rationality of values, a conspicuous feature is the high degree of generality—for example, attitudes toward plagiarism (Boudon 1995), and the evolution of opinions on the morality of life insurance are studied in the general case, with a view to a number of highly generic reasons which are invested with explanatory value. The approach is theoretical and pretty abstract, as it pays relatively little attention to the cultural framing and typical interpretation of actions in a given society or community, although contexts are taken into account. The basic insight is that following the rules of the game is a necessary condition of the appropriateness of the players' attitudes. Plagiarism is an example of rule violation in valued social interactions among partly autonomous actors, and the negative moral feelings prompted by plagiarism signal the underlying unlawfulness of the conduct. However, it can be difficult to identify what being a player in a game involves, who are exactly the players first of all, etc.

General concerns are undoubtedly important for the understanding and justification of action. They also play a crucial role in the social design of those standardized ways to act (or react) in which individual or collective control turns out to be based on the ability to provide justifications for actions. Moral values, such as justice or respect for truth, *are* such general concerns. They are usually mobilized in a highly abstract way in argument and justification. However, contextual elements also come into play, especially when it comes to interpreting actions in the light of relevant values—and this ordinarily involves difficult steps. Moreover, contexts are not imposed upon social agents in a truly irrepressible way, but rather with "near-irrepressibility" (in the words of Andler 1999, 284) in particular because, as agents, we can choose to ignore part of the information we are processing. This is good news for theorists like Boudon, who cherish individual freedom; but the analysis of the role of contexts has its cognitive complications, and the very nature of a "context" is quite difficult to grasp in a precise way (Andler 1999, 274).

Boudon's theory of axiological rationality (a component of his later-days "theory of ordinary rationality") leads to definite conclusions in important cases, for example, plagiarism and the intentional deception of other people. Is it, however, sufficiently grounded in social contexts, and in the structuring of action in a given society, with its recognized rules? For example, Boudon explains that plagiarism is easily recognized by social agents as an inappropriate kind of conduct, hence also that it comes as no surprise that it is widely condemned in social life. However, at given moments in history, for particular practices and in specific sociocultural environments, what can be described as "plagiarism" is often described in other, more flattering or less shameful terms, and condemnation is therefore lacking. Inductions about the direct relevance of underlying moral values—such as the rightful respect for personal originality—are not easy to perform; they can suffer from identification problems so long as a very rich analysis of contexts is missing.

This seems to apply to the variability of judgments about truthfulness in the claimed authorship of musical works or instruments, in some cases at least. In given settings, authenticity is required and controlled; the social arrangements about it are said to reflect a moral norm of reciprocal respect for each person's contribution. Boudon's analyses are fully relevant of course. Reflecting an exacting individual-based view of legitimate claims, they contribute to our understanding of the shifting frontiers of personal authorship and protected intellectual or artistic property rights (e.g., in the notoriously painful social, psychological, and legal transition from the world of local and community-oriented "blues" or "gospel" music in North America to the more commercial, international, and artist-based world of "rock" music and popular songs generally speaking). The time-consuming lawsuits about the alleged plagiarism of extremely rich and popular "rock" bands to the detriment of more confidential "blues" artists are probably fueled by moral concerns which suggest that public recognition matters, beyond the copyright-related legal claims which are amenable to side arrangements in most cases.

In the analysis of such cases, Boudonian methodology draws attention to the structure of social interaction, beyond intuitions and commitments. In the spectrum of the contemporary approaches to "context," this is a characteristic of his "realist" approach (Greenhalgh and Manzano 2022, about Boudon 2014). Such a structure—with its rules, its standards of rule-following, its enforcing mechanisms, etc.—is indeed crucial to understand the feelings and judgments of social actors, and the consequences in decision-making and evolutive rule-setting. Boudonian methodology takes us far beyond the commonplace intuitionist view about the alleged "obvious" nature of the right and the unlawful. However, the identification, signaling, and interpretation of trespasses is itself heavily context-bound.

This becomes apparent as soon as we pay attention to context-based variations which really matter. For example, in the small world of violin-makers, it is quite usual to use other people's labels and this does not usually amount to an objectionable attempt to deceive clients, sellers, or musicians. The frontiers of originality can be said to be blurred, and *prima facie* this is a concern to be sure. However, the practice is meant to receive a rich variety of mutually exclusive, and often *positive*, interpretations, in alternative contexts of interaction. Claiming a false identity can be an element in a forgery scenario and moral indignation must be expected in this case. When it is not clearly meant to cause error, however, it can be a means to pay tribute to an artistic tradition or school in instrument-making, with a fake label used as a decorative item for this purpose.

This occurs in an expertise-driven sphere of interaction, in which individual persons or clients are supposed to be well aware of the low informative value of labels in instruments; some people can be fooled, and indeed a number of victims *are* fooled—but this takes place in an environment which is structured in such a way that their lack of prudence is to be blamed, although the exact frontiers of expected prudence are an object of persistent disagreement. The practice can also be a component of an artistic copy process, which amounts to paying tribute to great masters of the past and acknowledging their time-enduring influence, and this is certainly not morally objectionable insofar as the copy gives clues to help people (at least, *competent* people) to differentiate the copy from the original. Again, some people can be fooled, unfortunately, and these ordinary practices (self-effacing copying or the use of decorative labels) can be frustrating for reasons beyond unfairness in selling operations; in particular, they make it difficult to know the origin, therefore also the building processes, of instruments which testify to truly excellent, sometimes significantly original, workmanship. Originality in itself isn't the central problem here, however, and social judgment does not appear to be dependent on serious attempts to check that no intention to deceive other people is present (the rules of the game are compatible with the tolerated deception of imprudent buyers).

In this example, authentic identification does not play as important a role as the one it assumes, for example, in science (where the cumulative nature of the activities and the interpretative importance of the correlation between scientific work and scientific traditions or schools of thought give true authorship a distinguished normative status) or literature (the interplay of personality and creation being a notable component of our literary experience as publishers or readers). It must be recognized that the underlying moral values or norms are put to use in a way which can hardly be severed from the contextual signaling and decoding habits and normative expectations in a particular *milieu*. It seems that analyzing the contexts which make sense of practices and decisions is required if we are to understand the operating rule-following conventions and the significance of compliance with rules in a relevant way. Similar observations can be made in the case of musical originality: sometimes it morally matters a lot (e.g., in the world of heavily shared and broadcasted popular songs nowadays), sometimes it doesn't (e.g., in musical performances in eighteenth-century *salons*), for reasons which have a lot to do with context-specific values and normative expectations.

How deep should a reference to "context" take us? Shouldn't we "contextualize" the analysis to a greater extent than in Boudon's approach?

The previous examples suggest that the normative aspects of interactive contexts are quite important in some cases, and must be taken into account in an explicit way. Specific social norms, however, take us a distance from overarching moral judgments which are given a guiding role in the elaboration of conduct. Presumably, two complementary approaches can be defended. On the one hand, the generality in Boudon's approach reflects the tradition and approach of comprehensive social science. The aim is not really to make general predictions on the basis of an abstract model but rather to use theory to shed light on important aspects of social life as it unfolds in the real world, starting from the theorist's understanding of human motivation (Coenen-Huther 2019). This ambition is less directly operational than one might expect, which can be frustrating when compared with some of the classic ambitions of the social sciences. However, correspondence with experience—in particular, with expressed reflective judgments—retains its critical scientific role. In *Le Juste et le Vrai* (chap. 5), the structured and recurrent empirical results about perceptions of fairness are treated as important evidence in favor of the existence of axiological rationality (clearly differentiated from an instrumental kind of rationality) and the relevance of transcultural and transcontextual reasons (such as those which pertain to following rules of the games we accept to play).

On the other hand, a simplified benchmark model calls for an explanation of the conditions under which the model can be used in a relevant way. The explanation should cover its hypotheses, the correspondence between a given context and these hypotheses (which can be checked), the ways of dealing with the possible discordance between the judgments of several actors in this respect, pluralism (or the lack of it) in the interpretation of socially influential rules, etc. The most essential task is undoubtedly to understand the kind of reality to which the simplified model mobilized by the theorist gives access. We can then envisage the possibility that the sociologist's reasoning gives access to important aspects of situations or problems. In addition, Boudon's insistence on the aggregation effects which result from individual actions in a continuous way and the precise notion of "habit" which can be elaborated in this perspective (following Simmel, see Boudon 1998, 184) provide resources to address "deep" contextual dimensions in the constitution of the framework of human action in given societies.

Boudon thought that a merit of the "cognitivist" model was a precise articulation of the universal and the contextual: interesting studies of normative attitudes are anchored in contexts, but a transcontextual analysis is possible (Boudon 1995, 243). In some discussions, he hints at a "contextual" objectivity of values: the good ways to mobilize values can differ across contexts (Boudon 1995, 290). Universality is not uniformity, and the availability to observers of transcontextual understanding is key to a proper understanding of it. Hence, the role given to contexts calls for measure and prudence; complexity theorists, for example, are blamed for giving contexts a role which makes it difficult to understand the feelings of justice beyond local phenomena (Boudon 1995, 221). His methodology is thus flexible enough for a rich treatment of contexts; a possible worry is the fact that in some cases, taking contexts seriously might lead us away from ordinary discourse about values, with its usually very general and encompassing characteristics.

Conclusion

Boudon's sociology is remarkable for the close association between action explanation and value-based justification it has uncovered. Thus, inquiring into the structure of action and its theoretical treatment is helpful when it comes to assessing Boudon's methodological choices and legacy in the tradition of methodological individualism. The present set of reflections about Boudon's methodology in *Le Juste et le vrai* and closely related writings has relied on the connection between reasons for action and the reasons which support axiological statements, in line with Boudon's central tenets. This connection, it has been argued, raises a query about the Boudonian treatment of contexts: while they play a major role in the analysis of social interaction and the associated individual good reasons, they play a rather minor role in the understanding of commitment to values. The explanation of social interaction gives a potentially important role to specific contexts, while the treatment of values appears context-independent, by and large.

This suggested asymmetry in the treatment of contexts appears helpful in the perspective of an assessment of Boudon's singular approach to axiology, which coincides with a significant contribution to the understanding of the methodological involvement of values in social science. It turns out that the Boudonian vindication of the role of values in scientific explanation is based on general moral views. Generality itself appears to play a central role because the most helpful moral beliefs (from a methodological point of view) are the most general ones in the first place. All in all, Boudon's contribution to axiology is closely linked to the actionism he sought to defend and to the conception of social interaction that underlies it. This correspondence is exemplified at the methodological level, and it fully makes sense in the context of an intellectual endeavor to understand social experience and the formation of individual judgment in one and the same framework. This being said, the correspondence between the logic of values and the analysis of interactions is not a direct and easy one. Problems of identification and contextualization do arise and their discussion is part of Boudon's very fruitful intellectual legacy. Indeed, the problems should not be treated as obstacles. They are, in themselves, of interest to readers of Boudon's work today, as they seek to make his theoretical contribution lively again, possibly along the path of a theory of normative justification as a built-in, partly contextual aspect of social life.

References

Andler, D. (1999). *Science et philosophie. Quinze essais d'épistémologie.* Palaiseau: Cahiers du Bibliothèque du CREA (Ecole Polytechnique).

Baechler, J., Chazel, F. and Kamrane, R. (eds.) (2000). *L'acteur et ses raisons.* Paris: Presses Universitaires de France (PUF).

Boudon, R. (1977). *Effets pervers et ordre social.* Paris: PUF.

———. (1979). *La Logique du social.* Paris: PUF.

———. (1984). *La Place du désordre.* Paris: PUF. Engl. transl. 1986. *Theories of Social Change: A Critical Appraisal.* London: Basil Blackwell—Polity Press.

———. (1995). *Le juste et le vrai: études sur l'objectivité des valeurs et de la connaissance.* Paris: Fayard. Engl. Transl. 2001. *The Origin of Values.* New Brunswick/London: Transaction.

———. (1998a). *Etudes sur les sociologues classiques.* Paris: Presses Universitaires de France.

———. (1998b). La rationalité axiologique. In: Mesure (ed.) 1998, p. 16–57.

———. (1998c). Au-delà du « Modèle du Choix Rationnel » ? In: Saint-Sernin et al. 1998.

———. (2003). *Raison. Bonnes raisons.* Paris: PUF.

———. (2007). *Essais sur la théorie générale de la rationalité: action sociale et sens commun.* Paris: PUF. Engl. transl. 2009. *Towards a General Theory of Rationality: A Defence of Common Sense.* Oxford: Bardwell Press.

———. (2008). How Can Axiological Feelings Be Explained? *International Review of Sociology* 18(3): 349–364.

———. (2009). *La rationalité.* Paris: PUF.

———. (2012). *Croire et savoir. Penser le politique, le moral et le religieux.* Paris: Presses Universitaires de France.

———. (2013). *Le Rouet de Montaigne: une théorie du croire.* Paris: Hermann.

———. (2014). What Is Context? *Kölner Zeitschrift für Soziologie und Sozialpsychologie* 66(1): 17–45.

Boudon, R. and Clavelin, M. (eds.) (1994). *Le Relativisme est-il résistible?* Paris: Presses Universitaires de France.

Boudon, R., Bouvier, A. and Chazel, F. (eds.) (1997). *Cognition et sciences sociales.* Paris: Presses Universitaires de France.

Bouvier, A. (1997). Argumentation et cognition en sociologie morale et juridique. In: Boudon et al. 1997, p. 91–120.

Bulle, N. (2020). Trois versions de l'individualisme méthodologique. *L'Année sociologique* 70(1): 97–128.

Cherkaoui, M. and Hamilton, P. (eds.) (2009). *Raymond Boudon, a Life in Sociology—Essays in Honour of Raymond Boudon,* 4 vols. Oxford: The Bardwell Press.

Coenen-Huther, J. (2019). Raymond Boudon et la compréhension sociologique. *Revue européenne des sciences sociales* 57 (1/2): 157–167.

Demeulenaere, P. (2003). *Les normes sociales. Entre accords et désaccords*. Paris: Presses Universitaires de France.

Di Iorio, F. (2020). Individualisme méthodologique et réductionnisme. *L'Année sociologique* 70(1): 19–44.

Forsé, M. and Parodi, M. (2010). *Une Théorie empirique de la justice sociale*. Paris: Hermann.

Goldthorpe, J. H. (1998). Rational Action Theory for Sociology. *British Journal of Sociology* 49(2): 167–192. https://doi.org/10.2307/591308.

Gravel, N. and Picavet, E. (2000). Une théorie cognitiviste de la rationalité axiologique. *L'Année sociologique*, 50(1): 85–118.

Greenhalgh, J. and Manzano, A. (2022). Understanding "context" in realist evaluation and synthesis. *International Journal of Social Research Methodology* 25(5): 583–595, DOI: 10.1080/13645579.2021.1918484. Link to this article: https://doi.org/10.1080/136 45579.2021.1918484.

———. (2020). Dignité et rationalité axiologique. L'héritage de Raymond Boudon. *L'Année sociologique* 70(1): 175–195.

Morin, J-M. (2006). *Boudon—un sociologue classique*. 2d. ed. 2020. Paris: L'Harmattan.

Picavet, E. (2015). Methodological Individualism in Sociology. *International Encyclopaedia of the Social and Behavioural Sciences*.

Rawls, J. (1971). *A Theory of Justice*. 2d. ed. 1999. Cambridge, MA: Harvard University Press.

Saint-Sernin, B., Picavet, E., Fillieule, R. and Demeulenaere, P. (eds.) (1998). *Les Modèles de l'action*. Paris: PUF.

Valade, B. (1996). *Introduction aux sciences sociales*. Paris: PUF.

Weber, M. (1922). *Wirtschaft und Gesellschaft*. Tübingen: Mohr.

Chapter 5

THE EPISTEMOLOGY OF BELIEFS IN BOUDON'S SOCIOLOGY: FROM THE SOCIAL SUBJECT TO THE EVOLUTION OF POLITICS, MORALITY, AND RELIGION

Nathalie Bulle and Jean-Michel Morin

The Epistemology of Beliefs in Boudon's Sociology

Epistemology is understood here in its broadest sense, as Raymond Boudon does from his earliest writings to his latest work (Boudon 2012, 2013). It pertains to the evaluation of any belief or knowledge to determine whether its endorsement by the social subject is justified and legitimate (Pouivet 2013, 17–18). In France, the term "epistemology" is often used in a much more restrictive sense. Since Bachelard, it has been reserved for a certain kind of philosophy of the natural sciences. As a result, political, moral, and religious beliefs are often discredited from the outset. They are declared out of scope *a priori* because they do not belong to the physical or biological sciences. The broader international definition is the one advocated by Boudon. For him, there is continuity between all areas of human adherence: natural sciences, but also rules of law or religious faith. In all cases, the individual believes that "an apple falls once it is detached from the tree" (natural science), "a red light means we should stop" (rule of law and conduct), or "our life continues (or not) after death" (faith). In all cases, sociologists must take these beliefs and knowledge seriously. They need to understand their epistemological foundations, especially from the point of view of the observed subject.

Does this mean that we should assimilate all beliefs? Certainly not. Boudon carefully distinguishes between individual and collective beliefs. He also separates, to better bring them together, descriptive and normative beliefs: the former are about the "true," and the latter are about the "right."

These categories have their importance: natural sciences are about the "true," whereas politics or morals are about the "right." But the dividing line is more subtle: Is religion about the "true" or the "right"? Here, once again, let's take the notion of belief in its broadest sense to grasp the whole picture. Following Kant, we can also distinguish between different kinds of beliefs: knowledge, opinion, and faith (Cuin 2022, 34–35).

- Knowledge: is objectively sufficient to achieve certainty for everyone. For example: "The battle of Marignano took place in 1515" or "2 + 2 = 4."
- An opinion: does not have this solidity. For example: "X is the best candidate for the next presidential election" or "Reducing working hours for some creates jobs for others."
- Faith: is subjectively sufficient to achieve conviction among those concerned. For example: "Something in us will outlive us" or "God exists."

Ultimately, in all cases, the subjects have their reasons for holding and sharing their beliefs, until there is evidence to the contrary that would challenge their personal convictions or even shared certainties.

This is therefore the thread we propose to draw from Boudon's work. Taking an interest in beliefs and their epistemological foundations seems crucial for the sociologist. First, because beliefs induce our actions. Second, because our beliefs are anchored both objectively in a context and subjectively in our reasons. And finally, because human history seems to be largely shaped by the evolution of our collective beliefs.

This is the journey we seek to retrace:

- First, by focusing on the social subject and its multiple, more or less shared beliefs.
- Then, by examining how the evolution of shared beliefs illuminates our common history, especially in its political, moral, and religious components.

The Role of Neo-Kantian Theory of Knowledge in Understanding the Social Subject and Its Beliefs

This section highlights the importance of the Kant-inspired theory of knowledge in Boudon's sociology, from the foundations of methodological individualism to the cognitive sociological analyses of the beliefs and values of social subjects (for a detailed overview of the sociologist's work, see Morin 2020). Boudon's form of neo-Kantianism, following in the footsteps of the great founders of methodological individualism to whom he refers, in particular Max Weber and Georg Simmel, can be seen as the cornerstone of his sociology. It is central to his conception of the workings of human thought, underpinning both his articulation of an "understanding" sociology with methodological individualism, and the methodological continuity of his approach to all forms of thought, ordinary as well as scientific, to all kinds of ideas, whether judged correct or dubious or false, and to different kinds of beliefs, whether descriptive (also known as positive) or normative (also known as prescriptive). We aim to elucidate these relationships, emphasizing their implications for the notion of causality, the treatment of the consciousness and unconsciousness of concepts, and the symmetry of Boudon's interpretation of descriptive and normative beliefs.

Generalized Kant: expanding and layering the "a priori" of knowledge

In particular, Boudon retains two main ideas from Kantian philosophy. The first is that knowledge requires the application of interpretive cognitive tools: the "*a priori.*" The second is that the interpretive nature of knowledge is also the basis of its validity: The notion of truth, like that of knowledge, depends on mediated access to reality through structures of meaning. Boudon credits Simmel with being the most explicit about the fact that truth and objectivity are accessible to the knowing subject not, as he writes, *although*, but *because* knowledge always expresses a point of view (Boudon 1990, 57). In this respect, however, it is essential to understand the consequences of the neo-Kantian generalization of the Kantian "*a priori,*" which does not possess the universality or fixity of the Kantian categories of knowledge, and even relativizes their *a priori* status. Simmel (1905/1907) expresses this generalization in a passage from his *Problems in the Philosophy of History*—a work translated into French by Boudon (1984a)—in which he discusses the inadequacy of the Kantian *a priori* to explain the possibility of subjective experience itself. He concludes that the Kantian *a priori*, which "makes experience possible in general," represents only the highest element in a series whose terms, which can be expressed in the form of propositions, refer to relative levels of abstraction. In relation to the higher terms, the elements of this series appear empirical, but in relation to the lower terms of the series, they appear *a priori*. Simmel notes that this generalization (and, we might add, relativization) doesn't change the function of the *a priori* itself, only its content. At various levels, *a priori* constructs serve an enterprise of selection, connection, and arrangement of data derived from experience in relation to the next level. This process contributes to their very power of shaping and applies to entire fields of knowledge.

To fully understand the epistemological and cognitive implications of Kantian and neo-Kantian developments in the theory of knowledge, we must remember that the associationist psychology of classical empiricism treats all ideas as merely combinations of elementary sensations, without differentiating ideas from their foundational sensations. As a result, it can have been relayed by twentieth-century behaviorism, where reference to the contents of consciousness disappears because, as William James explains, in associationism, ideas are treated just as "things" that the mind binds together (James 1950 [1890], 554). In contrast, with Kant, the activity ascribed to the knowing subject implies the attribution of meaning to experience, which, in turn, brings the contents of consciousness to the fore.

Recognizing both the sensory foundations of knowledge championed by the British empiricists and the type of rational knowledge of the Continental rationalists, Kant posited that our knowledge comprises two parts: one empirical, derived from our sensory faculties, and the other theoretical, derived from our rational faculties. It is because each of us brings a non-sensory meaning to the sensory information we perceive that an intersubjective space of beliefs of all kinds, both descriptive and normative and, within the former, whether scientific or not, is possible. However, the activity that Kant ascribes to the knowing subject refers to laws of thought shared by all individuals. In this respect, Kant's solution introduces two types of *a priori* categories of knowledge: the *a priori* forms of sensibility (external intuition—space and internal intuition—time) are the necessary conditions for all perception, while the "*a priori* categories" of understanding (quantity, existence, causality, etc.) serve to organize our sensory experiences, converting them into meaningful knowledge. Kant saw the theoretical component of knowledge as categorical and necessary, and not, as is the case, merely hypothetical. Given their *a priori* status, in an absolute sense independent of any particular experience, the uniformity of categories is deemed necessary, otherwise, our experiences of the external world would be radically different. However, this universal basis for the activity of knowledge can hardly explain the great divergences in beliefs among human groups (see Filmer Northrop 1966, chap. 5, which highlights Kant's contributions and limitations on these issues).

On the moral level, Kant's unitary conception of the moral law, which mandates individuals to act solely based on principles that can be universalized, has similar limitations due to its generality. On the normative level, however, Kantian moral law expresses the condition of possibility of social life. Boudon (1999, 59) explains that Kant sees the origin of normative beliefs in the binding principles of practical reason, analogous in this respect to the *a priori* that make descriptive beliefs possible. There can be no viable society without rules that ensure the coexistence of individuals and that are potentially accepted by all. Such rules apply to all only if they ignore the interests of each individual. This perspective contrasts with utilitarianism and supports Weber's distinction between instrumental and axiological rationality. But, just as the *a priori* categories do not account for the variety of descriptive beliefs, the submission of subjects to the moral law does not account for the contextualization of their thinking. It does not address their specific moral feelings, nor does it consider the positive commitment inherent in Boudon's notion of moral feeling. It does, however, have the great advantage of arguing that human beings have the capacity "to lay down principles, to self-assign values, and to draw up programs, albeit vague at the outset, that gain clarity through realization" (Boudon 2007, 30).

From neo-Kantian theory of knowledge to methodological individualism

The generalization and relativization of the Kantian *a priori* into stratified systems of concepts, beliefs, propositions, etc., within the neo-Kantian framework "à la Simmel," is fraught with implications for sociological understanding. In particular, there is an intrinsic link between the neo-Kantian epistemological approach described above and methodological individualism (MI), which, as Boudon repeatedly reminds us, rests on three pillars:

1. Individualism: The analysis should be traced back to individual behaviors responsible for a social phenomenon.
2. Understanding: The analysis should make it possible to understand these behaviors in terms of the actors' reasons for acting in their situation.
3. Rationality: Social actors generally have good reasons, personal and/or impersonal, for acting as they do.

From the outset, it is clear that "individualism," which only requires reference to individual behavior, should not be confused, as is often the case, with "methodological individualism," which includes all three pillars (individualism, understanding, and rationality). Especially, MI's assumption that human action is driven by subjective meanings sets it apart from any attempt to naturalize the human subject. Boudon (1984b, 40) formalizes the general structure of the MI explanatory model as follows:

> Let us consider any social or economic phenomenon, M, that we are trying to explain. M must be interpreted as a function $M(m_i)$ of a set of individual actions m_i. As for the individual actions m_i, they are themselves, under conditions and in a manner to be specified, functions $m_i(Si)$ of the structure Si of the situation in which the agents or social actors are found. The function (in the mathematical sense) $m_i(Si)$ must be interpreted as having for the actor i

a function *of adaptation* to the situation Si. Weber would have said that the action m_i must be *understandable*. The structure Si is, on its side, a function Si(M') of a set M' of data defined at a macrosocial level or at least at the level of the *system* inside which the phenomenon M develops. Explaining M is, in short, according to this general paradigm [Methodological Individualism], specifying the terms of $M = M \{m[S(M')]\}$.

In the stated equation, the "function" $m_i(Si)$, which conveys how individuals subjectively "adapt" to their situation, implies the three pillars above in light of neo-Kantian epistemology. Their interpretive activity, at the source of their action, is mediated by structures of meaning involving their own cognitive and social resources and the differentiated contexts in which they are embedded (see, e.g., Boudon 2012, 236). This implies individualism. Moreover, these structures, which underlie their interpretive activity by accounting for the construction of meaning, lead to the postulate of understanding—a common premise of both neo-Kantianism and Kantianism is the unitary nature of the foundations of human thought. Finally, while the intervention of irrational idiosyncratic factors is acknowledged, the postulate of rationality is intrinsically tied to the prior two, through the notion that individuals' interpretive activities justify their reasons (both personal and impersonal) for acting as they do.

The significance of the neo-Kantian theory of knowledge in MI is revealed in Boudon's assertion that one cannot truly understand the Simmelian notion of form without recognizing its "organic" connection to methodological individualism (Boudon 1984a, 12), since these forms, as organizing structures of knowledge, express the German philosopher and sociologist's neo-Kantian stance. They embody the relatively persistent and socially shared—institutionalized— nature of various kinds of "*a priori*" of meaning, inviting us to explain social phenomena in terms of the "mental" dimension of individual actions. Boudon identifies the roots of this epistemological approach in both Simmel and Weber. He also identifies its premises in the writings of other great sociologists, premises likely to inspire them MI-type analyses, even if they are not among its classical proponents, as in the case of Emile Durkheim. Boudon (2007, 211) quotes the Durkheim of *The Elementary Forms of Religious Life*, who states that logical thought is only possible when human beings have come to conceive of a whole world of stable ideals beyond their transient sensible experiences. According to Durkheim, the impersonality and stability of these intellectual constructs, which form a public realm and, as Boudon notes, tend toward coherence with reality, confusingly express the recognition that a notion of truth stands apart from sensible appearances. Durkheim's neo-Kantianism is expressed by the idea that, far from hindering access to the truth, the combination of elements of a theoretical nature with elements of a sensitive nature is a condition for it.

The structure of human knowledge

The conclusions that Boudon draws from the neo-Kantian theory of knowledge for the philosophy of science feed his recurrent critique of the premises of positivism, which, he explains, are based on an untenable principle, namely that scientific knowledge can do without bringing principles into play (Boudon 2013, 41). The discussion of these principles, because they cannot be justified within the disciplines themselves, is a favorite topic of philosophy: "While they [the positivists] advocated the liquidation of philosophy in favor of the positive disciplines, Simmel concludes that it is eternal, since its existence is the consequence of the very nature of human knowledge" (Boudon 1990, 424).

The implications for normative beliefs, which are supposed to be based on reasoning structured in the same way as descriptive beliefs, are of the same order as for the latter, implying both a multiplicity of possible viewpoints and a form of possible transsubjectivity in judgments. Central to *The Meaning of Values*, for example, is the idea that normative beliefs bring into play *a prioris* that imposes a form of circularity on them, subjecting them to the "Munchausen Trilemma." The latter, formulated by the German philosopher Hans Albert, expresses that the justification of any statement inevitably leads to one of three pitfalls: an infinite regression, circular reasoning, or dogmatism. The arborescent and hierarchical conception of knowledge stemming from neo-Kantianism justifies abandoning the search for ultimate principles, unless they are vague and undefined: In descriptive knowledge, it concerns respecting reality, and in terms of morality, it concerns respecting the human (Boudon 1999, 78). In this regard, the principle of dignity serves merely as an overarching guide, whose essence is continuously taking shape or being "realized" (on this principle, see Mesure 2023). Given this structure of knowledge, justifying normative beliefs requires intricate networks of argumentative systems. Boudon summarizes this in his idea of a rationalist-contextualist approach to moral sentiments (Boudon 1999, 71): "Both practical-ethical certainties and intellectual-theoretical judgments are based on extensive, loosely interconnected systems of reasons" (Boudon 1999, 202) so that value judgments are variable, but they involve principles with potential transsubjective validity:

> Two systems of equations have different solutions if their parameters are different. This does not mean that the equations are different. The same applies to the contextual variation of value judgments. In all cases, the solution derives from reasons that are binding because they are objective. It differs from case to case, because the context imposes different conditions. (Boudon 1999, 240)

The variability of theoretical viewpoints applied to understand the human world justifies Boudon's criticism of "monisms" and overarching theories anchored in a unitary explanatory principle that falsely claims universal applicability. He observes that these monisms share an inclination to naturalize the human subject in an attempt to support their foundational principle. In doing so, they wrongly appeal to hypothetical causes of a material nature, such as biological, sociobiological, memetic, structuralist, and culturalist interpretations, among others:

> Materialism is a valid postulate for the sciences of nature, but not for the sciences of man, for the reason that it is realistic in the former case, but not in the latter. It is realistic to see the natural world as the effect of material causes, and superstitious to see it as the effect of final causes. In the human sciences, the terms of this relationship are reversed. (Boudon 2008b, 18)

Subject model and concrete subject

In Weber's "understanding sociology," broadly endorsed by Boudon, the ideal type serves as a conceptual model that simplifies and accentuates certain features of a social phenomenon for the heuristic aims of analysis and comparison (i.e., bureaucracy, the ethic of conviction, etc.). From the outset, the ideal type is consistent with an epistemology based on the construction of interpretive hypotheses. Its relationship to observable reality can be deemed correlational, provided that "correlation" here bridges two distinct realms: the theoretical and the empirical. This correlational nature underlies Weber's concept of empirical or causal adequacy, which complements the requirement of adequacy in terms of meaning, referring to the postulate of understanding.

The hypothetical nature of the ideal type, along with its heuristic function, illuminates the relationship between the rational processes postulated by the explanation and the subjective experience of individuals. In particular, Boudon's references to this experience in no way imply that the subjects are in complete mastery of their ideas. What may strike the reader is Boudon's allusion to the "immediate data of consciousness," especially given his limited references to phenomenology. This is further compounded by his frequent recourse to the concept of "feeling" to describe their experience. Boudon evokes "perceived reasons," "feelings," and the "impression" that something is right or compelling. In this respect, both descriptive and normative beliefs are not only interrelated but also "experienced" in similar ways. For example, when we experience indignation at a criminal act, we have the impression that the act is objectively bad, not that we feel so out of personal appreciation, as

Boudon explains (Boudon, 1995, p. 34). He further notes, "It is not because values are experienced as well-founded that individuals clearly discern the underlying reasons. More often, they understand them intuitively and emotionally" (Boudon, 1999, p. 12)

This view of the subjectivity of the social actor and its relation to experience is close to Weber's perspective. In the first chapter of *Economy and Society*, Weber explains that the conceptual constructs of sociology are ideal types not only from an objective point of view but also when applied to subjective processes, since most actions in the real world often take place in a state of semi-consciousness, or even unconsciousness, of their "intended meaning": The actor typically has a vague "feeling" of this meaning rather than an understanding or knowledge of it, and actions often arise from impulse or habit. Weber points out that this should not prevent sociology from constructing its concepts on the basis of a classification of possible types of "intended meanings," as if actions were consciously oriented toward meaning. It is therefore crucial to distinguish between the theoretical, rational model of a social actor, which may elucidate implicit, or "metaconscious," beliefs and arguments for explanatory purposes, and the actual lived experience of the individual.

"Conscious" and "metaconscious"

The concept of the metaconscious, borrowed from Friedrich Hayek (1978, chap. 17), allows Boudon to distinguish references to mental processes rooted in implicit knowledge from hypotheses involving unconscious processes supposedly at odds with conscious motivations, as found in Freudian theory (Boudon 1990, 110). In reality, the ends and means of action are always partly conscious and partly metaconscious. Whether in routine daily actions or in more deliberate activities such as scientific research, we rely on various representations and propositions that are not immediately at the forefront of our consciousness. We take these propositions for granted, which is why they remain implicit (Boudon 1990, 423–424). In this respect, the implicit represents an essential component of social interaction (Boudon 1990, 13). But, if we accept the continuum between the conscious and unconscious, drawing a definitive line between the two may not offer significant explanatory insight. This is reflected in the analyses of Simmel (1905/1907), who considers that attributing an act to an unconscious motivation is merely an articulation of our ignorance of the true motive. The theoretical model of the social actor selectively simplifies the content of thought that is most relevant to the explanation, without concern for each actor's full mastery of the meaning of their action. As Simmel explains in *Problems*, this leads to the adoption of a "strangely fictitious" psychology, which he describes as "abstract." In this model, Figure 1 represents the individual's cognitive relationship with the external world.

Precisely because the neo-Kantian "*a priori*" implies a stratification of knowledge, with more abstract knowledge underpinning an activity of connecting more concrete knowledge, as illustrated especially by Boudon's metaphor of "points of view," the "perspectives" implied by the connecting activity itself tend to escape the subjects' consciousness. Simmel points out in *Problems* that Kant, in fundamentally separating *a priori* from empirical knowledge, did not fully recognize the extent to which forms of connection unconsciously dominate the data of the external world.

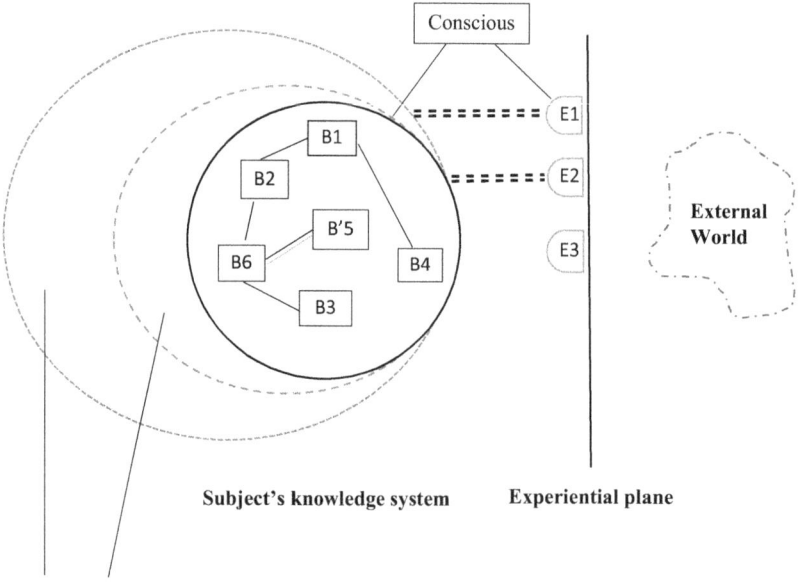

Metaconscious: diverse, intricate, levels of cognitive "*a priori*" of a linguistic, logical, epistemological, prescriptive or other nature, and other implicit elements of the subject's knowledge.

Bi: Beliefs, propositions, arguments of a descriptive nature

B'i: Beliefs, propositions, arguments of a normative nature

Ei: Elements of the subject's experience of the external world

==== : Cognitive links between normative and descriptive beliefs

= = = : Links between the subject's knowledge system and his or her more immediate cognitive experience of the external world

Figure 1. Overview of the subject's cognitive relationship to the external world in Raymond Boudon's theory of knowledge.

Here it is important to understand the unique status of both Simmel's concept of unconscious and Boudon's metaconscious, which, regardless of their experiential reality at the fringes of consciousness, refer to mental processes of meaning construction. This is why Boudon rejects the notion of psychic "forces" beyond the control of subjects. Again, such "control" doesn't necessarily involve their conscious, reflexive activity, but the meaningful mental activity that drives them. This activity is rooted in the whole stratified structure of *a priori*, admittedly more or less conscious, but implying the epistemological involvement of "final causes," motives, or reasons.

Rationality of false beliefs

The neo-Kantian theory of knowledge, along with the specific problem of the relationship between the conscious and metaconscious dimensions of thought, forms the backdrop to the various theses that Boudon puts forward to explain the subject's rational adherence to dubious or false ideas, as explored in works ranging from *The Analysis of Ideology* to *Montaigne's Spinning Wheel*, and including *The Art of Self-Persuasion.*

The neo-Kantian approach to knowledge presupposes an activity that becomes increasingly "meta-conscious" the more fundamental or abstract the *a priori* involved, especially when they are widely shared. As Simmel discusses in *Problems*, our consciousness focuses more on the external data it processes than on its own inner activity. This focus becomes even more pronounced when *a priori* propositions of a more universal nature are applied to various contexts, leading to a sense of familiarity and apparent self-evidence that makes them less noticeable. Often, this metaconscious nature is overlooked in explanations. In some cases, however, it can, as such, explain the adoption of questionable or false beliefs. Importantly, this does not undermine the postulate of rationality because these ideas result from the same processes that meaningfully produce "right" ideas. The cognitive role of the *a priori* in the process of knowledge acquisition can thus explain why individuals adhere to false beliefs, in a manner parallel to their adherence to true ones. As Boudon notes, "From the moment that these *a priori* lose their universal and unchanging character and approach what Popper calls conjectures—and what sociologists prefer to call frames— they can indeed easily create an illusion" (Boudon 1990, 57).

Boudon (1986) explains the phenomenon of ideology in terms of the typical processes of adherence to beliefs, involving both "positional" effects, which imply a specific social experience depending on the social situation of the actors, and "dispositional" effects, which imply the mobilization not only of experience but also of previously acquired and internalized knowledge, just as, he points out, a student internalizes the Pythagorean theorem: These are metaconscious dispositions that contribute to a meaningful understanding of the world. In *The Art of Self-Persuasion*, Boudon bases his analyses of misconceptions in philosophy and the human sciences on Simmel's intuition, set forth in *Philosophy of Money*, that the stratification of knowledge can lead subjects to draw valid conclusions from reasoning without realizing that these conclusions stem from the premises they are metaconsciously applying:

> If we want to think about the immense number of presuppositions on which the content of all knowledge depends, then it does not seem to be out of the question that we can prove a proposition A by B, but that B, through the truth of C, D, E., etc., can ultimately only be proved by the truth of proposition A. It is only necessary to admit a sufficiently long chain of argumentation—C, D, E, etc.—so that the return to the starting point escapes consciousness, just as the size of the Earth hides its spherical shape from immediate view, and creates the illusion that we can progress infinitely in a straight line. (Boudon 1990, 103)

Finally, the fact that all scientific knowledge rests on principles that are fundamentally unprovable and can only be validated through long-term application presents a challenge that, as Montaigne wrote, "puts us in a spinning wheel" and explains the persistence, at least in the short and medium term, of fragile or false beliefs that occupy a significant place in the public arena, such as astrology or certain conspiracy theories.

Evolution of Beliefs and Political, Moral, and Religious Thought

Evolution of beliefs: a process of "diffuse" rationalization

We have just evoked the transition from individual to collective beliefs. These collective beliefs seem to dynamically carry our shared history. The challenge is to understand how this happens. To elucidate this evolution, Boudon borrows Weber's notion of "diffuse rationalization" (*Durchrationalisierung*), which allows us to explain the emergence of long-term trends that become almost irreversible.

Looking back through history, it becomes evident that beliefs once deemed self-evident can no longer be taken for granted today. Tocqueville is astonished that Madame de Sévigné, an elegant, pious, and tactful woman of the seventeenth century, boasted in her correspondence of the great pleasure she derived from witnessing a particularly cruel capital execution (Boudon 2012, 2). It is true that some people today try to film gruesome scenes on social networks, but this is done clandestinely and no longer has the status of a matter of course, but rather that of a scandalous transgression. Fortunately, slavery has been abolished, a practice that didn't shock Seneca in antiquity or even Montesquieu in the eighteenth century (Boudon 2008a, 122). Admittedly, it is still practiced in some countries, but covertly and with broad condemnation. For millennia, our ancestors believed that the Earth was flat and that the sun revolved around it. Granted, 7% of the world's population still believes this. But everyone else knows it is wrong. The challenge now is to enlighten this small but significant fraction of the uninformed. That is over five hundred million people out of a total population of eight billion.

So, how is it that these world-driving beliefs evolve over time? So much so that we seldom encounter official advocates of cruel punishments such as quartering, the practice of slavery, or the notions of a flat and central Earth. This process of rationalization can be articulated in two phases (Boudon 2008a, chapter 5 on "normative progress"). The first phase is one of innovation: a novel idea emerges that competes with the multitude of preexisting beliefs. For example, what if every human being has an inherent dignity that should be respected? What if there is a single, transcendent God? What if the Earth is spherical and rotates within a galaxy? What if the separation of powers protects against excessive absolute power? The second phase is one of rational selection: through debate, examination, trial, and error, certain ideas gain acceptance and a growing number of believers, while others fade into obscurity. In the long run, this permanent decantation takes place: innovation-rational selection.

This process is reminiscent of Darwin's selection of species, which also operates in two stages to account for biological evolution. However, we must not confuse the neo-Darwinian mechanical process with the neo-Weberian rational process. In the neo-Darwinian model, a first stage may be environmental change, and a second, species adaptation through genetic mutations and natural selection. For example, in biology, (1) if a climate change causes trees to have only high-perched leaves, then (2) only long-necked animals like giraffes will survive and reproduce. Others will perish. This sequence-environmental change followed by species adaptation is ubiquitous in biology. Examples range from the tuskless elephant, which better evades poachers and thus has a higher survival rate, passing on its once-defective but now-protective genes, to the gray butterfly, which better camouflages itself in polluted air, avoiding predators and thus ensuring its survival and that of its offspring. This approach works less well in sociology. Consider the following: (1) since capitalists, as predators, lay off workers to increase profits by using only machines without the burden of wages, then (2) since labor is the only source of wealth, profits will decrease and the capitalists will dig their own grave. This is a well-known explanation by Marx, often presented in a very Darwinian light, depicting an economic landscape of predators and prey (Boudon 2008a, 74). But despite—or perhaps because of—the application of the Darwinian model, this theory falls short. Moreover, capitalism continues to flourish. Thus, the Darwinian process of environmental change followed by adaptation does not translate seamlessly into social contexts, such as the roles of capitalists and workers. It is more appropriate for natural phenomena like giraffes, elephants, or butterflies.

On the other hand, it is the rational process—consisting of innovation and rational selection—that best explains social phenomena. For example, if the new idea among capitalists is to replace humans with machines or artificial intelligence, this idea will inevitably meet with significant resistance, in part because of the looming fear of unemployment. But the idea will also find supporters. They might argue that machines actually create the jobs to make them; another point in their favor might be that machines often replace tedious tasks, allowing them to be performed more efficiently. In short, we can see how, over a long period of time, this innovation-selection process can lead to the rejection or adoption of an idea, by more and more people who support and trust it.

Boudon carefully distinguishes: On the one hand, what happens in the long run, with this process of rationalization, where, in the end, good ideas drive out bad ones; on the other hand, what happens in the short run. In the short run, "the diffusion of ideas obeys two fearsome sociological laws" (Boudon 2012, 37). First, a group outside the original transmitters of a new idea adopts it in a way that seems directly useful to them. Second, "the diffusion of ideas is often accompanied by undue simplifications" (ibid.). It is difficult to prevent lobbies and interest groups from appropriating these new ideas for their own benefit. Similarly, it is nearly impossible to prevent these ideas from being reduced, summarized, and oversimplified. But these short-term challenges should not obscure the broader reality: In the long run, you cannot fool everyone everywhere with superficial slogans and fragile or false ideas. In the end, discernment prevails. In his last, posthumous, work, *Montaigne's Spinning Wheel* (2013), Boudon warns that this long-term optimism does not provide full reassurance. The damage done by misguided beliefs can be profound, even catastrophic, during their prevalence, and persist until they are discredited enough to leave the "ideological" scene.

In France, Boudon primarily criticizes the flawed pedagogical theories that have led to the deterioration of teaching. He supports Nathalie Bulle's (1999) comparative study of the trajectories of the French and American educational systems, which are undergoing similar drifts, albeit with a time lag. Boudon's second thought concerns bad theories of delinquency that have led to a deterioration of security. He enviously refers to good criminological theories, such as those of Maurice Cusson in Canada. While it is reassuring to believe that in the long run things will inevitably improve after worsening, the interim damage, while temporary, cannot be overlooked. It is still too lasting for those who no longer have the time to wait for better days. They legitimately feel that their generation has been shortchanged, as if they were born at an inopportune time. It is not that there is some orchestrated "conspiracy" at play—instead, it is a process of rational selection from a plethora of reasons. But this selection is regrettably slow in fostering sound collective beliefs, especially in the face of those who suffer the tangible damage caused by bad ideas that are not discarded quickly enough.

In certain formulations of the rationalization process (Boudon 2008a; 2012), the author introduces an upstream and a downstream to the phases already presented. This aids in pinpointing factors that either facilitate or obstruct the process. Upstream, there is often a broad program that sparks new ideas. As a result, these ideas tend to surface when the conditions are conducive, even if they are already part of the zeitgeist. The aspiration for greater recognition of human dignity is a prime example of a program of this scope. Following Weber, Boudon traces its origins back to the epistles of Saint Paul. Once this expansive initiative was set in motion, subsequent innovations built upon it through the ages, leading to the contemporary interpretations of human rights that may still be subject to further refinement. Downstream, certain "historical forces" can thwart this evolution. Unfortunately, we know that civilization is periodically threatened by a resurgence of barbarism. Sometimes, the very emergence of new ideas can lead to misleading simplifications and perilous misappropriation. There is no point in giving examples here, for they are so numerous.

The process of rationalization that accounts for the collective evolution of our beliefs is not to be confused with immutable progress or systematic decline, and even less with a so-called law of history driven by an unyielding determinism. Rather, they are oriented trends underpinning a social phenomenon, which may gain or lose momentum, depending on the context. In his last book published in his lifetime, *Believing and Knowing* (2012), the author also emphasizes the ongoing tension between instrumental and axiological reasons in the selection of ideas, a preamble to the collective evolution of our beliefs. Individually, already: I want to protect the environment but find sorting garbage tedious; I am looking forward to retirement, but it would be nice to pass on a balanced budget to the next generation and therefore work a little longer; I am inclined to support political candidates whose programs are in the right direction for everyone, as long as their policies do not disadvantage me personally; and so on. The aggregation of these myriad personal motivations, torn within each individual between interests and values, given the right mix and context, gradually leads to the emergence of collective proposals that are likely to gain widespread support and thus become deeply held beliefs for a long time to come. This encapsulates the comprehensive rational process of idea innovation and selection and sheds light on the collective evolution of our beliefs, our institutions, and even our shared history.

Application to moral, religious, or political phenomena

The overarching process of rationalization, as elucidated by Weber and others, illuminates Joseph Schumpeter's insights into economic evolution as well as Thomas Kuhn's perspective on scientific evolution. In his later works, Boudon chose to focus his analysis on moral, religious, and political phenomena. To him, these phenomena seemed even more enigmatic than the others. As a result, the challenge of deciphering them and understanding their evolution seems great.

For his study of the evolution of moral sentiments in the context of globalization (Boudon 2012, chapter 4), Boudon draws on the World Values Survey, which has undergone five waves of measurement over 40 years: 1980, 1990, 2000, 2010, and 2020. For the data from the 1990s, he selects seven Western countries: France, Germany, the United Kingdom, Sweden, Italy, the United States, and Canada, as well as three countries that are more remote in this realm of values: Turkey, Russia, and India. He examines responses related to one's sense of right and wrong, perceptions of authority, trust in various institutions, and levels of tolerance. Tolerance is measured based on acceptance or rejection of neighbors characterized as immigrant workers, members of different ethnic groups, Jews, Muslims, homosexuals, people with AIDS, emotionally unstable people, drug addicts, or alcoholics (Boudon 2012, 139–146). In testing his explanatory model, both statically and then dynamically, by comparing the responses of the younger and older populations within each country, Boudon achieves conclusive results. First, responses seem to be driven more by principle or knowledge than by self-interest. To illustrate, individuals might tolerate emotionally unstable, potentially disruptive people because they understand that it is not their fault. Conversely, they might be less tolerant of an alcoholic who is equally annoying, but whom they perceive as responsible for their addiction. Hopefully, there seems to be a trend toward decreasing racism and homophobia, although Russia seems to be an exception. Second, the evolution of responses between young and old—which is further confirmed by analyzing successive survey dates—indicates a convergence, even for the three countries that were initially considered as *a priori* different. Across the board, people are increasingly rejecting blind obedience to orders without understanding and agreeing with them. There remains a clear demarcation between what is considered just and unjust, tolerance of difference is on the rise, and so on. These trends can be seen over time, although they have progressed at different rates depending on the country.

These results validate Boudon's explanatory model. What is more, they enable him to refute the popular yet flawed theories about "postmodern" globalization, which would plunge us into a society of "risk," where everything would be "liquid," leaving individuals lost, deprived of all reference points. The opposite is true: young people in England, France, Germany, or Russia hold highly structured personal values. They might not always recognize that these values are the collective result of a long, gradual process of rational sorting of ideas, but they certainly have firm convictions. Importantly, they often prioritize principles even if they occasionally conflict with their immediate interests, if the context permits. For instance, while some are committed to material growth, others lean more toward ecological and social progress. Some are deeply patriotic but still see themselves as citizens of the world, while others identify as cosmopolitan from the outset. In any case, this is a far cry from the unpredictable fluctuations of the so-called liquid globalization championed by some theorists who are unfortunately very much in vogue.

For the evolution of the relationship between religion and the state, commonly referred to as "laïcité," Boudon (2012, chapter 5) focuses on the case of France, especially as the country celebrates the centenary of its 1905 law on the subject. His demonstration is devastatingly incisive. Currently, the French have based their interpretation of secularism on a flawed system that is doomed to fail. It is time for them to embrace a more viable long-term model. At the heart of the current system are two misjudgments. First, the philosophy of the Enlightenment, epitomized by figures like Rousseau, seeks to replace traditional religions with a kind of civic religion that elevates the republic to the status of a "supreme being." Second, Comte's positivism seeks to replace religious belief with science, while maintaining a structure reminiscent of the Catholic Church. All this has produced nothing but tension and failure. You do not change beliefs by decree or revolutionary force. The core of the system that would be more promising is also twofold. First, with Tocqueville (1835), we must admire the American flexibility of a modern and religious country, where the decentralization of both the state and religions allows local adjustments to be made without escalating conflicts between church and state. This prevents such conflicts from reaching a national impasse, a recurring problem in France. Then, with Durkheim (1912), religious believers must be taken seriously. They have their own reasons for believing. This should be respected, even if we do not share their faith. It is therefore misguided to dismiss them as heirs of ancient superstition or as deluded individuals in need of enlightenment. From Boudon's perspective, the tensions of the past two centuries have prevented a process that has spanned several millennia from unfolding harmoniously.

Other countries seem better positioned to foster a more constructive form of secularism. Unusually, Boudon's argument here is supported entirely by French sources. He omits to mention Marx's characterization of religion as the "opium of the people" in negative theories, or Weber's powerful explanations in examples of sound theories of religious belief.

Regarding the political evolution of the consideration of popular sovereignty in representative democracy, Boudon (2012, chapter 6) once criticizes a sociological predecessor he usually admires the most: Tocqueville (1840). Tocqueville was concerned that universal suffrage in a representative system could lead to a "tyranny of the majority." By winning only 51% of the vote, a party could oppress 49% of the population throughout its term in office. As a member of parliament and later as a minister, Tocqueville proposed a system of "intermediate bodies," in the form of associations, to balance the interests between individuals at the bottom and their representatives at the top. In the twenty-first century, this leads to calls for a more "direct," "deliberative," and "participatory" democracy. All of these terms amount to challenge representative democracy and entrust popular sovereignty to more local, decentralized, grassroots bodies. While the idea is appealing, Boudon finds it dangerous. Local budgets may be safely managed by a neighborhood committee, but perhaps not national defense, the future of pensions, or the ecological transition. Our author calls on two sociologists who, in his opinion, are not used enough to warn against this. According to Robert Michels, any party left to its own devices, no matter how self-managing and egalitarian, is a machine for creating an oligarchy. It is the active partisan minorities that become tyrannical, and not the majorities, which often remain silent and passive. A second author, Mancur Olson, explains why. In unorganized large groups, everyone tends to benefit from the collective strength while minimizing their contribution, hoping to be able to count on the others without this passivity being noticed. But because everyone thinks the same way, no one does anything. In short, in large groups on common issues, everyone runs the risk of behaving like a "stowaway"; as a result, a motivated minority can take advantage of this inertia, leading to "the exploitation of the many by the few." Boudon's trenchant conclusion suggests that in a "participatory" democracy, only a few committed lobbyists with vested interests participate in discussions, while the majority remains silent or uninvolved. The central state then adopts the results of this "deliberation" as if it were a collective consensus. On the whole, it is preferable to perfect the existing representative system, the fruit of a great process of rationalization that for centuries has valued respect for the dignity of each individual and the separation of powers. Of course, a majority can win for a while. But this will lead to a change if the results are too disappointing. In any case, we will avoid tyrannies of 20% over 80%, or even 5% over 95%, when effective active minorities infiltrate supposedly "participatory" assemblies. Once again, a false good idea slows down a process that is excellent in the long run: The march toward a democracy in which the people are truly represented.

Back to Epistemology in the Social Sciences

The explanation for moral, religious, or political phenomena put forth is grounded in a precise static and dynamic analysis. This spans from individual reasons to the collective evolution of our beliefs. As we can see, such a method of analysis makes it possible to achieve certain explanatory "breakthroughs" (Boudon 2012, prologue). It also implies making "ruptures" (Boudon 2012, epilogue) with rival explanations that are insufficient but influential. In conclusion, it is appropriate to return to Boudon's epistemology. For him, it is a permanent reflection, no longer on the results obtained, but on how to obtain solid results with maximum guarantees. He often says that we are moving from the shop window of sociology to its workshop.

The "breakthroughs" are due to two sets of principles. The first concerns "sociology as a science" (Boudon 2012, 278). It consists of three principles:

1. The principle of "singularity" refers to the object under observation. For meaningful analysis, this subject must be clearly defined and offer a precise point of inquiry. It may be too much to try to explain all of humanity or all of history at once. Robert Merton (1949) recommended concentrating on "intermediate theories." Montaigne (1595) warns, "I fear we have eyes larger than our bellies, and more curiosity than capacity: we embrace everything, but we clutch at the wind" (quoted in Boudon 2012, 256–257). Moreover, it is inherently more difficult to locate an object or phenomenon at the macrosocial level than it is to do so at the meso or microsocial level. Put simply, it is often easier to identify a specific group or organization than to characterize a broad social movement. Yet, as we have seen, our author relishes the challenge of delving into such complex issues as morality, politics, and religion.

2. The principle of "neutrality" refers to the observer. A sociologist must set aside personal biases, interests, and passions, for he runs the risk of being blinded by them, of having the answers before the questions. Such premature conclusions are all too common. Instead of starting with the observed phenomenon and tracing it back to the underlying beliefs, then to the reasons, in relation to the context, we often invoke a ready-made explanatory variable—be it social class, gender, ethnicity, or age, among the most commonly cited. This approach mirrors Molière's

doctors, who prescribe remedies before making a proper diagnosis. In the realm of theater, the comic effect of an uninformed character repeatedly recommending a solution is undeniable. In sociology, however, this widespread practice of the pre-established leitmotif—"class," "gender," or "age"—is anything but amusing. It often predetermines outcomes and provides only superficial insights. When personal passions or interests intervene, the result is often a denunciation of dominant economic, sexual, or cultural groups, highlighting well-known and real inequalities. To truly delve into explanations, it is essential to start with a clearly defined phenomenon (as per Principle 1) and to adhere to the neutrality (as per Principle 2) advocated by scholars such as Weber and Durkheim.

3. The principle of "methodological individualism" refers to the approach that guides an observer in explaining the observed object, in this case, human beings within communities or societies. At its core is the near-postulate that individuals, though constrained, possess agency. Thus, understanding individuals becomes central to explaining collective beliefs and actions. The robustness of an explanation can be judged by its results rather than by its underlying assumptions. But let us remind that ontology inherently refers to the object of study. Consequently, it is admissible to analyze human actions or beliefs differently than we would a stone, molecule, or planet. These objects have different properties. As Weber pointed out, in nature, we can only grasp the behavior of objects functionally, and then determine it according to the rules of their course, with "because" explanations. For example, sick people have fevers because they have the flu. In contrast, social actions are driven by final causes, intentions, or reasons—explained as "in view of" motivations. Patients take medicine with the intention of getting well. They trust the effectiveness of the medicine and the doctor who prescribed it. They hope to regain their health. Conversely, a person's taking of a medicine is not caused by temperature, unconsciousness, habitus, or productive forces—in short, by any material cause or functional law. It is a common but fundamental misinterpretation to look exclusively for explanations in the social sciences from such causal perspectives. In fact, the patient just has reasons for wanting to be cured in this way.

The second set of principles details precisely this method, which Boudon refers to in his latest books as the "theory of ordinary rationality." He formulates it in four principles (2012, 39–41):

1. Ideas or beliefs drive the world, more than interests alone.
2. Such beliefs arise from our individual "reasons" for thinking or acting in certain ways. This rationality includes cognitive, axiological, and

instrumental facets. To the believer, a "reason" always feels justified, even if it seems irrational or illogical to an outside observer. We have seen how the neo-Kantian theory of knowledge sheds light on the importance of understanding the meaning individuals give to their actions and provides fruitful ways of explaining both their most well-founded reasons and their beliefs that seem most incomprehensible to the observer. It is the responsibility of that observer to try to understand them. This even suggests that there are no innate cognitive "biases" in the human brain. People may hold tenuous, questionable, or incorrect beliefs for a period of time, but these are eventually subject to revision and correction—a dynamic different from inherent "biases."

3. A two-step "rationalization process"—innovation, selection—accounts for the collective evolution of our beliefs, given our reasons, in our own context. This has been extensively illustrated.

4. A "continuity" exists between descriptive and normative beliefs. Both types are grounded on reasons, and both evolve through the rationalization process. In essence, it is erroneous to think of physics–chemistry–biology as domains where advancements in knowledge can be observed and to think of politics–morality–religion as merely a fabric of superstitions and illusions that may never be fully understood or explained. Numerous examples of this continuity have been provided. At times, we see the theology of grace being expounded in a highly rational manner (Quilliet 2007), while biological laboratory research seems conducted in a rather rudimentary, even arbitrary manner (as presented by Latour and Woolgar 1979, who draw from it an undue relativism).

The necessary "ruptures" in the epistemology of social sciences are now evident. We must exercise caution with explanations that do not respect either the three principles of sociology as a science or the four principles of the theory of ordinary rationality.

References

Boudon, R. (1984a). Introduction. In: Simmel, G. (ed.) (1907/1984) *Les problèmes de la philosophie de l'histoire* [*Problems of the Philosophy of History*] (pp. 7–52). Paris: PUF.

———. (1984b). *La place du désordre: Critique des théories du changement social*. Paris: PUF [Transl. 1991. *Theories of Social Change: A Critical Appraisal*. New York: Polity Press].

———. (1986). *L'idéologie: L'origine des idées reçues*. Paris: Fayard [Transl. 1989. *The Analysis of Ideology*. New York: Polity Press].

———. (1990). *L'art de se persuader. Des idées douteuses, fragiles ou fausses*. Paris: Fayard. [Transl. 1994. *The Art of Self–Persuasion: The Social Explanation of False Beliefs*. New York: Polity Press].

———. (1995). *Le juste et le vrai: études sur l'objectivité des valeurs et de la connaissance*. Paris: Fayard. [Transl. 2001. *The Origin of Values*. New Brunswick/London: Transaction].

———. (1999). *Le sens des valeurs*. [*The Meaning of Values*] Paris: PUF.

———. (2007). *Essais sur la théorie générale de la rationalité: action sociale et sens commun*. Paris: PUF [Transl. (2009). *Towards a General Theory of Rationality: A Defence of Common Sense*. Oxford: Bardwell Press].

———. (2008a). *Le relativisme* [Relativism]. Paris: PUF.

———. (2008b). Mais où sont les théories générales d'antan? [But where are the general theories of yesterday?] *European Journal of Social Sciences* 140: 31–50.

———. (2012). *Croire et savoir. Penser le politique, le moral et le religieux*. [*Believing and Knowing. Thinking Politics, Morality and Religion*]. Paris: PUF.

———. (2013). *Le Rouet de Montaigne: une théorie du croire* [*Montaigne's Spinning Wheel: A Theory of Belief*]. Paris: Hermann.

Bulle, N. (1999). *La rationalité des décisions scolaires. Analyse comparée de l'évolution des systèmes d'enseignement secondaire français et américain au XXᵉ siècle* [The rationality of school decisions. A comparative analysis of the evolution of French and American secondary education systems in the twentieth century]. Paris: PUF.

Cuin, C.-H. (2022). *Sociologie des croyances et de la foi* [*Sociology of Belief and Faith*]. Paris: PUF.

Durkheim, E. (1912). *Les Formes élémentaires de la vie religieuse*. Paris: PUF. [Transl. 2008. *The Elementary Forms of Religious Life*. Oxford: Oxford University Press].

James, W. (1890/1950). *The Principles of Psychology*. New York, NY: Dover Publications.

Hayek, F. (1978). *New Studies in Philosophy, Economics and the History of Ideas*. London: Routledge and Kegan Paul.

Latour, B. and Woolgar, S. (1979). *Laboratory Life. The Construction of Scientific Facts*. Berverly Hills: SAGE Publications.

Merton, R. (1949). *Social Theory and Social Structure*. Glencoe: The Free Press.

Mesure, S. (2023). Dignity and Axiological Rationality: The Legacy of Raymond Boudon. In: Bulle, N. and Di Iorio, F. (eds.), *The Palgrave Handbook of Methodological Individualism*. London: Palgrave Macmillan, 251–270.

Montaigne, M. de. (1595). Essais. Paris: Gallimard, réédition 2007. [Transl. 1958. *Complete Essays of Montaigne*. Stanford: Stanford University Press].

Morin, J.-M. (2020). *Boudon. Un sociologue classique* [*Boudon. A Classic Sociologist*]. Paris: L'Harmattan, 2ᵉᵐᵉ éd.

Northrop, F. S. C. (1946/1966). *The Meeting of East and West. An Inquiry Concerning World Understanding*. New York: Collier.

Pouivet, R. (2013). Epistémologie des croyances religieuses [*Epistemology of Religious Beliefs*]. Paris: Cerf.

Quilliet, B. (2007). L'acharnement théologique: histoire de la grâce en Occident, IIIe-XIXe siècle [*Theological Relentlessness: History of Grace in the West, 3rd–19th Century*]. Paris: Fayard.

Simmel, G. (1905/1907). *Die Probleme der Geschichtsphilosophie: Eine erkenntnistheoretische Studie* [Transl. 1977. *Problems in the Philosophy of History: An Epistemological Essay*. New York: The Free Press].

Tocqueville, A. de. (1835–1840/1986). De la démocratie en Amérique. Paris: R. Laffont (commentaires de Jean-Claude Lamberti) [Transl. 2000. *Democracy in America*. Chicago: University of Chicago Press].

Chapter 6

SOME THEORETICAL DEDUCTIONS FROM BOUDON'S MODEL OF SOCIAL MOBILITY

Renaud Fillieule

In a series of works published during the early 1970s, and especially in *L'inégalité des chances* (1973a), Boudon introduced a new method for studying intergenerational social mobility. He developed a *simulation model* that explains the attainment of social status through the interplay of one's social background and academic accomplishments. In this model, each individual within a given generation goes through *two selection agencies*, first the school system to attain a certain level of education, and second the labor market to secure a social status linked to the type of employment acquired. The comparison between the attained status in the workforce and the status of one's parents measures social mobility. Within a set of specific, well-defined assumptions, this model computes the trajectory of a particular generation from its point of origin (parents' status) to its eventual position (offspring's status), thereby determining the resultant intergenerational mobility. During the period around 1970, when Boudon was engaged in writing on these topics, all computations required by the model had to be executed manually. However, in this paper, we capitalize on the computational capabilities of spreadsheets to yield instantaneous results. Consequently, we are able to conduct a more comprehensive analysis of the influence on social mobility of various sets of parameters, particularly focusing on the two crucial parameter sets: the demand for education and the class structure.

The first section provides a concise overview of Boudon's model, while second section delves into his index of intergenerational mobility. Subsequent sections explore the effect on school attainment and social mobility of different values of the parameters of the model. The third section investigates the consequences of changes in demand for education, the fourth section, of changes in class structure (from a less to a more egalitarian society), and the fifth section, of changes in the degree of "meritocracy" (a more "meritocratic" system is understood here as a system in which an advanced educational level increases the likelihood to reach a higher social class). The sixth section addresses the classic Boudon–Bourdieu debate on the impact and significance of "cultural inheritance" on intergenerational mobility. Last, in the final section, we analyze the relevance of what Boudon calls the "language of systems," and the limits of the "language of correlations," in the study of social mobility.

The Basic Elements of the Model

The core idea of Boudon's theory is that intergenerational mobility stems from a process that runs through two selective agencies. The first agency is the educational system, which delivers various educational attainments and is characterized by a high degree of inequality of opportunity tied to one's social class of origin. The second agency involves the labor market, in which the status reached is strongly influenced by the individual's level of education. Boudon's theory uses a simulation model to formalize the distribution of status achieved by offspring (destination social class) based on their parents' social status (origin social class). Although this model is highly simplified, it offers a relevant overview of the status-acquisition process within a country.

Class structure. The social system considered comprises three social classes, C1, C2, and C3, denoting high, average, and low status, respectively. Table 1 shows the distribution of individuals across these classes within a sample size of 10,000 for a generation born in a given year. Boudon assumes that 10% of individuals belong to C1, 30% to C2, and 60% to C3. It is worth noting that his class breakdown is not too different from the much more recent classification used by Thompson and Hickey (2005) for the United States. The latter delineates an upper class and upper middle class at 16%, a lower middle class at 32%, and a working class and lower class at 52%. In Table 1,

Table 1. Class structure for a representative sample of 10,000 persons in the workforce.

	Parents (social origin)	**Children** (social destination)
C1	1,000	1,000
C2	3,000	3,000
C3	6,000	6,000
Workforce sample	10,000	10,000

Table 2. The demand for education as a function of the social class of the parents (Boudon 1973a, 170).

Social origin	Demand for education (%)
C1	80
C2	61
C3	40

the class structure is the same for the two generations, but this hypothesis will be lifted in Section 4. For simplicity, each couple is represented by a single parent, and each parent has just one child in the given generation so that the samples of both parents and children maintain the same size.

One of the central postulates of Boudon's model is that *the class structure is stable while the educational structure changes a lot over time.* Even if the class structure evolves, the educational structure changes much faster. Consequently, the disparity between the two structures intensifies in the long run, leading at the aggregate level to unexpected and undesirable outcomes (such as a costly and inefficient inflation diploma).

Educational levels. The three educational levels considered are denoted as S1, S2, and S3, respectively. These correspond to a bachelor's degree or higher (S1), between high school and bachelor's level (S2), and high school education or lower (S3). While Boudon takes a much larger number of education levels into account (a total of 9), the three main levels suffice for the purposes of this paper.

Demand for education. Table 2 displays the variation in educational demand across different social classes. It formalizes a widely recognized sociological finding, indicating that *the demand for education strongly depends on the social class of origin*: the higher the class, the more intense the demand for education. This demand is formalized in this context as the probability to keep studying in order to attain a higher educational tier rather than stopping and entering the workforce. With the data employed by Boudon (inspired by the study of Girard and Clerc 1964), families belonging to class C1 have an 80% propensity of educational pursuit[1] (parameter of the model). When children with a C1 background reach one of the two major bifurcation points of our simplified educational framework (end of high school and end of college), their likelihood to *keep on studying* in order to reach the next level is 80%. Conversely, their probability of concluding their educational journey at those points and transitioning into the labor force (or opting for a short vocational training) is calculated as $(1 - 80\%) = 20\%$. Families

---

[1] The calculation leading to this value of 80% is presented in Section 6.

from C2 have a lower demand (in this instance, 61%), and families from C3 have an even lower demand (40%). The demand for education is much higher nowadays, a trend that will be explored in Section 3.

These significant differences between social classes are observed in empirical studies and Boudon (1973a) explains them through Merton's (1957) theory of group reference and study-related expenses. Children from higher classes are integrated into a reference group comprising parents, relatives, peers, and others, where heightened educational attainment is almost assumed. Any achievement falling short is perceived by the family as a failure, thus prompting the family to actively support and motivate the child to go as far as possible within the school system. Conversely, when the origin status is lower, children reach quicker a satisfactory educational level for themselves and their families. The financial burden of studying puts an additional brake on the educational aspirations of children from less advantaged backgrounds, thus providing a more comprehensive account of the structural pattern delineated in Table 2.

Educational attainment. Table 3 computes the probability for children from various social classes to get one of the three educational tiers. A person with a C1 parent has a $(1 - 0.8) = 0.2$ probability to stop at S3, a $0.8 (1 - 0.8) = 0.16$ probability to reach S2 and stop there, and a $(0.8)^2 = 0.64$ probability to attain S1 (the cumulative sum of these three probabilities is 1). For individuals from C2 and C3 backgrounds, the base probabilities used are 0.61 and 0.40, respectively, reflecting their comparatively lower demand for education. Figure 1 illustrates the educational journey of children from C1 origin.

Table 4 presents, not the probabilities, but the numbers of children from each origin reaching each educational level within the 10,000 sample of the second generation. Suffices to multiply the educational probabilities of Table 3 by the size of the origin classes from Table 1.

The educational composition outlined in Table 4 (S1 27%, S2 23%, S3 50%) is *endogenous* to the model, shaped by the demand for education from the various classes. These results are derived from Boudon's assumptions,

Table 3. Educational attainment: probability to stop at the different levels as a function of the social origin (S1 bachelor and above, S2 between high school diploma and bachelor, and S3 high school diploma or below).

Children	Educational attainment (percentages by origin)			
Social origin	S1	S2	S3	Total
C1	64	16	20	100
C2	37	24	39	100
C3	16	24	60	100

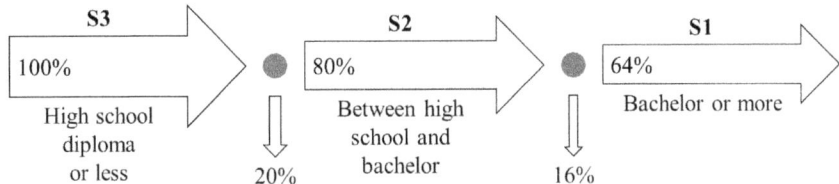

Figure 1. Educational journey of the children from C1 origin: out of 100% entering the school career, 20% will end up with S3, 16% with S2, and 64% with S1.

Table 4. Educational attainment as a function of social origin in a sample of 10,000 individuals from the same generation: out of the 1,000 children from social class C1, 640 get the highest level of education S1, 160 get the average level S2, and 200 get the lowest level S3. Then, 1,116 of the 3,000 children from social class C2 get S1, etc.

Children		**Educational attainment (headcounts)**			
Social origin		S1	S2	S3	Total
	C1	640	160	200	1,000
	C2	1,116	714	1,170	3,000
	C3	960	1,440	3,600	6,000
	Total	2,716	2,314	4,970	10,000

which draw from data going back to the 1960s. Today, the demand for education has risen, leading to a more pronounced distribution toward S1. Recent measurements in Western countries reveal the following proportions, with S1 bachelor's and above, S2 between high school diploma and bachelor's, and S3 high school diploma or below:

- Model (Table 4): S1 27%, S2 23%, S3 50%
- France[2] 2021: S1 36%, S2 13%, S3 51% (individuals having completed their studies between 2018 and 2020)
- Canada[3] 2016: S1 35%, S2 24%, S3 41% (age group 25–34)
- USA[4] 2021: S1 41%, S2 26%, S3 33% (age group 25–34)

Status acquisition. Table 5 displays the individuals' acquisition of social status as a function of their educational level. It operates on a *70% priority or weightage offered by the educational level on the acquired status*, illustrating a *meritocratic* system of

---

[2] INSEE (2021).
[3] *Education Highlight Tables*, 2016 Census, Statistics Canada (statcan.gc.ca).
[4] *Educational Attainment in the United States*, 2021, United States Census Bureau (census.gov).

Table 5. Status acquisition as a function of educational attainment, with a 70% priority given to the educational level: among the 2,716 individuals of the second generation having reached S1, 700 get the C1 status, 1,411 the C2 status, and 605 the C3 status. Among the 2,314 having obtained S2, 210 get the C1 status, etc.

Status acquisition		Children (headcounts)			
Children		C1	C2	C3	Total
	S1	700	1,411	605	2,716
	S2	210	1,112	992	2,314
	S3	90	477	4,403	4,970
	Total	1,000	3,000	6,000	10,000

status achievement. In this context, "meritocratic" denotes a strong association between educational level and attained status. The cells are filled up sequentially, from left to right and top to bottom. The process begins with the distribution of S1 individuals into appropriate categories. There are 1,000 slots in C1 (and 2,716 individuals with S1), so 70% of the 1,000 slots (= 700) are allocated to S1 individuals. This leaves $(2,716 - 700) = 2,016$ S1 individuals unassigned. Moving to C2, which has 3,000 slots, the dynamics shift. In the previous case, the number of individuals was greater than the number of slots, so the 70% priority had to be applied to the number of slots. The situation is now reversed. Since the number of slots (3,000) is superior to the number of remaining individuals (2,016), the 70% priority must logically be applied to the number of individuals. As a result, 70% of the remaining 2,016 S1 individuals (= 1,411) get into class C2. The remaining S1 individuals get the C3 status $(2,716 - 700 - 1,411 = 605)$. The second row of the table (S2 individuals) is populated following the same principles. The third row (S3 individuals) is then entirely determined by the cells already filled up and the cumulative values found in the "Total" row (reflecting the class structure of the second generation).

Intergenerational mobility. Last, we have Table 6, which represents the matrix of social mobility. It combines the information from the two previous tables and shows the intergenerational mobility between parents and their children. From Table 4, the 1,000 children from a C1 background reach the educational attainments (S1 640, S2 160, S3 200). From Table 5, the probabilities of transitioning to C1 status are as follows: for S1, it is (700/2,716); for S2, it is (210/2,314); and for S3, it is (90/4,970). Suffices then to multiply the Table 4 numbers by their respective Table 5 probabilities to determine the number of individuals coming from C1 and acquiring the C1 status: 640 (700/2,716) + 160 (210/2,314) + 200 (90/4,970) = 183. Therefore, 183 individuals from a C1 background achieve C1 status. The remaining cells of Table 6 are computed in exactly the same way.

Table 6. Intergenerational mobility: out of the 1,000 children from the highest background C1, 183 in turn get the highest status C1, 429 get C2, etc.

Social mobility		Children (headcounts and percentages by origin)			
Parents		C1	C2	C3	Total
	C1	183 (18%)	429 (43%)	388 (39%)	1,000 (100%)
	C2	374 (12%)	1,035 (35%)	1,591 (53%)	3,000 (100%)
	C3	443 (7%)	1,536 (26%)	4,021 (67%)	6,000 (100%)
	Total	1,000	3,000	6,000	10,000

Boudon's Index of Mobility

The question now is: what is the degree of mobility exhibited in Table 6? Boudon (1973a) does not make use of a synthetic quantitative index. However, in his mathematical analysis of social mobility (1973b), he develops such an index. This index will prove valuable thereafter for contrasting the mobility intensity among different configurations. Boudon's mobility index is denoted as M_B and here is its rather intricate formula:

$$M_B = 1 - \frac{\sum_i n_{ii} - \sum_i \max(n_{.i} - n_{\sim i.}, 0)}{\sum_i \min(n_{i.}, n_{.i}) - \sum_i \max(n_{.i} - n_{\sim i.}, 0)}$$

This index ranges from 0 to 1, reaching 1 when mobility is maxed out and dropping to 0 when the social system is immobile. Its complexity comes from the fact that it measures the "pure" mobility, that is, the mobility that is not "forced" by a lower number of slots for the offspring than for the parents. To illustrate, if the parents' generation has 6,000 C3 slots and the children's generation sees a decline to 4,500 C3 slots only due to workforce changes, a "forced" upward mobility of 1,500 C3 children occurs. This index does not count these 1,500 "forced" movements in its assessment of mobility.

In the formula, n_{ii} is the headcount at the intersection of row i and column i of the mobility matrix, $n_{.i}$ is the total of column i, $n_{i.}$ the total of row i, and $n_{\sim i.}$ the sum of the totals of the rows other than i. There is no need here to delve into the comparison with other indices, such as the Glass index and the Yasuda index, since they are less satisfactory (see Boudon 1973b, Chapter 1).

The mobility index should be conceived as a measure of distance, minimum (= 0) when there is social immobility and maximum (= 1) when social mobility is at its peak. For Table 6, the Boudon index M_B is 0.595 = 59.5%. Table 7

Table 7. Complete social immobility (maximized diagonal): mobility index $M_B = 0$.

Total immobility		Children			
Parents		C1	C2	C3	Total
	C1	1,000	0	0	1,000
	C2	0	3,000	0	3,000
	C3	0	0	6,000	6,000
	Total	1,000	3,000	6,000	10,000

Table 8. An example of maximum social mobility (minimized diagonal), where children tend to get a status as far away as possible from their parents': mobility index $M_B = 1 = 100\%$.

Max mobility		Children			
Parents		C1	C2	C3	Total
	C1	0	0	1,000	1,000
	C2	0	0	3,000	3,000
	C3	1,000	3,000	2,000	6,000
	Total	1,000	3,000	6,000	10,000

depicts a completely immobile social system and the calculation shows that $M_B = 0$. Table 8 illustrates the opposite case of maximum mobility and $M_B = 1$.

Boudon's index measures mobility across the whole spectrum between complete immobility and maximum mobility. However, the most relevant configuration is not maximum mobility, but rather "random" mobility. The "random" table is the one in which *the acquired status is independent of the origin status*. In other words, the social class of the parents has no influence whatsoever on the social class of their children (Boudon (1973a) employs the random mobility or independence hypothesis in a different context in Chapter 1). Table 9 illustrates this "random" mobility, wherein the statuses attained in the second generation are merely proportional to the number of available slots in each destination social class.

The concept of "random" mobility helps us build a simple index, derived from Boudon's M_B index. Rather than being measured between immobility and max mobility, mobility is measured between immobility and "randomness." We call this index the Boudon-Random index, denoted as $M_{B\text{-}Rand}$. It is simply

Table 9. "Random" mobility: the status acquired by the children is not influenced at all by the status of their parents. Whatever their origin, children acquire a status in proportion to the number of slots available in each class, so 10% end up in C1, 30% in C2, and 60% in C3: mobility index $M_B = 0.675 = 67.5\%$.

Random mobility		Children			
Parents		C1	C2	C3	Total
	C1	100	300	600	1,000
	C2	300	900	1,800	3,000
	C3	600	1,800	3,600	6,000
	Total	1,000	3,000	6,000	10,000

the ratio between the Boudon index of the "observed" mobility table and the Boudon index of the "random" table:

$$M_{B\text{-}Rand} = \frac{M_B(\text{"observed" table})}{M_B(\text{"random" table})}$$

The Boudon index M_B for the "observed" Table 6 is 0.595, while for the "random" Table 9, it amounts to 0.675. Consequently, the Boudon-Random index is $M_{B\text{-}Rand} = (0.595/0.675) = 0.882 = 88.2\%$. The closer this index is to 1 or 100%, the closer the social system is to a situation where status attainment is just "random" in the sense that it is unaffected by the educational level or social background (the Boudon-Random index can theoretically go above 1 but not within any real social system). With the 88.2% value, we see that the mobility of the social system described in Table 6 (generated by Boudon's parameters) closely approximates a system that randomly assigns the social class to the second generation. This outcome is paradoxical. A social system characterized by (i) a strong impact of social origin on educational attainment and (ii) a significant connection between education level and acquired status turns out to exhibit a social mobility that is much closer to randomness than to immobility. This paradox requires further exploration. It is addressed in the last section, using a slightly different model from the one outlined above.

Changes in the Demand for Education

There are *three sets of parameters* in the model:

- The demand for education (C1 0.80, C2 0.61, C3 0.40)
- The class structure (C1 1,000, C2 3,000, C3 6,000)
- The "meritocratic" priority of educational attainment in the access to status (70%)

Thanks to the spreadsheet formalization, it is very easy to change these parameters and assess their effect on social mobility. The changes in demand for education are addressed in this section.

Importance of the differential demand for education between social classes

The difference in the demand for education across the three classes plays a crucial role in the model. What would happen if the demand for education was the same for the three social classes? The spreadsheet immediately answers. If instead of (C1 0.80, C2 0.61, C3 0.40) we insert the same probability for all classes, for instance (C1 0.80, C2 0.80, C3 0.80), the result is the "random" mobility table (Table 9), leading to $M_{B\text{-}Rand} = 1$. In this scenario, the origin no longer influences the social prospects of individuals, as status distribution aligns with the available positions within each class.

This outcome remains consistent even when the other two kinds of parameters are altered. Let us assume that the demand for education is the same across classes, with (C1 0.80, C2 0.80, C3 0.80). If the class structure changes at the second generation, shifting from (C1 1,000, C2 3,000, C3 6,000) for parents to (C1 2,000, C2 3,000, C3 5,000) for offspring, the resulting social mobility remains random, yielding an $M_{B\text{-}Rand}$ of 1. The children's allocation now conforms to the new class proportions of 2:3:5 instead of the 1:3:6 structure of their parents (see Table 10). Similarly, if the priority "meritocratic" coefficient shifts from 70% to any other value while all classes hold identical demands for education, the resulting mobility is still purely random. In the model of Section 1, *if the differences in demand for education from the various classes are eliminated, then the structure becomes purely "random" in the sense that the acquired statuses are independent of social origin.*

Table 10. Random mobility with different class structures for the two successive generations: the class acquired is independent of the social origin.

Random mobility		Children			
Parents		C1	C2	C3	Total
	C1	200	300	500	1,000
	C2	600	900	1,500	3,000
	C3	1,200	1,800	3,000	6,000
	Total	2,000	3,000	5,000	10,000

Effects of a narrowing and a widening of the differential in demand for education

What happens when the gap between classes widens or narrows? After the conclusion of the previous subsection, the answer becomes apparent. Stretching the probabilities—for instance, transitioning from (C1 0.80, C2 0.61, C3 0.40) to (C1 0.90, C2 0.61, C3 0.30)—*reduces* social mobility: the Boudon index decreases from 0.595 to 0.555 (down 6.7%) and the Boudon-Random index from 0.882 to 0.822 (down 6.8%). Conversely, if the probabilities approach each other, for instance, substituting (C1 0.80, C2 0.61, C3 0.40) with (C1 0.70, C2 0.61, C3 0.50), social mobility *increases*: M_B rises from 0.595 to 0.633 (up 6.4%) and $M_{B\text{-}Rand}$ from 0.882 to 0.937 (up 6.2%). In these examples, the impact is more significant in the C1 and C3 rows compared to the slight movement in the C2 row. The overall effect on mobility of a widening or conversely a narrowing of the demands for education is depicted in Figure 2.

In terms of educational attainment, there is a shift from (S1 27.2%, S2 23.1%, S3 49.7%), as shown in Table 4, to (S1 24.7%, S2 20.6%, S3 54.7%) with wider gaps between educational demands. With less S1 and S2 and more S3, the widening or divergence between the demands, therefore, *reduces the overall educational achievement* of the social system. The detailed data show that this widening significantly favors children from C1 in terms of school attainment, and this advantage translates into a lower mobility that also benefits

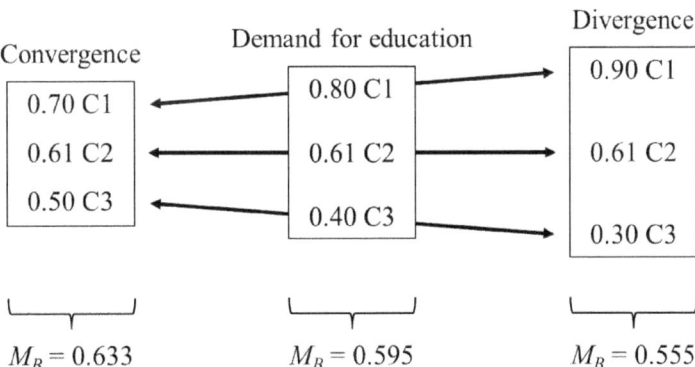

Figure 2. Social mobility (measured by the Boudon index M_B) increases when the demands for education from the social classes converge and decreases when they diverge.

individuals with a C1 origin. The consequences are reversed in the case of narrowing or convergence between educational demands: overall school achievement improves, children from C3 tend to get better diplomas and they benefit the most from the higher mobility.

Effects of a translation upward and downward of the demand for education

If the demand for education is translated upward, for instance, adding 0.10 to all the probabilities, shifting from (C1 0.80, C2 0.61, C3 0.40) to (C1 0.90, C2 0.71, C3 0.50), calculations reveal that mobility *decreases*: M_B slightly declines from 0.595 to 0.590. A similar result follows if the upward adjustment is smaller, like adding 0.01 or 0.05. When, conversely, the probabilities are translated downward, such as subtracting 0.01, 0.05, or 0.10 from the initial probabilities, mobility *increases*. Figure 3 illustrates this pattern.

In the case of an upward adjustment (e.g., adding 0.10), there is a notable increase in educational attainment across all classes. However, the likelihood of reaching C1 status diminishes for children from all backgrounds. As a result, the proportion of C1 children staying in C1 falls from 18% to 16% (more mobility), the percentage of C2 children remaining in C2 rises from 35% to 36% (less mobility), and the percentage of C3 children remaining in C3 also rises from 67% to 68% (less mobility). As C2 and C3 encompass larger segments of the population compared to C1, their impact on the index is more substantial, ultimately resulting in lower overall mobility. The effects are nevertheless quite small.

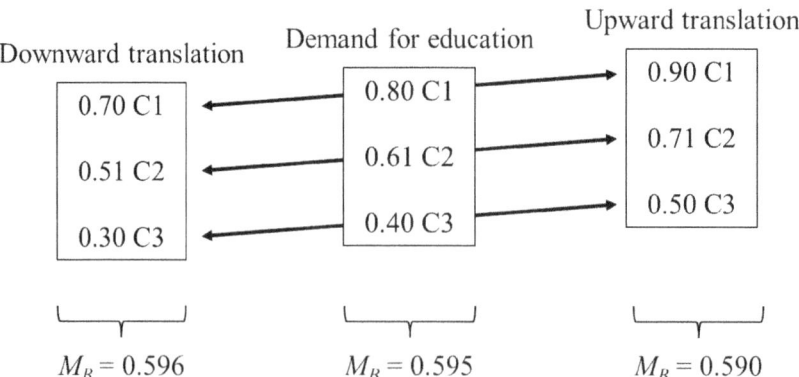

Figure 3. Social mobility decreases when the demands for education are translated upward.

Effects of the long-run increase in the demand for education

Boudon (1973a) extensively investigates the major historical trend of the rising demand for education. In his model, he examines what happens during four successive periods (T_0, T_1, T_2, T_3). The transition from one period t to the next $(t+1)$ involves an increase in each of the probabilities p representing the various demands. This rise is formalized by the following formula:

$$p_{t+1} = p_t + 0.1(1 - p_t)$$

The closer the probability p to 1, the smaller the increment $(1 - p)$ from one period to the next. In other words, the demand for education from a lower class rises by a bigger increment than from a higher class, which is to be expected since the former group has a larger margin of progression. It is important to note that in this formula, the "period" is not necessarily a single year but can instead encompass any number of years. For instance, if one period corresponds to 5 years, then the four consecutive periods from T_0 to T_3 span over 20 years.

Within our dataset, the demand for education from C1, for instance, would shift from 0.80 in T_0 to 0.82 in T_1, further to 0.84 in T_2, and ultimately reach 0.85 in T_3. Table 11 compares the structure in T_0 (which corresponds to Table 6: C1 0.80, C2 0.61, C3 0.40) and the structure in T_3. In the latter, the respective demands for education derived from the formula above are (C1 0.85, C2 0.72, C3 0.56). The higher probabilities in T_3 than in T_0 reflect a general increase in the demand for education—a phenomenon that has been widely observed over the past decades. Yet, the two mobility structures in T_0 and T_3 exhibit very small differences. The percentages in Table 11 are indeed quite similar between these two periods. Boudon (1973a, 257) concludes that there is almost no change in social mobility. There is, however, a small

Table 11. Intergenerational mobility before (T_0) and after (T_3) an increase in the demand for education.

Social mobility		Children (percentages by origin)							
		Period T_0 (mobility 0.595)				Period T_3 (mobility 0.617)			
Parents		Size	C1	C2	C3	C1	C2	C3	Size
	C1	1,000	18%	43%	39%	14%	41%	45%	1,000
	C2	3,000	12%	35%	53%	11%	34%	55%	3,000
	C3	6,000	7%	26%	67%	9%	26%	65%	6,000
		10,000	1,000	3,000	6,000	1,000	3,000	6,000	10,000

increment in social mobility: the Boudon index M_B rises from 0.595 in T_0 to 0.617 in T_3. This observation is corroborated by the fact that the probabilities of individuals remaining in the same class between T_0 and T_3 diminish (see the values of the diagonal): from 18% to 14% for C1, from 35% to 34% for C2, and from 67% to 65% for C3.

The (minor) change in mobility observed in Table 11 stems from two sources: (i) a higher demand for education across all classes and (ii) a narrower gap in demand for education between the classes. Translating the probabilities upward without narrowing them *decreases* social mobility (see Figure 3). Narrowing the probabilities, on the other hand, *increases* mobility (see Figure 2). The mobility witnessed between T_0 and T_3 in Table 11 is therefore the result of two opposite influences, with a dominance of the narrowing effect.

Another notable effect of the rise in demand for education is the evolution of the educational structure. In T_0, the school system delivers 27% S1, 23% S2, and 50% S3 (see Table 4). In T_3, the heightened educational demand leads to a distribution of 42% S1, 22% S2, and 36% S3.[5] While mobility only undergoes a minor alteration, the simulated structure of degrees changes significantly, a much higher number of individuals getting S1 and a much lower number getting S3. Despite the marked increase in S1 accomplishments, the available slots in C1 do not correspondingly increase, ultimately resulting in stability at the aggregate level (on the incongruence between the class structure and the educational structure, see Section 7).

The educational democratization that takes place between T_0 and T_3 in this example can be seen as a Boudonian explanation of *diploma inflation*. Although the quantity of higher-level diplomas increases a lot, their value for upward mobility diminishes correspondingly (given the modest rise in social mobility). Simultaneously, the value of lower-level degrees depreciates even more. Between T_0 and T_3, the probability of getting to C1 with an S1 educational level decreases from 26% to 17% (divided by 1.53), the probability of getting to C2 with S2 drops from 48% to 28% (divided by 1.71), while the probability of getting to C3 with S3 increases slightly from 89% to 90%. Overall, the value of educational attainment, measured in terms of mobility, experiences a substantial decline. This phenomenon explains in part the surge in demand for education. If individuals do not want to fall behind on the social ladder, they must strive to attain increasingly higher educational levels over time (Boudon 1973a, 299). In this manner, the escalation in educational demand can be attributed, in part, to the consequences of this very escalation, forming a circular causality.

---

[5] These data are similar to those observed in the United States in 2021 for individuals between 25 and 34 years old according to the US Census Bureau: S1 41%, S2 26%, S3 33%.

Changes in the Class Structure

The difference in class structures can appear (i) between distinct social systems (one of them more hierarchical and the other more egalitarian) and (ii) between consecutive generations (the first one more hierarchical and the next more egalitarian). The two cases are going to be investigated in turn.

Comparison between a more hierarchical and a more egalitarian society

Up until this point, a single class structure has been used, namely (C1 1,000, C2 3,000, C3 6,000). Let us now compare this initial social system with a more egalitarian alternative in which the class structure is (C1 2,000, C2 3,500, C3 4,500). In this second arrangement, individuals are much more evenly distributed across social strata. The demand for education remains unchanged at (C1 0.80, C2 0.61, C3 0.40). According to the Boudon index, the significantly more egalitarian society exhibits a *reduced* level of mobility: the M_B metric declines from 0.595 to 0.567. The difference in educational structure is rather limited, with (S1 27%, S2 23%, S3 50%) in the more hierarchical society and (S1 33%, S2 22%, S3 45%) in the more egalitarian society. Table 12 displays the two mobility matrices. In the more egalitarian society (compared to the more hierarchical counterpart), mobility is notably lower for C1 origin, a bit lower for C2 origin, and much higher for C3 origin. Given the larger numbers within C1 plus C2 in contrast to C3, their diminished mobility exerts a dominant influence, resulting in an overall reduction in total mobility.

Table 12. Comparison of intergenerational mobility between a more hierarchical society (C1 1,000, C2 3,000, C3 6,000) and a more egalitarian one (C1 2,000, C2 3,500, C3 4,500).

Social mobility			Children (percentages by origin)						
			More hierarchical society $M_B = 0.595$			More egalitarian society $M_B = 0.567$			
Parents			C1	C2	C3	C1	C2	C3	
	C1	1,000	18%	43%	39%	31%	39%	30%	2,000
	C2	3,000	12%	35%	53%	22%	36%	42%	3,500
	C3	6,000	7%	26%	67%	14%	32%	54%	4,500
		10,000	1,000	3,000	6,000	2,000	3,500	4,500	10,000

Table 13. Social mobility when the class structure of the 2nd generation is more egalitarian than the class structure of the 1st generation: $M_B = 0.500$.

Social mobility		Children (headcounts and percentages by origin)			
Parents		C1	C2	C3	Total
	C1	366 (37%)	359 (36%)	275 (27%)	1,000 (100%)
	C2	747 (25%)	1,083 (36%)	1,170 (39%)	3,000 (100%)
	C3	887 (15%)	2,058 (34%)	3,055 (51%)	6,000 (100%)
	Total	2,000	3,500	4,500	10,000

The evolution from a less to a more egalitarian class structure

Let us now consider the scenario of Table 13 where the class structure evolves *between the two successive generations*, shifting from a less equal society for the parents (C1 1,000, C2 3,000, C3 6,000) to a more equal system for the children (C1 2,000, C2 3,500, C3 4,500). The mobility index is $M_B = 0.500$, lower than all our previous values. This outcome arises due to the measurement of only "pure" mobility, while "forced" mobility occurs here: (6,000 – 4,500) = 1,500 individuals move out of C3 and end up in the 500 additional slots in C2 and 1,000 additional in C1. The educational structure is not at all affected since it only depends on the demand for education (C1 0.80, C2 0.61, C3 0.40) and the class structure of the parents (C1 1,000, C2 3,000, C3 6,000) (see Table 4). Although the overall "pure" mobility is quite low (because C1 and C2 origins have higher reproduction rates than in the previous cases), the C3 origin has the smallest reproduction rate encountered thus far (51% from C3 to C3). The upward mobility opportunities are therefore the best so far for children from C3, which is understandable on account of their "forced" mobility out of C3.

Changes in the "Meritocracy" Coefficient

Until now, a 70% weightage has been assigned to prioritize the attainment of social status based on educational accomplishments (see Table 5). This priority or "meritocratic" coefficient will now be modified, everything else equal. The results are summarized in Table 14. Elevating the level of "meritocracy" *reduces social mobility*. However, it has no effect on educational attainment, as the priority is applied after the completion of the school career. Children from C1 background have the same educational attainment independently of the priority coefficient. Nevertheless, with an 80% status priority instead of 70%, they benefit from a higher probability

Table 14. Increasing the priority coefficient of status acquisition reduces social mobility. Parameters: class structure for both generations (C1 1,000, C2 3,000, C3 6,000) and demand for education (C1 0.80, C2 0.61, C3 0.40).

Priority coefficient	Mobility index M_B	Probability of coming from C1 and reaching C1	Probability of coming from C2 and reaching C2	Probability of coming from C3 and reaching C3
50%	0.633	15%	32%	64%
60%	0.613	16%	33%	65%
70%	**0.595**	**18%**	**35%**	**67%**
80%	0.579	20%	35%	68%
90%	0.565	22%	36%	70%

to get to C1 with S1, and their downward mobility is reduced. A similar but smaller effect occurs for individuals of C2 origin. Since more C1 and C2 destination slots than before are already occupied, individuals of C3 origin encounter fewer opportunities to climb up the social ladder and their mobility is therefore reduced too. Mobility is curtailed for all classes in a more "meritocratic" regime.

The Weak Influence of "Cultural Inheritance"

Boudon (1973a) employs a more elaborated version of the model than the one presented in Section 1. Instead of relying on just three probabilities representing the demands for education from the three social classes (see Table 2), he uses the left and right tables detailed in Table 15. These tables are filled in with data adapted from the survey by Girard and Clerc (1964).

Table 15. *Left* (cultural inheritance): academic results according to social origin. 60% of C1 children have good results, 30% of them have average results, etc. *Right*: demand for education according to social origin and school results. 85% of C1 children with good results benefit from the best school orientation, 75% with average results benefit, etc.

Academic results	R1 good	R2 average	R3 weak	Total	Demand for education	O1	O2	O3
C1	60%	30%	10%	100%	C1	85%	75%	65%
C2	50%	30%	20%	100%	C2	70%	60%	40%
C3	30%	40%	30%	100%	C3	60%	40%	20%

Table 15 (left part) shows the academic achievements based on the original social class. It encapsulates the fact that *children from higher social origin tend to get better grades*. Surveys have long highlighted a positive correlation between school performance and social strata (see, for instance, the meta-analysis by Sirin 2005). An explanation is that families from higher strata tend to pass on to their children a *cultural inheritance* that equips them with the skills necessary for navigating the school environment (in terms of vocabulary, syntax, familiarity with literature, and other subjects covered in school curriculum). Conversely, children from lower social strata tend to be socialized within a cultural context that may not be fully aligned with the demands of the educational system. As a result, they tend to be less successful when going through academic testing.[6]

Table 15 (right part) shows the probabilities to embark on a trajectory that ultimately leads to a more advanced diploma. This table illustrates two main trends: (i) the higher the social origin, the higher the probability of pursuing an advantageous path (rows) and (ii) the better the academic results, the higher the probability (columns). For instance, children of C1 origin having good academic results (O1) benefit from the best orientation in 85% of the cases. If they have average results (O2), they benefit in 75% of the cases, and so on. Regardless of social class, students with better grades tend to follow a more favorable academic path.

Hence, three main components interplay in the process of inequality formation throughout the school career: (i) the higher the social origin, the better the grades (cultural inheritance), (ii) the better the grades, the more favorable the school orientation, and (iii) the more elevated the social origin, the stronger the incitation and desire to reach a superior academic level (demand for education).

The probabilities of the demand for education used in the preceding sections (C1 80%, C2 61%, C3 40%) are extracted from a combination of the left and right parts of Table 15. It is assumed that 60% of children from C1 achieve good grades, 30% attain average grades, and 10% low grades. Furthermore, for the C1 origin, those with good grades benefit from a favorable orientation in 85% of the cases, those with average grades in 75%, and those with low grades in 65%. In total, these C1 children benefit from a favorable orientation with the probability: $(0.60 \times 0.85) + (0.30 \times 0.75) + (0.10 \times 0.65) = 0.80$. This figure corresponds to the 80% demand for education attributed to C1.

---

[6] This theory aims at explaining the impact of social class on academic performance "everything else equal," that is, independently of the fact that rich and poor children attend different types of schools, experience different classroom compositions, are taught with different types of academic methods, and so forth.

A similar calculation methodology provides the two other probabilities found in Table 2, namely 61% for C2 and 40% for C3.

To assess the relative importance of the two effects (cultural inheritance and demand for education), suffices to neutralize in turn each one of them and compute the resultant social mobility.[7]

- First scenario: *The difference in "cultural inheritance" is canceled.* The academic outcomes of C1 children are attributed to children across all classes: (good results 60%, average results 30%, and weak results 10%). The calculation indicates that mobility increases from 0.596 to 0.618 (up 3.7%).
- Second scenario: *The difference in demand for education is canceled.* The demand from C1 families is extended to families from all classes: (O1 85%, O2 75%, O3 65%). The calculation reveals that mobility increases from 0.596 to 0.670 (up 12.4%).

Mobility increases much more when the disparity in demand for education is eliminated than when the difference in "cultural inheritance" is neutralized. Among these two factors, the most influential by a wide margin is therefore the demand for education. Consequently, it is the difference in demand for education, rather than in "cultural inheritance," that limits mobility the most. With this kind of finding, Boudon could claim victory against Bourdieu and Passeron (1964), who primarily emphasized cultural inheritance to explain the role of the school system in the reproduction of society. It also validates Boudon's (1973a) call for a more meritocratic school system, in which student orientation closely aligns with their academic achievement. Bourdieu and Passeron (1964) advocated instead for a "rational pedagogy" that they never took any trouble to explain.

Furthermore, it is worth noting that the results of the complete model utilizing Table 15 closely mirror those of our simplified model built upon Table 2. The mobility matrices and corresponding indices are almost the same in these two versions, which justifies our use in this paper of the simple 3 × 1 Table 2 instead of the much more complex 2 × 3 × 3 Table 15.

The Language of Systems versus the Language of Correlations

One of the first results that Boudon draws from his model is a solution to the following paradox. Empirical surveys show that (i) social origin strongly

---

[7] The usual parameters are applied: class structure (C1 1,000, C2 3,000, C3 6,000) and a 70% "meritocratic" priority.

influences the level of education attained and (ii) the educational level in turn greatly impacts the achieved social status. It might seem justified to conclude, with a syllogistic deduction, that social destiny will be closely correlated with social origin, leading to weak intergenerational mobility: (origin class → school attainment) and (school attainment → destination class), therefore (origin class → destination class). However, this conclusion is contradicted by empirical investigations. Observations reveal that despite the correlations (i) and (ii), mobility is in fact quite strong and typically much closer to a random assignment of status than to a rigid social system that identically reproduces society (Boudon 1973a and see Section 2). For Boudon, the explanation of this paradox[8] comes from the discrepancy between the educational attainment structure and the class structure. This discordance can adequately be taken into account in the language of systems but cannot be captured in syllogistic reasoning.

To assess the validity of this explanation of the paradox, we need a model in which the educational attainment structure is *exogenous* instead of endogenous. We can use another model developed by Boudon (1973a, Chapter 1), in which the educational achievements are treated as parameters and allocated with a priority coefficient. This priority operates similarly to the 70% "meritocratic" priority of diplomas for access to status. In this model, not only the class structure but also the educational structure are parameters. Boudon sets the priority coefficient for educational attainment at 80%. This means that individuals of C1 origin are accorded an 80% priority in obtaining the highest educational levels. For the successive educational levels S1 and S2, they either occupy 80% of the available slots (if the number of available C1 children is greater than the number of slots) or 80% of them are allocated to the category (if the number of slots is larger than the number of available C1 children). The remaining individuals from C1 get S3. The individuals of C2 origin are then allocated to the remaining slots of S1 and S2 with 80% priority (the remainder are placed in S3), and the individuals of C3 origin get the remaining available slots in S1, S2, and S3.

Table 16 presents the acquisition of the educational levels with an 80% priority based on origin, in the case where the educational structure (S1 2,000, S2 3,000,

---

[8] This paradox is similar to but not the same as the "paradox of Anderson" (Anderson 1961). In the latter, the fact that the child reaches a higher educational level than the parent does not improve on average the chances of upward social mobility (in spite of the importance of the educational level for status acquisition). Solving this puzzling paradox is a major achievement by Boudon (1973a, Chapter 1). He uses a model that integrates the educational level of the parents, but that cannot be presented here for lack of space.

Table 16. Educational attainment determined by an 80% priority of social origin within the parameters of class structure and educational structure.

Children		Educational attainment (headcounts)			
Social origin		S1	S2	S3	Class structure
	C1	800	160	40	1,000
	C2	960	1,632	408	3,000
	C3	240	1,208	4,552	6,000
	Educational structure (exogenous parameter)	2,000	3,000	5,000	10,000

S3 5,000) is different from the origin class structure (C1 1,000, C2 3,000, C3 6,000). It showcases a very high degree of inequality of educational opportunity between the social classes (80% of C1 reach S1, against only 4% of C3).

Now, the question arises: does mobility increase as the discrepancy between the class structure and the educational attainment widens? The answer is affirmative. Let us start with an educational structure that is the same as the class structure (S1 1,000, S2 3,000, S3 6,000) and (C1 1,000, C2 3,000, C3 6,000). We find a mobility index $M_B = 0.389$, a value that is by far the lowest among those calculated in this paper. We then progressively shift the educational structure further away from the class structure. The more these two structures diverge, the higher the mobility, as evidenced in Table 17.

Table 17. As the discrepancy between the class structure and the educational attainment increases, mobility rises at first, reaches a plateau, and then rises again.

Class structure does not change: C1 1,000, C2 3,000, C3 6,000			
Educational structure			Mobility
S1	S2	S3	M_B
1,000	3,000	6,000	0.389
1,500	3,000	5,500	0.457
2,000	3,000	5,000	0.493
2,500	3,000	4,500	0.508
3,000	3,000	4,000	0.506
3,500	3,000	3,500	0,488
4,000	3,000	3,000	0.505
4,500	3,000	2,500	0.555
5,000	3,000	2,000	0.594

A wide discrepancy between these two structures can therefore explain in part the quite high mobility observed.

Moreover, this discrepancy cannot be taken into account in the syllogistic reasoning based on the two initial correlations. Despite facing criticism from empirical sociologists such as Robert Hauser after the publication of his book (see Fillieule 2018), Boudon is justified in asserting that the language of empirical correlations or "factors" is not well suited to the analysis of mobility. The attainment of status is not just the outcome of a succession of simple causal forces, but rather the result of a complex interaction between the demand for education, the acquisition of education, and the array of available opportunities on the social ladder. This intricate interplay can only be effectively formalized through a theoretical model that uses typical data (instead of empirical data that inevitably vary from case to case) and highly simplified yet relevant processes. The theory takes a step back from the immediate empirical reality, but only to then be able to *satisfactorily explain it.*

Conclusion

This paper has extended Boudon's model of social mobility in various directions with the help of spreadsheet computing, illustrating its fruitfulness and relevance for this subject matter (see also Bulle 2009). While our approach has been deliberately theoretical, it is worth emphasizing that a notable strength of Boudon's work on this topic lies in his constant return to data gathered in various countries concerning education and mobility. He formulates his assumptions with a view on these data and then always uses the theoretical models built on these assumptions to explain real-world typical regularities. Boudon's model stands out to us as one of the best ever developed in sociology, notably due to its powerful combination of theoretical and empirical insights. It is all the more regrettable that his model seems nowadays to have fallen into neglect. This unfortunate situation may come from the dominance of empirical measurement in contemporary studies of intergenerational mobility. Prominent recent references, such as those of Black and Devereux (2011) and Chetty et al. (2020), focus on the empirical study of the phenomena and they list factors that either favor or hamper mobility, such as family structure, neighborhood quality, health and health-care access, race, and so on. While these investigations provide valuable findings, they are confined to the "language of factors" that Boudon questioned, rather than the "language of systems" that he championed. These recent studies never provide an integrated theoretical overview of the mobility process, which lies at the core of Boudon's pioneering contribution.

References

Anderson, C. A. (1961). A Skeptical Note on the Relation of Vertical Mobility to Education. *American Journal of Sociology* 66(6): 560–570.

Black, S. E., and Devereux, P. J. (2011). Recent Developments in Intergenerational Mobility. In: Ashenfelter, O. and Card, D. (eds.), *Handbook of Labor Economics*, Vol. 4B. Amsterdam: Elsevier, Chapter 16, 1487–1541.

Boudon, R. (1973a). *L'inégalité des chances. La mobilité sociale dans les sociétés industrielles*. Paris: Armand Colin. English translation: *Education, Opportunity, and Social Inequality: Changing Prospects in Western Society*. New York: Wiley, 1974.

———. (1973b). *Mathematical Structures of Social Mobility*. Amsterdam: Elsevier.

Bourdieu, P., and Passeron, J.-C. (1964). *Les héritiers. Les étudiants et la culture*. Paris: Les éditions de Minuit.

Bulle, N. (2009). The Actuality of Education, Opportunity and Social Inequality. In: Cherkaoui, M. and Hamilton, P. (eds.), *Raymond Boudon: A Life in Sociology*. London: Bardwell Press, 357–378.

Chetty, R., Hendren, N., Jones, M. R., and Porter, S. (2020). Race and Economic Opportunity in the United States: An Intergenerational Perspective. *Quarterly Journal of Economics* 135(2): 711–783.

Fillieule, R. (2018). *L'inégalité des chances*: apports théoriques, réponses aux critiques et postérité. *Revue européenne des sciences sociales* 56(2): 65–83.

Girard, A., and Clerc, P. (1964). Nouvelles données sur l'orientation scolaire au moment de l'entrée en sixième. *Population* 19: 829–872.

INSEE. 2021. France, portrait social. INSEE Références—Édition 2021.

Merton, R. K. (1957). *Social Theory and Social Structure*. Glencoe: The Free Press.

Sirin, S. R. (2005). Socioeconomic Status and Academic Achievement: A Meta-Analytic Review of Research. *Review of Educational Research* 75(3): 417–453.

Thompson, W. E., and Hickey, J. V. (2005). *Society in Focus*. Boston: Pearson Education.

Chapter 7

FOR A CRITIQUE OF "CRITICAL SOCIOLOGY": RAYMOND BOUDON'S TOOLS FOR THE INTELLECTUAL REBUILDING OF THE DISCIPLINE

Alexander Riley[1]

Two decades ago, I read Raymond Boudon's *Pourquoi les intellectuels n'aiment pas le libéralisme*. The book struck me as marvelously insightful about a pathological condition he saw already invading the discipline of sociology. I wrote a review of the book that was enthusiastic but not uncritical and pitched it to a few mainstream sociological journals.

It was rejected in all of them, and on the same grounds. Boudon, I was told by one of these journal's book review editors, is not well known in the English-speaking scholarly community. Though I gathered this was true, I was hard-pressed to see this as a legitimate reason not to review an informative book by a little-known author. Such a review might better acquaint readers with a writer they ought to know. But the editor insisted. Boudon, he claimed, "repeats a good deal of crass, confused, ignorant conceptualisations of the people he attacks.[…] Such views appear in […] opinion pieces in newspapers.[…] They do not advance theoretical debate." More, he continued, "we […] do not see any merit in asking our readers to spend time on this book and would not want to encourage anyone to buy it." No substance whatsoever was offered on precisely what in Boudon's view of the discipline was "crass, confused [or] ignorant," though I requested examples. It was asserted as something self-evidently true, requiring no argument or evidential support.

---

[1] Several paragraphs in this essay contain modified versions of text contained in two other published texts by the same author: a book review in the *International Journal of Contemporary Sociology* and an online cultural politics site *The Postil*.

It is my impression that Boudon's reputation among English-speaking sociologists is likely no more widespread now than it was 20 years ago. This is to the detriment of those sociologists. I will suggest in this essay a major reason why Boudon's ideas, especially those that have to do with the knowledge-producing propensities of social science intellectuals, are not likely to get much traction in this demographic group. It is because he is correct about the disinterest in scientific knowledge of that group and about the increasing power they exert in shaping the entire discipline.

My view, then and now, is that Boudon's perspective on the process by which intellectuals, and specifically sociologists, tend to cobble together frameworks for understanding the world is full of useful insights. It would, if engaged with and understood by sociologists in the United States and elsewhere in the English-speaking world, enable those intellectuals to better fulfill their social functions as intellectuals and avoid the serious missteps they are currently making.

The Dominant American Sociological Worldview: Contemporary Critical Sociology (CCS)

I intend in this essay to use the term "Contemporary Critical Sociology," or CCS for short, to describe the dominant perspective on the study of society in American sociology. By this term, I mean the newly emergent tradition of thought in sociology (which has been adapted in whole or in part in some other contemporary academic disciplines as well) in which the entirety of human social organization and interaction is made sense of fundamentally by reference to a set of *a priori* principles regarding invisible but inescapable structural relations of domination among social groups. This framework is frequently cloaked in the language of science, but it is shot through with highly simplified moral *a prioris*. It is claimed that these social groups can in nearly every case be neatly divided into two categories: the dominant/advantaged/privileged and the dominated/disadvantaged/unprivileged. CCS purports to be both a sociological theory, offering alleged insights into the workings of society, and a politics, a moral standpoint on what is to be done to advance a utopian project for perfecting social organization and interaction. The scientific and moral projects are explicitly linked in CCS, and efforts to try to distinguish the two activities are typically looked at with suspicion by those who adhere to the ideology.[2]

---

[2] Christian Smith (2014), in *The Sacred Project of American Sociology*, has very effectively sketched out how this stitching together of "scientific" and political projects operate for the proponents of CCS.

CCS exists in a familial relationship with other, earlier bodies of so-called critical theories, including Marxism, feminism, and various race-centered conflict theories. The baseline that unites all these theoretical approaches is the reduction of all social life to relations of domination and dominance based on group membership (with the emphasis on different groups in different theoretical strands) and the refusal of any efforts on any grounds to protect scientific inquiry from unregulated moral and political motivations. CCS differs from them in its more holistic effort to account for domination. It uses the language of "intersectionality" to present a calculus of the degree of dominance or domination of the members of any specific group. This calculus combines various identity categories considered of the utmost salience to social life in CCS, the most important of which are racial and ethnic group identity, gender, and sexuality.

CCS asserts as a moral requirement a deep concern about social injustice and discrimination. This call for concern about injustice is consistently made in a utopian manner entirely decontextualized from historical, comparative, and situational context. "Concern about social injustice" in, say, the Jim Crow South of the 1930s is something most in the contemporary US would recognize as morally desirable. But when the concern expands to a belief that, for example, using pronouns to describe an individual that match his or her biological sex when he or she prefers different pronouns is a form of "violence" that causes "trauma," we are in a substantively different space, with much more likelihood of disagreement about the claim of injustice. CCS typically does not recognize any significant distinction between these kinds of interactional situations. Any situation in which members of a recognized dominated group can make a claim to unfair or unequal treatment, however tenuous, is a *de facto* proof of the unfair or unequal treatment. For this reason, among others, CCS is reasonably classified an utopian perspective.

CCS operates as a moralizing discourse about inequality and justice that routinely exaggerates in this manner and simultaneously attempts to mobilize sociological frameworks of thinking to show how the inequalities are being illegitimately produced and how to undo them. In this way, a purportedly scientific mode of analysis is used as epistemological support for the utopian moral/political project. That moral/political project is predicated on a utopian belief that a society without hierarchy, inequality, and discrimination is not only imaginable but practically feasible, if only we will all set to work to achieve it—and a first step in that process will involve accepting CCS's claims about how society works as uncontestably true. CCS has thus rejected any real commitment to the realm of science—which is founded on systematic disputation of analyses with rigorous adherence to the empirical as the judge between theories—and fully immersed itself in that of politics, while surreptitiously mobilizing scientific authority in order to give undue weight to its polemical and moral claims.

CCS and "Structural Racism" in American Sociology

The concept of "structure" and its purported causal effects on social outcomes is the most important theoretical tool in CCS. "Structure" is a venerable concept in the social sciences, with a wide range of utilizations over the years. It must be admitted that a very great deal of the usage of the concept "structure" in sociology is ill-considered, non-rigorous, and intellectually sloppy. The term is wielded to attempt description and/or explanation of a dizzying array of social phenomena, quite frequently with no attempt whatsoever to carefully define it and rigorously demonstrate its existence and action in the real world. Elder-Vass, citing an earlier text, characterizes much of the deployment of the term "structure" in sociology as "strikingly nebulous and diverse" (Elder-Vass 2010, 77).

Though I can advance no systematic account of the concept "structure" here, my view is that "structure" is in some limited applications a useful conceptual term in the social sciences. There are certainly continuities over time in any human society regarding both the institutional and the relational aspects of those societies. Cultural norms, though constantly changing, typically do so slowly and especially over short periods of time exhibit consistent stasis. The same is true of the networks of relationships among individuals in a society, for example, with respect to the hierarchy and relational structure of occupations. In both cases, these structures provide a field of options to individuals, sometimes relatively large, sometimes considerably smaller, and we can feasibly talk about such structures as limiting ranges of outcomes to some degree. It is, however, always exceedingly difficult to formalize precisely how and how much they do so, and any rigorous usage of the concept "structure" has the responsibility of taking up that difficult task, especially when "structure" is used as a central conceptual term in the analysis.

CCS takes this widespread theoretical negligence on "structure" to extraordinary lengths. Here, the term is taken as doxa, an already-established truth. It operates as a kind of shibboleth, a token of membership in a moral and political community. Any serious effort to define and delimit it scientifically is seen as irrelevant, and anyone who requests such a definition is identified as outside the moral community.

There are, in the various bodies of sociological thinking that make up CCS, analyses of numerous different structures, each of which is often taken to be a component of a broader structural apparatus. Among the specific forms of structure that are taken as primary by CCS practitioners are those that affect social outcomes by, respectively, gender or sex and race. Structures of social class are, of course, of primary importance in Marxian theoretical frameworks, and many varieties of CCS still include it in their overall perspective on structure, though typically as considerably less important than race and gender. But the two structural apparatuses of the patriarchy and structural/systemic racism, or white supremacy, have become the most important in CCS, and in the discipline generally.

Given the constraints of space faced in this essay, I will examine only the example of structural racism in its incarnation in CCS. The argumentative logic is exactly parallel to what one finds with respect to the patriarchy, even though the specific axis of domination differs in its details. In this sense, it is clear that a monolithic, hyper-simplistic model for human social life is utilized by CCS to understand virtually every empirical phenomenon asserted by its practitioners to be of sociological interest.

I have for some years used an article written by a former president of the ASA as exemplary of the kind of argumentative logic commonly found in sociology today on the matter of structural racism. The article is Eduardo Bonilla-Silva's "The Structure of Racism in Color-Blind, 'Post-Racial' America," which was published in *American Behavioral Scientist* in 2015. It is a particularly useful example to analyze because it gives evidence of the extent of influence of CCS in American sociology, as its author is a well-respected member of the American sociological profession. He has published frequently in mainstream journals and presses, and he has numerous prizes from its national organization, even serving as that organization's elected president.

The first point that must be made about the article is that none of its key conceptual terms are effectively defined. "Race" and "racism" both go without rigorous definition. "Race" is claimed to be a nonexistent entity, created as a fiction by practices of "racism." The latter is presented as the entirety of practices that produce the fiction "race," which is nothing more than the hook on which a racist society hangs all its efforts to distinguish between dominant and dominated groups. In the details, it turns out that just about everything that happens in American society is evidence of "racism."

There is also no concentrated effort to describe how structural racism, or any other structure, can be demonstrated to exist and to have particular causal effects on other aspects of the social body. The argument of the piece in brief, which is perfectly consistent with how the CCS framework on race is presented elsewhere in the discipline, is that American society, while historically becoming less racist by some evidence, is just as vigorously racist as it ever was. Indeed, it is more effective now at discriminating along racial lines because the mechanisms for doing so have evolved so deviously and ingeniously.

In place of the earlier methods for racist exclusion, which relied on empirically observable acts of discrimination and prejudice by real individuals, structural mechanisms for racist exclusion have been created. Yet the operation, and the very existence, of these structures is argued for by Bonilla-Silva only by description of their purported causal effects.

The flaws in Bonilla-Silva's reasoning are often so glaring that one finds it difficult to believe he has not seen them himself. He complains constantly here and elsewhere, for example, of a "ruling sociological elite" that rejects CCS, that is, as an entity oppositional to the intellectual worldview he presents. Yet, as noted above, he has been substantially feted and rewarded by the profession. He received the ASA's Cox-Johnson-Frazier Award for sociology directed to "social justice" in 2011. Two years earlier, one of his books received an award from the ASA's Section on Racial and Ethnic Minorities. In 2018, he was elected the president of the ASA. The claim that Bonilla-Silva and his work have been rejected by some reactionary "elite" inside the discipline is absolutely baseless. It is, on the contrary, much more reasonable to see him as a full member of that elite, which adheres firmly to CCS.

Racism produces racist ideology, which, Bonilla-Silva claims, is not simply a body of ideas. It is "a material force" operating on racial minorities. This astonishing claim is not argued but simply asserted. The ideology's "force," it is inferred, is to be seen in a number of observations. "Racial structure" imposes "common social locations" on members of racial groups. No specifics are given, but presumably this means that those recognized as white are placed by these structures in elevated positions in the hierarchy, while those defined as non-white are situated in lower strata. What do we make, though, in this analysis of the sizable black middle and white lower classes? What of the substantial numbers of blacks in the American business, political, and cultural elites? Bonilla-Silva has nothing to say in response to such questions (Bonilla-Silva 2015, 1360–1362).

The racist structures are, in Bonilla-Silva's view, evident in the mere existence of racial inequality. This perfectly anti-scientific claim—X exists, and merely by virtue of its existence, we therefore know Y is its cause without any need to test the relationship or evaluate other potential causes—has been still more boldly stated for a larger audience by figures such as Ibram X. Kendi. The claim constitutes a complete bypassing of the scientific process of endeavoring to demonstrate cause as a relationship between two phenomena.

Again, it is true that there exist racial disparities in various social outcomes. Housing segregation by race exists. Blacks as a group have lower per capita incomes and savings than whites. Educational outcomes differ by race, as does the likelihood of being involved in the criminal justice system as an offender. These and other empirical claims are made by Bonilla-Silva and left to stand as *de facto* evidence of the causal power of racial structures and systemic racism. But the social scientist recognizes immediately that cause cannot be carelessly imputed in this way without theoretical and methodological precision and proof.

Myriad factors can be posited as potential contributors to the disparities observed. Individual-level discrimination might be a factor, but evidence for it, as Bonilla-Silva admits, has become considerably scarcer than it was a half-century ago. Other factors to be considered in their effect on outcomes are particular behaviors and cultural beliefs that inform those behaviors of the different racial groups. And what is the causal structure of behavioral predilection and cultural belief themselves? That is, why do individuals and groups tend to hold the values they hold and behave in the ways that they do? Certainly, aspects of human nature shared among the entire species and historical elements of group experience will factor in here in a substantial way. Much in the way of the basics of human behavioral predilection and propensities for particular kinds of beliefs is shared by all of us. But differences in groups in terms of the distribution of given abilities, skills, and psychological profiles could play a role too. This latter is a topic on which we still know much less than we would like and need to know, though research is constantly yielding more and more in this regard. It is presumptive and anti-scientific to dismiss such things as potential causal factors in advance of possession of more thorough knowledge, as sociologists who favor structural racism models universally do.

The likely scenario in explaining any particular outcome of racial inequality in societies like this one is that it is some complicated combination of all or some subset of these factors that produces the relevant disparities as outcomes. Science is frequently messy and complex in this way. The structural racism argument endeavors to erase scientific difficulty and complexity by making *a priori* claims based on no careful analysis and nonexistent theoretical sophistication.

Here is an illustrative example of Bonilla-Silva's argumentative strategy in the article. When he looks for empirical evidence of the "new racism," he purports to find it in, for example, the "persist[ent] [...] discrimination in the housing and lending markets" (ibid., 1362). It may well be that, considered in just their statistical propensities, black and white prospective home buyers are not treated precisely the same by lenders. But Bonilla-Silva gives no indication he has given serious thought to the potential causes of that differential treatment. He knows, as he has provided it as yet more evidence of structural racism, that blacks as a group are poorer, with less net wealth, than whites. They also have higher rates of mortgage default, even when one controls for social class of the loan recipient. The emergence in the 1970s of a concerted social justice effort by the federal government to ensure that home loans were extended even to black buyers most unsuited in economic terms for responsibly managing a mortgage raised the already high rates of black default on mortgage loans.

A full scientific theory on differential access to home loans by race would need to make room for understanding these facts. Why would we expect, absent political force and penalties for refusing, that loan agents would extend loans to a poorer population at the same rates they grant them to a wealthier population, given that they are desirous the loans be paid back? And, if we take a theoretical step back to questioning why the two populations are situated differentially in terms of wealth, we have the full panoply of potential causes illustrated above that must be considered before we can make anything like a confident statement about its causes. That is, why are the two groups situated differently in terms of earnings and wealth? Claiming "structure" does it before any analysis of ground-level behavior and beliefs of individuals is a moral move, not a scientific one.

Bonilla-Silva explicitly attacks what he calls "abstract liberalism" (ibid., 1364). This view—which he never clearly defines but which appears to encompass both the analytic view that individuals are the only entities in the human world that can act and thus that they should be the focus of our scientific efforts to understand human action, and the moral/political view that individuals are the proper focus of polities and the sole possible bearers of rights—is denounced in the most visceral terms. The catchphrase for which Bonilla-Silva is well known among sociologists is "racism without racists," which is a definitional implementation of the structuralist, anti-methodological individualism Boudon decried throughout his career. Whatever the claims to scientific and/or political philosophical primacy of "abstract liberalism"— and Bonilla-Silva makes no effort to thoroughly investigate or substantively critically engage with them—it can in the CCS view adequately be summarized as racism.

Bonilla-Silva is but one exemplar of the CCS position in American sociology with respect to questions of racial inequality. It may well be that CCS is in fact the dominant perspective in the discipline on this matter. In early 2023, the American Sociological Association released a statement on "race and racism" that purports to identify the aspects of "systemic or structural racism" in the United States (American Sociological Association 2023). Its logic is precisely that of the Bonilla-Silva article. Astonishingly, this 17-page, single-spaced document produced by a team of sociologists who specialize in the sociological study of race and racism and bearing the imprimatur of the entire professional organization does no better in making the causal argument regarding structural racism than Bonilla-Silva does. It gives readers not a single word on the all-important question of demonstrating cause in structural analysis. The entire discussion of "systemic racism" is dedicated to a ritualistic repetition of the familiar litany of supposed examples of the phenomenon— housing segregation, differences in educational outcomes, health disparities, and policing. Nothing is presented in the way of a scientific demonstration that the facts discussed can be shown to be caused by structures rather than the behaviors of individuals, which, once again, are informed by a number of sources including predilections given by human nature, cultural values and norms, and interactional and other characteristics of human social life.

The Anti-Liberal Bias of Intellectuals: The Roots of CCS in a Radically Anti-Individual Worldview

In a 2004 book, Boudon gave an account of the intellectual distaste for liberal social institutions and practice that outlines much of the intellectual framework of CCS without explicitly naming it as such (Boudon 2004a). Classical liberal psychology, which Bonilla-Silva attacks with his notion of "abstract liberalism," presents human beings as basically rational animals, not fully autonomous to be sure but capable in situations of real-world action of using a reasoned consideration of interests drive decision-making and action. A liberal sociology would operate out of methodological individualism, recognizing that groups and collectivities are but conglomerations of individuals, and that the former are mere theoretical constructs while the latter are the only entities in a society that empirically exist.

Sociology in its dominant anti-liberal incarnations, for example, CCS, rejects this idea of the subject and the study of society entirely. Instead, humankind is presented as a fundamentally collective creature. Human thought and action are in this view determined by forces beyond the control of the individual. The liberal notion of autonomy is an invention with no relationship to reality and no utility in explaining what happens in the world. The study of society cannot take as its key concept a fiction, so the anti-liberal sociologist looks to collectives as the agents of action in the human world.

Boudon suggests a useful taxonomy of the intellectual class. Intellectuals can be subcategorized into three groups: (1) those intellectuals who pursue a pure love of knowledge; (2) those driven by an "ethic of conviction," who turn away from intellectual matters to politics; and (3) those who seek fame (Boudon 2004a, 77–78). Each type relies to some degree on social environment for sustenance, even if there are basic psychological profile differences in individuals that go a long way to explaining which of the three categories best describes a given intellectual. The last two types are those most generally dominant in the contemporary field of sociology, and indeed in academia more generally, for reasons having to do with how academic training and the scholarly profession have been altered.

Anti-liberal ideas increasingly dominate in the intellectual world, according to Boudon. But how could this be, given their demonstrable falsity? The answer is their utility. Boudon shows, using Pareto as a source, how ideas can be categorized along two distinct descriptive binaries. There is the axis of truth and falsity, and that of utility and non-utility. In the constant competition of ideas, a specific idea may win out either because of its truth or its usefulness toward some other purpose. Utility is comparatively the more powerful criterion, even among intellectuals. Those ideas that are both untrue and useless are quickly dismissed. True but practically useless ideas can be accepted, but their path to wide acceptance is much steeper than that of ideas that are useful but false, which can easily win adherents (ibid., 117, 164).

Why are false, anti-liberal ideas—for example, in CCS, that the full and sole cause of all racial inequality is racism, whether individual or structural—so useful to the intellectuals? The answer for Boudon has to do with the rise of the mass university. He is trenchantly critical of this institution. Indeed, it is not too much to say that he sees its rise as a harbinger of the possible end of real intellectual life. Contrary to the popular notion foisted upon us by its advocates, the mass university is not populated by a student body whose intellectual level is increasing. Standards, Boudon argues, have to drop as the idea of university enrollment comes to be seen as an entitlement shared by all or nearly all in a given society (ibid., 140–141). He is writing in the days before the flourishing of Diversity, Equity, and Inclusion (DEI) apparatuses on campuses around the country, but he could well be describing the contemporary landscape in higher education. The emergence of the ideological categories of democracy and equality as evaluative mechanisms for intellectual work creates a move away from the hard business of science and toward the easier production of moralistic judgment. Knowledge is made only painstakingly and requires demonstrable intellectual skill and merit, whereas moralizing can be done by anyone and with minimal exertion. It is moralizing then that takes on the greatest value as capital in the mass university (ibid., 147–148). If Boudon were still with us, he would doubtless point to the countless efforts on campuses to link all scholarly research to moralizing DEI ideals as verification of his argument.

Against the rising tide of anti-liberalism in the universities, Boudon reiterates the need for a defense of the liberal individual and the social and political order that best accommodates that individual. He calls for a return to the classical tradition in sociology, to the intellectual frameworks of men such as Alexis de Tocqueville, Max Weber, and Georg Simmel. These thinkers, all classical liberals in Boudon's estimation, embody the true critical spirit of intellectual life. The anti-liberal intellectuals, on the other hand, who never stop talking about "critique," are in fact rigid conformists to the anti-scientific ideological edifice that has been erected in replacement of the classical university (ibid., 192, 213).

Boudon on Tocqueville's Analysis of Religion and Democracy: A Critique of CCS Before the Fact

Raymond Boudon spent a good deal of his scholarly career defending a properly scientific view of the discipline of sociology against deviations such as the CCS phenomenon. In so doing, he explicitly took up the banner of the classical tradition of the discipline and championed the rigor and commitment to objectivity found in the best of the founding generation of sociology. The perspectives and work of Tocqueville, Weber, and Simmel especially were mined by Boudon for insights into the construction of a contemporary sociology that would yield accurate information on the workings of the social world.

Boudon's *Tocqueville for Today* (2006) makes a persuasive case for recognizing the author of *Democracy in America* as one of the most important founding and still most formidable figures in the sociological investigation of the human world. In both his studies of American democracy and of the causes and consequences of the French Revolution, Tocqueville presented a framework for the study of human social organization of unique power and precision that holds up two centuries on.

Among the profound insights of Tocqueville noted by Boudon are his accounts of the sociology of religion and the long-term tendencies of democratic culture. Tocqueville viewed Christianity as a driver of profound cultural and religious transformation, and he believed some of that transformation might even involve a dissipation of religious belief. This was due to the fact that Christianity was a "religion of the end of religion" (Boudon 2006, 22) that contained the seeds of its own destruction in some of its central tenets. The insistence of Christianity on the moral value of the human individual *per se*, and of the total equality of all humans in this regard, distinguished it from previous religious traditions in a profound way. These ideas proved tremendously attractive and spurred the spread of the religion that embodied them. Yet, once sufficiently radicalized, they could undercut basic moral and epistemological structures of the faith, and indeed of all religion.

Tocqueville's insights on religion here can be usefully expanded to discuss historical developments since his death. CCS, as well as some of its offshoots outside the academy, can be analyzed in intriguing ways as an evolutionary descendant of the Protestant Christianity that produced the Social Gospel and Liberation Theology. Though CCS, like most sociology, presents itself as a secular worldview, there is no doubt whatever that the moral vocabulary at its core—innocent and sacred victims terrorized and discriminated against by evil victimizers, merciless structures of oppression produced by malevolent institutions—invokes the same symbolic territory inhabited by Christianity broadly speaking. The body of ideas that makes up CCS is an ideological development perfectly consonant with the overall drift of Christianity in the West over the past 500 years since the Protestant Reformation produced fundamental shifts in the nature of Christian belief and practice.

The Reformation was an all-out assault on ritual and on the preexisting Christian recognition that sacredness was located not only outside the world in God's majesty but also in the earthly realm that humans inhabited. The Church that the Reformation challenged understood that sacredness manifests on a continuum. God represents the polar, pure absolute of sacrality. Angels, saints, and holy relics, which are all sacred entities, are at some distance from that purest form of sacredness, and they reside somewhere closer to the profane pole at which humans who are uncleansed by ritual reside. The Protestants established a stark, total, and unalterable distance between God and man, the sacred and the profane. All religion recognizes the magnetic repulsion of sacred and profane. Yet in primitive religions as well as in the Christianity dominant in Europe before the Reformation, entities are able to move through the power of ritual from one category to the other. Sacred things can inhabit the profane world without catastrophe or contradiction.

For the most radical among the Reformers, however, this was a central blasphemy of the existing Church. In the radical view, God and the sacred are unchanging and ever-lasting, forever beyond the ken and the approach of man. Mysteries by which miracles such as transubstantiation can be made to occur with prescribed rites and prayers, or mortal humans can become saints by actions of the Church, were seen as anathema. Historically, the Roman Catholic Church has been effective at incorporating elements of indigenous faiths based on animistic principles into Christian practice, and the pantheon of the saints has been an effective mechanism for doing this. The Marian cult, for example, has proven an efficacious means of bringing populations with local indigenous beliefs concerning sacred mother figures, real and mythical, into the Church.

Protestantism rejected all of this. CCS embraces the same exaggerated, exclusivist binary system established by the radical Protestants, though moved into the secular sphere of cultural politics. The thrust of Protestantism, especially in the mainline denominations in the United States, has been toward individualism and the desacralization of the world. Sociologists have long recognized that an evolution of religious practice in a direction that deemphasizes collective ritual and the mystical properties of sacred things is close to a guarantee that the religious body in question will decline in its ability to attract members. Religions that become indistinguishable from the surrounding culture lose the elements of belonging and meaning production sought after by those seeking religious goods (Finke and Stark 1992). Some of the Protestant denominations unabashedly embraced the secularizing momentum and turned the evangelizing, otherworldly project of traditional Christianity into a this-worldly political project of the progressive left.

These mainline Protestant groups explicitly built social justice into their church doctrines. They have been shrinking in membership for decades. Some have all but disappeared. Their existing membership skews heavily toward the social elite as defined by education and income. The processes of rationalization eliminated the glue of their former religious denominations, but these social classes still had the innate human need for a symbolically meaningful universe. They therefore left their old churches and transferred the symbolic categories of those faiths into the new schema present in ideologies such as CCS.

Boudon sees Tocqueville's position on religion as admirably objective. He notes that a "scientific position" on religion is often taken in the social sciences to mean something like Marx's perspective, or, earlier, that of Voltaire and similar Enlightenment thinkers. But Boudon argues that true objectivity does not constitute a partisan criticism or rejection of a phenomenon. It has to do with an effort to understand it without bias, in both its functional strengths and weaknesses. Boudon reads Tocqueville as an agnostic who nonetheless is capable of understanding and accepting the full historical legacy of Christianity as a cultural force in the West.

Some of the most compelling analyses in Tocqueville's study of the causes of the French Revolution deal with the growth of hostility to religion among important segments of the intellectual classes of the Old Regime. The "cult of Reason" (ibid., 117–120) was widely embraced by intellectuals. Tocqueville even describes the enthusiasm with which these intellectuals embraced the cult as bearing evidence of a kind of new religion, in just the way I discuss CCS as in a genealogical relationship with radical Protestantism. Rousseau's civil religion, which gave birth to the French Revolution's Cult of Man under Robespierre, is a precursor of the moral framework of CCS, endeavoring to marry a secular political philosophy with the emotional power of religion. Auguste Comte's religion of humanity is still another early template.

The general trend in democracy toward ever-increasing emphasis on equality and on a socially decontextualized freedom was another central concern in Tocqueville's writing. Equality was consistently seen by Tocqueville as a potentially dangerous belief if carried to the extremes to which it tends to lend itself. Democracy reduces future orientation and promotes individualism, cultural decline, and the dissolution of the family. It also tends to drive the ideology of equality. The doctrine of hell becomes harder to accept in a democracy, and it is such a belief, Tocqueville argues, that is precisely what is needed to make it likely that there will emerge a broad mass morality capable of enforcement. As equality becomes more widespread, religious belief tends to decrease. Tocqueville states this as a kind of sociological law, which Boudon finds compelling.

Boudon on the Logic of Social Action: The CCS Retreat from Logic

Boudon was for his entire life a staunch defender of the rationality of a wide range of everyday human action. Everyday social actors are not dupes, he argues, and they employ a significant amount of logic when they make decisions about action. In Boudon's framework, individual actors typically achieve rational understandings of their situations and act in ways that take those understandings and their relevant goals into careful account.

It is hardly a simplistic atomism Boudon proposes in theoretical terms, as individuals consider a wide range of contextual and interactional factors. But in his view, it is certainly a grave theoretical error to attribute causal power to invisible forces that cannot be carefully delineated in their effects. Boudon accepts Herbert Simon's notion of subjective or bounded rationality as the most useful conceptual tool for defining sociological action. Rationality is never, in empirical situations of human decision-making, unbounded and unconstrained. There are limits on the knowledge of any actor, but this does not mean the actor acts irrationally (Boudon 1994, 235–237).

By contrast CCS assumes that social actors are in all cases guided entirely by structures beyond their control. White subjects will come to embrace racist ideas by their mere presence inside what Bonilla-Silva calls (without demonstrating their existence) "racial structures." Their very efforts to express their individualism with respect to such structural arguments about racism, by, for example, claiming to be capable of evaluating other individuals on information other than their race, is itself evidence in CCS of their inability to escape the structure. Non-whites too are trapped in a structural mechanism that exceeds their control, though presumably they become capable of escaping at least some of its elements when they fully embrace CCS principles and beliefs.

Boudon argues that common sense reasoning has been devalued in sociology. The critique of common sense presumes *a priori* that everyday reasoning must proceed from false premises, given their non-intellectual origins. In this view, common sense is the antonym of good sense. The masters of suspicion—Marx, Nietzsche, and Freud—are three of the major sources of this view on common sense. People are deluded about basic elements of their own lives and the world in which they live, as a result of immersion in some form of false thinking, whether capitalist false consciousness, *ressentiment*, or the delusions foisted on the mind by the unconscious (Boudon 2004b, 166–167).

It is not only these standard sources of the academic left, though, who Boudon sees at the origin of this condemnation of common sense. Others more typically understood as not on the radical left, David Hume and Auguste Comte, come under criticism too for their attacks on context-independent judgment. Hume argued that tradition is the only stable justification for some of our most epistemologically important knowledge, while Comte's law of the three states presents the idea that the rules of thought are variable (ibid., 167–170). This shows Boudon's consistent positioning of his own view of knowledge as somewhere other than the various positions on left and right that posit determinism of knowledge by social and historical context.

CCS adheres to a vision of common sense that is broadly aligned with that of Marx. For Marx, all social classes understand the world from the perspective of their position in the class structure. In capitalist society, the ruling knowledge is produced by the bourgeois classes. This knowledge serves—at least until the moment that revolutionary possibility coalesces—to delude members of the working classes into misunderstanding their own interests and the reality of the social structures in which they are trapped. For CCS, the common person—and this is true of both dominant and dominated classes, though there is a greater possibility for those in the latter to potentially see through some of the structures of domination—in a white supremacist society believes he or she knows all kinds of things about the social world, but all or nearly all of that supposed knowledge is corrupted by the structures of racism. Any common sensical attitude that, for example, it might be a good idea to avoid certain parts of town at certain times of day, or that one should as a member of a non-white group work hard to advance individually and invest little if any energy in collectivist philosophies of action cannot be reasonable forms of calculation based on experiential data and background social knowledge. They are by definition deluded and in fact consonant with racist structures.

The task of the sociologist in trying to understand the motivations for action and their consequences is difficult in the extreme, according to Boudon. Humans typically assume effects have causes in their actions, and sociologists too must seek relations of cause and effect in the social world. But cause is "an inexorably obscure notion" (Boudon 1994, 148). And individuals can certainly go astray in their working through of the logic, given a confusing array of variables from which to select those most relevant.

Boudon gives a fine example from Steinberg's study of American teachers in which the latter demonstrates how easy it is to move from a tight correlation in American education between area of study and religious identity—with Jews, Protestants, and Catholics presenting distinct profiles—to a belief in a causal relationship between the two. As it turns out, though, here the historical shape of the disciplines at the time at which different religious groups gained mass entry into universities or were the dominant religious groups represented there explains the relationship much more fully (ibid., 165–170).

Boudon discusses as an admirable exemplar of the logic of social action and also the logic of the social analyst the methodology of Georg Simmel in *The Philosophy of Money*. Simmel's theory is relativist but not skeptical. This is not the radical relativism of, for example, philosophers of science such as Paul Feyerabend who deny the very possibility of making defensible truth claims that can be separated from subjective positions. Boudon defines relativism here simply as the rejection of realism (ibid., 263). Contrary to those like Feyerabend and the postmodernist and poststructuralist veins of social analysis, Boudon argues that relativism does not require incompatibility with objectivity and truth. A proper relativism simply posits that we cannot imagine that knowing subjects operate with a fully accurate copy of reality in their minds as they act. Per Simon, they act according to a bounded rationality that is relative to their knowledge and lack of knowledge.

Simmel, in Boudon's view, offers a nuanced, sensitive methodology for understanding the nature and causal power of money over social relations. Money both liberates and alienates, and the actions of actors with respect to it must be understood as producing both, with no logical precedence given to either. Both are true. In the end, Boudon says Simmel "cling[s] tightly to the notions of truth and objectivity [while] giv[ing] up trying to achieve absolute knowledge [...] the gentle move from substantialism to relativism should forewarn us against fanaticism and dogmatism" (ibid., 277). The latter descriptives perfectly map the attitude of CCS on the questions it purports to study.

In contrast to his celebration of the method of Simmel, another celebrated figure in the classical tradition of sociology is criticized by Boudon for failing to rigorously adhere to the necessary logic of social analysis. He describes Durkheim's use of a logical error to ground his argument on religion. Durkheim begins *The Elementary Forms of Religious Life* by making the case for his view of the origins of religion. The structure of his argument is well-known in the discipline. There are at the time of Durkheim's writing two existing main competitor theories for religion's origins: the naturalist theory—personalized forces of nature were the first religious objects—and the animist—religion has its beginnings in primitive theories of the soul.

Durkheim works through both, rejecting each in turn, then presents his own sociological/totemic theory as the logical alternative. But, as Boudon notes, this assumes only three possible explanations. How do we know there are no others superior to all three of those Durkheim presents? We do not, and so the logical form on which the case rests is unsustainably shaky (ibid., 116–123).

The CCS method of assuming the delusion of social actors with respect to what it presents as the reality of race—which is that race has no reality beyond its role as a tool in racial domination, and that there are no conceivable biological grounds on which reasonable distinctions between human subpopulations might be made—is far more egregiously illogical than Durkheim's argumentative *faux pas* in *The Elementary Forms*. In order to assert this claim, nearly all evolutionary biology must be ignored, though a few cherry-picked biologists whose radical politics self-evidently inform their view—for example, Richard Lewontin, who in addition to denying all potentially sociologically meaningful genomic differences between human groups has written a manifesto for the Marxian organization of biology (Levins and Lewontin 1985)—are repeatedly cited.

CCS purports that human populations that recognize distinctions among different populations that they associate with different places of origins are operating solely on the basis of falsehoods linked to discriminatory intentions. But there exists much work in evolutionary biology that supports the existence of real genotypical differences among human populations that are reflected in phenotypical differences easily discernible by those unaware of genomic information, some of which directly refutes the reasoning of those select biologists cited by CCS sociologists (e.g., Edwards 2003; Reich 2018). Just as Durkheim invalidly presumes only a small subset of possible answers to the question he asks, the CCS sociologists presume in advance that their preferred answer is the only possible one. They refrain even from mentioning the arguments from scholars in the relevant field that run against the grain of their preference.

This returns us to Boudon's argument about the staying power of ideas that are false. It is the usefulness of CCS ideas on race, in the context of a cultural effort by many elites to move American society in a particular policy direction on the problem of racial inequality in which racism is presumed the cause of everything and only broad transformation of the entire society is sufficient to address it, that fuels the success of such ideas. CCS sociologists, in assuming the inability of actors to behave rationally because of the supposed existence of invisible structures, present themselves not as scientists attempting to understand action, but rather as moralists whose sole task is to evaluate the action according to an *a priori* ethical model.

The Stakes

Raymond Boudon died almost exactly 10 years ago from the time I am writing this essay. He was clearly one of the most prominent figures in sociology in his native France. His theoretical statements and his ardent defense of rationality in both everyday social action and in the production of social science knowledge make him a writer who one hopes with some confidence will continue to be read, both in France and elsewhere.

Boudon's perspective on the proper building of social scientific knowledge was once widely shared in the discipline in the United States and elsewhere. Indeed, it is not too much to say that he was one of the most consistent sources in his lifetime in affirming the core of the classical tradition in sociology, which was firmly attached to the project of a scientific sociology that would carefully distinguish social science from partisan politics. In that classical generation, Durkheim provided a model approach in his separation of sociology from politics. In his sociological study of the origins and nature of socialism, he defined the latter as "a cry of grief, sometimes of anger" (Durkheim 1962, 41). Whatever one's position on the justice of that cry—and it is of relevance that Durkheim himself identified as a socialist, so he was not excluding from the category of science a politics with which he was unsympathetic— it does not constitute an objective effort to understand the world. The two things—a moral stance and the sociological effort to understand that moral stance—must be recognized as categorically different.

As the socialist project in Durkheim's day, so is the CCS project today. That contemporary sociologists have largely, unlike Boudon, refused to recognize Durkheim's distinction has led to an intellectual deterioration of the discipline and of its reputation outside the circles of activist sociologists.

And this will certainly continue in the foreseeable future, for there is almost no chance that Boudon's criticisms of the way of doing sociology that is expressed in CCS will produce the ends he hoped. Boudon's endeavor was to contribute to the intellectual recovery of sociology from an irrationalist malady that threatens to reduce a once vibrant and respected academic field to a branch of moralizing and partisan politics viewed with derision by those with real scientific credentials. But the perspective he represents is disappearing in American sociology and it is difficult to imagine how it can be revived in the current context for the training of professional sociologists.

Boudon's greatest inspiration among the classical generation, Weber, famously described the inevitable disappearance of the work of the scientist, given a properly functioning scientific community: "In science each of us knows that what he has done will be antiquated in ten years [...] whoever wishes to serve science has to resign himself to this fact" (Weber 1946, 138).

The scientific sociologist, that is to say, must hope—though this hope personally grieves him given his commitment to his own work and reputation—to see his work disappear under the advance of progress in knowledge. But what if there is no scientific progress because the community of scientists has given up the project of science in the name of politics under the guise of scholarship? Then, Weber notes, we will find ourselves in a truly dismal situation, for almost none of the professors in universities are in any way fit to provide moral and political models: "[O]f a hundred professors at least ninety-nine do not and must not claim to be [...] masters in the vital problems of life, or even to be 'leaders' in matters of conduct" (ibid., 150).

Boudon would be unhappy to see where we are a decade after his death, though he would not be surprised. For we are now in a world where the scientific sociologist cannot even hope to disappear under the wave of progress after making his momentarily crucial contribution to objective knowledge. In our world, such a sociologist is likely never to be heard from to begin with, and we can well imagine a time when such figures will no longer exist at all. With gratitude, however, we can still read Raymond Boudon.

References

American Sociological Association, "Race and Racism in the United States: A Sociological Guide for the Public," online document, January 2023. https://www.asanet.org/wp-content/uploads/2023/01/race-and-racism-in-us-soc-guide-asa-2023.pdf.

Bonilla-Silva, E. (2015). The Structure of Racism in Color-Blind, "Post-Racial" America. *American Behavioral Scientist* 59(11): 1358–1376.

Boudon, R. (1994). *The Art of Self-Persuasion*, translated by Malcolm Slater, Cambridge: Polity Press.

———. (2004a). *Pourquoi les intellectuels n'aiment pas le libéralisme*. Paris: Odile Jacob.

———. (2004b). *The Poverty of Relativism*. Oxford: The Bardwell Press.

———. (2006). *Tocqueville for Today*, translated by Peter Hamilton. Oxford: The Bardwell Press.

Durkheim, É. (1962). *Socialism*. New York: Collier.

Edwards, A. W. F. (2003). Human Genetic Diversity: Lewontin's Fallacy. *BioEssays* 25: 798–801.

Elder-Vass, D. (2010). *The Causal Power of Social Structures: Emergence, Structure, and Agency*. Cambridge: Cambridge University Press.

Finke, R. and Stark, R. (1992). *The Churching of America, 1776–1990: Winners and Losers in Our Religious Economy*. New Brunswick: Rutgers University Press.

Levins, R. and Lewontin, R. (1985). *The Dialectical Biologist*. Cambridge: Harvard University Press.

Reich, D. (2018). *Who We Are and How We Got Here*. New York: Pantheon.

Smith, C. (2014). *The Sacred Project of American Sociology*. Oxford: Oxford University Press.

Weber, M. (1946). *From Max Weber*. New York: Oxford University Press.

Chapter 8

RAYMOND BOUDON'S SOCIAL THEORY AS A GENERAL RESEARCH PROGRAM: APPLICATIONS OF BOUDON'S WORK SINCE HIS DEATH (2013–2023) AND FUTURE PERSPECTIVES

Christian Robitaille

Raymond Boudon's career as a social scientist started with an inquiry into the mathematical approach to the study of social facts and the problems of the structuralist perspective in mid-twentieth-century sociology (Boudon 1967; 1971 [1968]). He then turned his scientific attention to the study of inequalities in education, publishing a book (Boudon 1974 [1973]), which has put his work at the center of academic discussions as he reached conclusions which were significantly at odds with that of Pierre Bourdieu and Jean-Claude Passeron (1990 [1970]). Afterward, from the 1980s on, Boudon studied topics such as social values (Boudon 1995; 2001), ideology (Boudon 1989 [1986]; 1994 [1990]), and democracy (Boudon 2003; 2006). But, from that moment on, something had changed. Although he always was interested in epistemological issues, his *focus* became increasingly theoretical rather than topical. He aimed at discovering the proper general foundations of social scientific analyses *through* the study of the specific topics he was addressing. As a consequence, these empirical/topical concerns were increasingly brought together in order to illustrate the fruitfulness of what he termed the "general theory of rationality" (Boudon 2007; 2011).

Indeed, a large portion of his academic work from the 1980s up to his death in 2013 aimed at carefully building this theory based either on a rethinking of classical and contemporary social theories (Bulle and Morin 2015) or on empirical/topical insights. If a special concern with the problems of ideology, values, democracy, and political sociology indeed permeates his work, his analyses nevertheless all aim at clarifying the general research program he is trying to delineate for the social sciences.

It is no coincidence, however, that the analysis of the topics of ideology, values, and politics were put at the front as convincing illustrations of his own theory. Values, politics, and ideas are indeed complex things which can neither be fully explained using the instrumental approach of rational choice theory (RCT) nor using any of the various fashionable irrationalist approaches of the day. It is very easy to dismiss opposing ideas, values, or thoughts as being merely the result of brainwashing, false consciousness, crowd mentality, panopticism, habitus, the patriarchy, systemic racism, the heterosexual matrix, and so on. It is also quite easy for social scientists to dismiss points of view diverging from their own out of consideration by arguing that they are merely the result of the combining forces of the quest for power and wealth of some elite (instrumental rationality) and of the docile gullibility of soulless and powerless masses (irrationality). But it is also unscientific. One fails to *explain* by accusing and stipulating. If Lavoisier's refutation of Stahl's phlogistic theory merely consisted in accusing him of wealth-seeking or gullibility, the grounds on which the chemical revolution now rests would become shakier. It is rather Lavoisier's careful consideration of the good reasons why Stahl and other scientists believed in the existence of phlogistons that helped him understand why they were wrong and provided contemporary chemistry with the solid foundations it now enjoys.

Likewise, social theory cannot merely rest on the accusation that opposing views are the result of instrumental or irrational forces. This does not mean, of course, that instrumental rationality and "brainwashing" never play a role in the realm of politics, values, and ideas. But if and when, for instance, brainwashing *does* occur, social scientists must explain the reasons why it is done and how/why it works. To do so, they must contextualize ideal typical actors to assign them plausible reasons explaining why they believe what they believe or do what they do. Boudon's sociology aims precisely at illustrating the fruitfulness of his general theory of rationality by making it clear that these complex and controversial topics are badly addressed by contemporary social theory. In other words, taking on these complex topics and showing how his theory of rationality can be used to explain them is the best way to demonstrate the *generality* of his own approach. Indeed, if his theory applies to these complex topics, then it is not difficult to imagine that it can also be applied to other social phenomena.

But simply because Boudon himself used some of the most complex examples to illustrate the scope of his theory does not mean that social scientists should restrict themselves to the study of the same phenomena tackled by Boudon. On the contrary, Boudon aimed at providing the social sciences with a *general research program* which can be pursued by scholars interested in any social topic whatsoever. And indeed, many scholars have attempted to apply Boudon's theory to a wide variety of topics.

This chapter aims precisely at demonstrating the generality and richness of Boudon's work by compiling some of these recent applications of his seminal social theory. It will be divided into two main sections: the first section will refresh the reader's mind on Boudon's approach and general theory, while the second section will focus on some applications of his methodological individualism and general theory of rationality to various topics including education, relative frustration, gambling, policy evaluation and legal studies, radicalization, terrorism and security studies, and conspiracy theories.

The following by no means exhausts all of the work using Boudon's insights; it nevertheless provides a good idea of what types of studies can be conducted using his sociology as a foundation. It shows, in other words, that Boudon's social theory constitutes a properly *general* research program, that is, a research program which allows for a wide range of social phenomena to be explained and studied successfully. Hopefully, this chapter will convince you that there are many good reasons to use Boudon's work for your own research endeavors.

Boudon's Approach to the Study of Social Phenomena

To contextualize Boudon's work, I wish to make a few preliminary remarks on his general approach to the study of social phenomena before tackling the main task of this chapter. This contextualization will allow readers who are not fully knowledgeable about Boudon's theoretical work to find a basic sketch of his main ideas as well as a few references for further reading. This section will first briefly delineate Boudon's classical influences and discuss his engagement with RCT before culminating in an exposition sketching his very own general theory of rationality.

Building on classical sociology and rational choice theory

Boudon's work is characterized by a constant concern for the elaboration of a general theory which stands on the shoulders of giants. This is the reason why his theoretical work heavily engages with the insights of Tocqueville (Leroux 2014), Durkheim (Besnard 2003, chap. 12; Leroux 2020; Demeulenaere 2022), Simmel (Robitaille 2020), and Weber (Leroux 2019). Boudon is indeed an *heir*. He reinterprets the work of his eminent predecessors and contemporaries in order to build his own theory on solid grounds. His main concern is to find a general and systematic manner by which one can attempt to understand as many intriguing social phenomena as possible. In this quest, Boudon mainly mobilizes Weber's typology of social action (Weber 2019 [1921], 101–103), Simmel's model of social forms (Simmel 1971), and Ludwig von Mises's principle of methodological singularism (Mises 1998 [1949], 44–46); he also exemplifies his own theory with evidence from Durkheim's *Suicide* (1951 [1897]) and *Elementary Forms of Religious Life* (2001 [1912]), from Tocqueville's *Democracy in America* (2000 [1835/1840]), as well as from the work of many other classical theorists.

In addition to his reliance on classical theories, Boudon built his general theory of rationality in dialogue with contemporary social scientists who attempted to study the social world by focusing on the actor's rationality. It is hence by analyzing the concepts and applications of the rational choice theories of prominent social scientists such as James Coleman (1986) and Mancur Olson (1971) that Boudon formulated a sharp criticism of RCT and presented his own approach as a better alternative.

Indeed, Boudon (2003) explains that RCT is adopting a conception of human rationality which is narrowly instrumental and utilitarian. In brief, it is based on the assumption that individual actors wish to increase their wealth (more-or-less subjectively conceived) by reflecting on the appropriateness of various means to reach this goal. Once this assumption is accepted, then every intriguing collective action should in principle be understood by decomposing this action in utilitarian ends and instrumental means of achieving these ends.

Public choice theory, for instance, was confronted with an intriguing phenomenon: in spite of the fact that no individual vote can have any impact on the outcome of an election, the number of voters at any given election is far from zero. The assumptions here are that rational voters would wish to increase their well-being by having the candidate whose platform conforms better with their interests win and that they will aim at finding the best means of getting this candidate elected. The paradox is hence obvious: the best means cannot possibly be "voting" as individual voting has, in elections involving a large number of voters such as national elections, a probability close to zero of having an impact on the final outcome but nevertheless has a nonzero opportunity cost. Yet, participation rates remain high in Western elections. How can we explain this problem?

RCT, to explain such a behavior, can only save its assumption that people are rational by reevaluating what the utilitarian goal behind voting could be. If it is not to elect a candidate, what can the goal of voting be? Various attempts have been made to save RCT: voting is the expression of extremely high risk aversion from a majority of voters (Ferejohn and Fiorina 1974, 535) or is a way to signal trustworthiness to others by self-interestingly demonstrate at little cost an interest for the common good (Overbye 1995, 376).

These explanations are deemed unconvincing by Boudon (1998). Indeed, they do not conform with the reasons most *real* individuals claim to have for voting.

Most voters do not claim to vote because of some self-interested high risk aversion nor because they wish to maintain their reputation as a trustworthy individual by signaling some interest for the common good. Most people vote because they think it is the right thing to do. As such, for this particular problem as well as many others predominantly involving values or cognition (rather than predominantly involving narrowly defined utilitarian interests), RCT is not a proper approach to make sense of collective actions. This is why Boudon thought it important to take a step back and to consult the work of classical thinkers, in particular of Weber, in order to keep the good aspects of RCT while correcting the bad aspects.

The general theory of rationality

What is wrong with RCT, according to Boudon, is the assumption of universality of the role that instrumentalism and utilitarianism play in *specific* reasoning processes.

In a fundamental sense, it is true that every *action* involves thought processes about which means would be best suited to achieve given ends; it is also true, in a basic sense, that these "given ends" are indeed always expected to increase the actor's *ultimate* pleasure or reduce his or her *ultimate* pain. In this sense, then, it is true that reason is *ultimately* instrumental and utilitarian.

However, social scientists are not only interested in the *ultimate* form of action (the means–ends relationships *as such*, emptied from specific empirical content); they typically aim at clarifying *specific* phenomena by seeking an understanding of the *specific* actions that brought them about. In this perspective, one must be more specific in terms of the means and ends chosen. If all actions stem from a desire to improve the actor's *subjective* well-being, such an improvement can take various empirical forms: one may indeed seek to increase one's material wealth or one may seek to increase one's spiritual or psychological well-being by acting in conformity with what one believes to be higher values. If both can be categorized as actions aiming at improving the actor's well-being, they nevertheless remain categorically distinct in the empirical form we seek to understand.

This is why Weber's typology of social action can be useful, as it distinguishes between *value* rationality and *purposive* rationality. Boudon terms them, respectively, *axiological* rationality and *instrumental* rationality. True enough, voting is done as a means to increase one's well-being; but not usually one's material well-being (by seeking to obtain a better deal with the elected candidate in office). It is rather one's psychological well-being resulting from acting in conformity to one's perception of what one's duty is that explains why so many people vote. Boudon indicates that, if one believes that democracy is a *just* system of governance and that any alternative is *unjust*, then one's vote *does indeed count* (in the actor's mind), not toward the achievement of electing a particular individual of course, but in contributing to the performance of one's duty in preserving a system deemed as just. It makes sense, then, that in a particular country in which democracy is largely perceived as the only fair political system, there are high participation rates in spite of the fact that any individual vote has an almost null probability of affecting the outcome.

All of these reasoning processes about values and the best means to act in conformity to values are also accompanied by reflections about *truth*. Indeed, if one votes because one believes that one's vote counts toward the achievement of performing one's duty, one must also think that this is *true*. That is, one must believe that it is true that voting contributes to fulfilling one's duty. One does not necessarily have an "interest" in believing this to be true, nor is it a belief rooted in one's values, but a belief rooted in what one perceives as being *true*. These reasoning processes—those which are neither about interest nor value—are rooted in what Boudon calls "cognitive rationality." In other words, an individual who votes typically does so because (1) he or she believes it is his or her *duty* to help preserve democracy (axiological reflection process); (2) he or she believes that voting is a good instrument to help in the achievement of the valued goal of performing his or her duty (instrumental reflection process aimed at increasing his or her psychological well-being through the axiological performance of his or her duty); and (3) he or she believes that it is *true* that voting constitutes a good means to achieve the goal of acting in conformity to value (cognitive reflection process).

This was just an example to illustrate a general principle. In brief, most social actions can be explained by a complex combination of these three types of reflection processes. Empirically, the social context in which the actor is located is what allows social scientists to plausibly apply weights to these different types of reasons to think and act. In this case, as Boudon points out, it seems clear that the main typical motor for the act of voting is rooted in the actor's axiology; it is a reflection on values which predominantly guides what is to be done, as compared to possible alternatives, in order to reach a greater psychological satisfaction.

With this typology of rationality, we are now equipped with the basic tools of a general research program, that is, a program which aims at applying weights to these types of reasoning processes to ideal typical actors involved in *any* social phenomenon of interest in order to explain it. The goal of social explanation can be seen as decomposing a macrosocial problem or paradox in terms of the typical individual actions and motivations which caused it in order to analyze *how* these three types of rationality operated in light of the typical social and cognitive contexts of the actors involved.

This is what allows us to reconstruct the problem or paradox in an intelligible manner; how we can provide, in other words, *social explanations*.

Applications of Boudon's Work Since His Death (2013–2023) and Future Perspectives

Now that the reader has a better idea of what Boudon's general research program involves, it is time to turn our attention to *how* this program has been applied. In order to present a manageable number of analyses, the following will be constrained to studies made after Boudon's death in 2013. As for the methodology used here, the following literature has been obtained by typing the keywords "Raymond Boudon" on Google Scholar, restricting results from 2013 up until June 2023 (when this chapter was completed) and collecting every result, which was then individually analyzed in order to identify the extent of Boudon's influence. Those with only minor mentions, tangential remarks, or brief quotations of Boudon were excluded (there were many). Only a subset of illustrative studies using Boudon's work as a main theoretical foundation was retained, thus reducing the material analyzed to a manageable number which can be discussed in more depth. Master's and PhD theses were also excluded, although there were many of them, which may indicate that Boudon's research program will lead to further publications in the near future. Finally, works in French were also excluded for the purpose of both reducing the scope of an already ambitious endeavor and adapting to the anglophone audience to whom this book is addressed. These restrictions have the inconvenience of making it seem like Boudon's work has been applied to a few studies, but they have the advantage of allowing us to discuss them in more depth and to show how exactly Boudon's program *can* be implemented. This should nevertheless, I hope, provide the reader with a broad range of possible applications and potential research ideas.

The sociology of education

Throughout his career, Boudon presented original contributions on which scholars from various thematic perspectives have since built. One area which Boudon studied early in his career and for which he gained much prominence was the sociology of education. His analysis of the educational system and its role in social mobility, particularly in his book *Education, Opportunity, and Social Inequality* (Boudon 1974 [1973]), has indeed attracted much attention. Consequently, this is perhaps the area in which his work is most used in contemporary social scientific investigations. As this is the most well-known aspect of Boudon's work (and as many studies heavily rely on his work), I will only provide a brief outline of the impact of his work since his death to leave space to discuss less well-known applications in more detail.

Although Boudon's contribution to the sociology of education dates from 1973, many studies are still citing him and building upon his work. Most of these studies are framing their analyses using Boudon's distinction between the primary (class socialization) and secondary (socially influenced aspirations motivating concrete decision-making) effects of social origins on educational attainment and his rationalist perspective which gives a prominent role to positional decision-making based on varying aspirations.

In particular, some have sought to build new, more robust, indices to measure unequal access to education (see in particular Bulle 2016) in order to see the extent to which Boudon's results on social mobility can be maintained.

Others have focused on complementing Boudon's findings on how social or policy changes have impacted the democratization of education over time (Bulle 2019) and the effects it has had. Attempts have been made to change slightly the focus from educational outcomes as such to inequalities in the acquisition of *skills* (Green and Kaye 2022) or to the special sociological analysis of children considered "at risk" of obtaining "poor educational outcomes" (Becker and Tuppat 2013) and of special groups of children and adolescent such as refugees in Germany (Will and Homuth 2020). Some scholars have drawn upon Boudon's analysis of educational inequalities to see if his approach and results also apply to educational systems in locations such as Chile (Ceron et al. 2022), Spain (Valdés 2022), Germany (Blossfeld 2018), Québec (Labrosse et al. 2017), contemporary England (Thompson and Simmons 2013), China (Liu 2019), or Indonesia (Arifin 2017). They all demonstrate that Boudon's insights, either through the use of theoretical simulation models or through the application of his framework to specific social contexts, can successfully explain educational inequalities and their impact on social mobility.

There are too many studies related to the sociology of education which use at least in part Boudon's seminal work to list them exhaustively here or to go in much depth in their presentation. However, one can already see the generality of Boudon's research program. Delineating geographical specificities and developing additional measures of educational inequalities (or improving existing ones) relying on Boudon's work on education prove to be promising research endeavors for interested scholars.

Relative frustration

One of Boudon's major contributions to our understanding of social enigmas is linked to his study of perverse effects of social action. In his book *The Unintended Consequences of Social Action* (Boudon 1982 [1977]), he presents a chapter (Ch. 5) on what he terms "the logic of relative frustration" where he finds a way to explain the following paradox: when more opportunities are available within a social group, it sometimes brings more resentment toward those who succeed, and frustration on the part of individuals who do not succeed, than when there were fewer opportunities.

Relevant and convincing social analyses have been conducted on this topic before Boudon. One may think, in addition to Tocqueville's or Durkheim's work cited by Boudon (ibid., 109), of Ludwig von Mises's explanation of the anti-capitalistic mentality (Mises 2008 [1956]) or of Helmut Schoeck's sociological analysis of envy (Schoeck 1987 [1966]). Boudon adds to this by providing a rational explanation for the understanding of why, in a social context in which there have been much more opportunities for individuals such as is the case in most Western countries since the Industrial Revolution, there is nevertheless an increasing amount of frustration within the population.

Boudon (1982 [1977], 106) argues that, in order to understand envy, one must understand the context of the envious individual. The idea is that an individual who believes the wealth and prestige of another individual *is attainable to him or her* will be more resentful than when he or she believes these goals to be unattainable (ibid.). This makes intuitive sense as, to take a simple example, while realizing that the King is wealthier and more powerful than them, peasants were not frustrated by this situation as they were aware that such wealth and power is simply inaccessible to them; they cannot enter in the competition for this wealth and power. But when workers are told that there are a certain number of promotions available and that they perceive their coworkers as equals, then they are likely to enter the competition, and if some of these coworkers get a promotion which they don't get themselves, then it likely leaves them frustrated. Likewise, if opportunities for promotion increase within a firm, then applications for promotion will likely increase, and those who are not promoted will be frustrated about the fact that many whom they consider to be their equals (or even their inferiors) have been promoted but not them (ibid., 109–110).

In other words, the context in which inequalities are perceived matters to understand the reaction they will trigger. This illustrates quite well that, when we perceive others as our equals (or our inferiors), seeing them win the competition provides us with good reasons to become frustrated. Fixed stratification structures hence paradoxically can make people less frustrated (ibid., 122): the perception of higher classes being unattainable to the common person reduces frustration when compared to a situation in which reaching higher classes is perceived as a goal which can realistically be attained and when a sufficient increase in opportunities to compete for a place in these higher classes occurs.

Boudon tried to modelize a version of this paradox using game theory. He postulated a certain number of equally competent coworkers who can choose whether or not to invest in the chance of obtaining a promotion (ibid.). This investment is hence costly. With the number of promotions available increasing and the number of coworkers remaining constant, it is expected that more people will make the investment (as the expected reward outweighs the cost). If the number of promotions, although increased, remains lower than the number of employees who chose to invest in the chance of getting the promotion, then, assuming equality among employees' ability, promotions will be randomly distributed among those who chose to invest (ibid., 110–111). This will leave non-promoted investors *worse off* than they would have been had they not initially invested, thus rendering them frustrated. The number of frustrated individuals is hence expected to increase when promotions increase up to a certain point (after which the number of promotions is high enough to reduce the number of those who will be worse off) in some "inverted-U" shaped curve. In other words, there is a particular number of increased opportunities which maximizes frustration. By analogy, Boudon argues that there are situations in society when opportunities rising are also accompanied by an increase in frustrated individuals.

This modelization of relative frustration had an impact on recent empirical studies; some have indeed attempted to explore the scope and limitations of Boudon's theoretical model. Berger and Diekmann (2015) used an experimental setting to verify with three experiments how actors would react to an increase in opportunities. They found out that, with increased opportunities, there was also an increase in the number of investments in attempting to be rewarded (ibid., 729). However, they noticed more caution than they expected in terms of investment toward obtaining an opportunity when there was an intermediate number of opportunities available, thus limiting the relative frustration at these intermediate levels (ibid., 731–732).

The authors suggest that these results do not support as clearly as anticipated Boudon's theory. They nevertheless suggested that, by enlarging the focus from only those who chose to invest and lost to both these same "losers" *and* those who chose not to invest at all, then perhaps the experimental results could confirm Boudon's theoretical insights (ibid., 732–733). Using the Gini coefficient to measure inequalities, it was observed that when opportunities are initially increased, resulting inequalities are increased. It was hypothesized that, when inequalities increase, due to inter-personal comparisons, frustration on the part of those who did not participate *and* of those who lost while competing for these opportunities increases. Hence, the experimental results seem to support the following claim: when opportunities initially increase at a low rate, more people are frustrated until we reach a point in which there are sufficient opportunities to reduce this rate of frustrated individuals (ibid., 734).

Now, interpreting the Gini coefficient correctly requires contextualization. Here, all students who participated in the experiment had equal chances to become winners if they invested. A low Gini coefficient is hence reasonably connected with low frustration (and vice versa). In fact, only a highly stratified society *within a context in which there is perceived equality* can be seen as "frustrating" as those who invest and lose do not see the reason why they lost, and those who do not invest may regret not investing when observing the final outcome.

Although this study obviously has many limitations, as is the case for all experimental approaches in the social sciences, it does help in clarifying the broad theoretical considerations put forward by Boudon. One could imagine future experiments in which we compare equal systems with unequal ones. There remains the problem that frustration is here associated to a quantitative measure. There is no reason to believe that the Swiss students participating in this experiment truly were "frustrated" at the outcome, as their reasons for participating in the study are not the same as the reasons why individuals who apply for promotion do. Failing at the latter is clearly more frustrating than "failing" in the context of a controlled experiment.

Otten (2020) has also used computer simulations to incorporate something left out of Boudon's model. In Boudon's model, when there were more promotions than people investing in the chance of getting a promotion, the remaining promotions were simply not allocated to anyone. Otten redistributed these randomly to non-investors (ibid., 2). It is argued that this scenario often fits real cases in which, when there are not a sufficient number of qualified individuals applying for a role or promotion, this role is sometimes given to individuals who are less educated (and who would not normally have competed for it). The predictions made from the computer simulations were that it is when the cost of investing in the promotion is low and that the number of promotions available moves from a "low" level to an "intermediate" one that deprivation increases while opportunities increase (ibid., 5). If the cost of investing is too high, then the promotion does not bring much difference between those promoted and those who did not pursue a promotion, which is likely to lead to fewer investments. The empirical experiment made with students supported most of what the simulations predicted (ibid., 8–10).

A possible way to specify Boudon's model in light of the above experiments is to conceive of frustration as not only being the result of *absolute* loss (as in the case of those who invested time and money in an unsuccessful attempt to obtain an opportunity), but also *relative* loss (i.e., being frustrated by the fact that one has less than others). Boudon does show that frustration may occur as a result of comparisons *after* the competition is over, but Otten (2022) indicates that the anticipation of this comparison must also be taken into account *during* the competition (i.e., should matter to the actor's decisions). He has therefore integrated into Boudon's model an assumption of "inequity aversion" (ibid., 4) to verify how this would change the behavior of actors. Using similar experiments to Berger and Diekmann, Otten finds that adding this assumption further nuances the results (ibid., 13–14). Boudon's model may prove to be too simplistic here. But experiments may also not be the best way to capture effects linked to relative deprivation and frustration as the opportunities provided in laboratory contexts do not really matter; students may not really care about the outcomes as this experiment is not a defining feature of their life. On the other hand, there clearly are situations in society in which obtaining an opportunity has great importance in the eyes of competitors. Using alternative methods to empirically evaluate Boudon's theoretical claims would likely improve our knowledge of relative frustration further.

Gambling

As an example of a topic which has not been addressed by Boudon, but for which Boudon's social theory contributed to shed light on empirical data, we can take the case of gambling. Indeed, Savard et al. (2015) have attempted to understand the phenomenon of gambling among adolescents using Boudon's general theory of rationality. Rejecting deterministic accounts of gambling as a "vice" or an "illness," they argue that the phenomenon of teenage gambling could be explained more profitably by focusing on the motivations of the actors involved (ibid., 47). After evaluating various models' more-or-less deterministic attempts at explaining gambling behaviors in a population of adolescents, the authors indeed suggest that few of these models succeed in their endeavor as a result of the fact that they do not take into account the social position of actors within a context in which gambling provides them with *meaning* (ibid., 45).

Although this first article only delineates a *path* that researchers could follow to understand the phenomenon of adolescent gambling, the same authors have also later tried to apply these insights to the empirical analysis of the phenomenon (Savard et al. 2018). Using semi-structured interviews with 31 adolescents who gamble (secondary data analysis), they categorize their reasoning processes in relation to their social environment into Boudon's typology (see previous section of this chapter).

Some of the reasons provided by the participants for why they were gambling involved stress alleviation, the capacity to celebrate a win by buying things (including clothes, drugs, and alcohol), or the feeling of relief linked to the repayment of debts. Other mentioned benefits related to the creation of social bonds or, even, to a perception of climbing within the social hierarchy by looking "cool" and standing out of the crowd (ibid., 591–592). Hence, to some participants, gambling is an easy, convenient *instrument* to obtain money which then allowed them to obtain goods and an enviable social status. However, due to what most would consider to be enormous potential costs (e.g., getting involved in illegal activities to repay debt, family disputes relating to money, loss of social and romantic relationships, or issues at work and school), it is doubtful that most participants simply considered the benefits as higher than the costs. We can then speculate that the values linked to friendship and the development of skills were also factors explaining why some of these adolescents choose to continue to gamble in spite of the *recognized* heavy costs associated with it (ibid., 596).

There are therefore, according to this study, cognitive and instrumental reasons involved, which are mostly linked to the *belief* (held as *true*) that gambling is a proper tool for making easy money and maintaining social ties invoked to justify the action of gambling. There are also axiological reasons invoked by participants such as the value put in creating a community and in facilitating or maintaining friendships (ibid.). Moreover, various goals linked to gambling are valued in our society (wealth, power, status, etc.); some forms of gambling are also seen positively (skills relating to poker or other card games). Many adolescents hence do not see their behavior as being something which goes against the values they were taught to cherish. Simply, they have chosen a quicker but riskier path toward what seem like perfectly valid and valued life goals. The authors then identify paths toward social change (ibid., 598): if intervention focuses on changing or specifying the values on which these adolescents act, it may also reduce perceived social problems linked to adolescent gambling.

There are clearly research opportunities to explore in more detail what these cognitive, instrumental, and axiological reasons are specifically. Perhaps a study design taking the Boudonian theoretical framework as a basis for the questions asked during interviews would allow researchers to reach more solid conclusions in this respect. The authors of this study, however, faced limitations due to their use of secondary data; they nevertheless initiated a potent research area which could eventually lead to a much deeper understanding of adolescent gambling. Other research opportunities also come to mind here. Attempting to apply a general theory of rationality to other activities considered as "vices" in society such as heavy alcohol consumption and tobacco or drug consumption (or drug dealing) could contribute to shed a new light on the explanation of the social phenomena they trigger. They also constitute "difficult" and controversial cases, as they are often perceived as irrational behaviors. Applying a rationalist perspective to their understanding can therefore become an important contribution in illustrating the generality of Boudon's theory.

Policy evaluation and legal studies

Another way in which Boudon's social theory can be used is as a theoretical framework for policy and legislation analysis. Indeed, by focusing on the contextualized actor's reasoning processes, one can better make sense of why a certain policy is linked to a certain set of consequences.

Patok (2019), for instance, relying on Boudon's methodological individualism and on his theory of rationality, explored the experience of Polish immigrants in blue-collar jobs in France in the context of the EU's free movement of labor policy. In particular, she takes a closer look at what characterizes their integration in the workplace given the climate of tension linked to fears about this policy affecting negatively local blue-collar workers (ibid., 20). After interviewing 60 Polish immigrant workers and observing them at work, she concludes that they are often considered as good workers when compared to the French blue-collar workers by clients and employers (ibid., 29); this context provides them with reasons to work harder so that they meet expectations. This can, however, also create tensions with the French who, because of this, also have reasons to believe, from their own perspective and context, that these immigrants are "stealing" jobs from the locals (ibid., 28). Patok uses Boudon's social theory to present a picture of complex relationships which shape the identity of blue-collar Polish workers.

Future studies could very well draw on these insights to analyze other social groups. For instance, interviewing employers or clients to see their perspective on immigrant workers could enhance the results of this study and, once again, using Boudon's theoretical program as a basis for the analysis would allow us to shed light on the complex set of relationships between immigrant workers and local workers, employers, or clients, as well as their social impacts. This study shows, in brief, that the evaluation of the effects of policies can benefit from using Boudon's social theory.

As legislation provides a contextual framework in which actors develop their thinking and acting, Boudon's social theory is well suited for studies focusing on such legislation and their social origins and effects. To understand how legal plurality (defined as the coexistence of statist and non-statist legal frameworks within a given society) is managed and negotiated by various actors, Leclair (2023) relies directly on Boudon's social theory of the actor as an autonomous being who nevertheless acts and thinks in relation to his or her social context (ibid., 65). The legal pluralism in this case constitutes such a social context which influences how actors behave and think. For instance, the degree of legitimacy enjoyed by statist legal systems in the eyes of the individuals has a considerable impact on how non-statist legal systems can emerge and what place it can take within a given society (ibid., 72).

In turn, this degree of legitimacy is grounded in *the reasons* for social actors to accept a particular statist or non-statist legal framework (ibid.). For example, if a deeply religious community establishes norms of conduct for their community, individuals who are part of this community are less likely to believe that any statist law which goes against their community's legal framework is justified. The competition between local, national, transnational, and international actors for the imposition of legal frameworks over individuals must hence be understood as a competition for legitimacy in the eyes of contextualized social actors (ibid., 135). Although this is indeed a complex phenomenon which involves many actors interplaying and reacting to one another, Leclair clearly shows that using Boudon's conception of the social actor as having good reasons to believe in the legitimacy of a particular legal framework as compared to another brings insightful results. His study uses empirical evidence from a variety of countries, especially from Africa but also from Canadian Indigenous communities or the Roma community in Romania, thus showing the general applicability of his approach.

His paper is broad and focuses on state actors, non-state elite actors, as well as ordinary individuals and their interactions within legal pluralism. This is hence a good basis for future research using Boudon's social theory as the theoretical framework for an analysis of the interactions within competing legal frameworks. As Leclair (ibid., 160) makes clear, there is still a lot of space for empirical research to clarify these mechanisms and to reduce the number of plausible, yet speculative claims made about these complex processes.

Radicalization, terrorism, and security studies

Radicalization, terrorism, and security studies in general have often been conducted on the basis that actors are either irrational beings who get corrupted by their emotions, by charismatic leaders, and by madness or on a conception of actors as instrumentally rational beings who seek to gain something out of these violent acts (such as a sense of belonging to a group, a place into heaven, or power and prestige otherwise inaccessible to them). But as a growing interest in understanding the motivations behind violent extremism and crime can be observed in the social scientific literature since the beginning of the century (McLaughlin 2023), many studies have relied to a great extent on Boudon's general theory of rationality to make sense of these phenomena. Indeed, as Boudon's theory presents a complex contextualized rational actor who can not only reason instrumentally but also cognitively and axiologically, it has the potential to be usefully applied to the understanding of complex phenomena such as violent extremism.

In his extensive review of the literature on the social scientific analysis of radicalization, Marlière (2022, 57–59) shows that Boudon's concept of relative frustration has been used to understand radicalization processes in the West. Indeed, against the pathologizing tendencies of holistic approaches to the study of radicalization, a focus on why socially situated individuals become radicalized through their own reasoning within their social contexts allows for a better explanation of radicalization processes. It is not because one is deprived or unstable *per se* that one becomes more likely to radicalize oneself. It is rather because, given the promises of equality, freedom, and prosperity permeating the public discourse of contemporary democracies, individuals who do not feel equal, free, and prosperous have good reasons, from their perspective, to reject the system altogether (ibid., 58, 66).

Radical theories hence become more appealing as they provide a logical explanation for why these individuals think they were fooled; they allow these social actors to make sense of their situation and of that of the world surrounding them; they get rid of the contradictions that are so obvious to those who feel left out of the promises of democracies (ibid., 63–66). This, as Marlière points out in his conclusion (ibid., 70), is not sufficient to provide a general explanation of radicalization but can indeed apply to specific cases and hints toward the possibility of developing typologies which will then allow us to understand the phenomenon in its generality.

This is again quite in line with Boudon's (2012) very own approach rooted in methodological singularism, a concept borrowed from Austrian economist Ludwig von Mises, according to which complex historical problems can only be interpreted in their singularity, that is, we must decompose general problems in various singular parts to make sense of them. The difficulty here is that radicalization is *not* such a singular problem; it must be decomposed and analyzed using more specific ideal types. And this is precisely what has been attempted by McLaughlin and Robitaille (2021).

Following the academic debate on whether cognitive radicalization is a necessary condition for behavioral radicalization and vice versa (i.e., is it necessary to believe in a radical violent ideology in order to act on its basis and does believing in such an ideology make one more prone to act on it?), McLaughlin and Robitaille developed a typology in order to dehomogenize the phenomenon in question and to apply a methodologically singular analysis of each type of radicalization. Using explicitly Boudon's typology of rationality, they have indicated many insights and paths forward for future empirical research wishing to analyze various types of radicalization (and the process of radicalization or de-radicalization) (ibid., 13–19).

They created three "pure" types to guide empirical research: radicalized warriors (individuals who are both cognitively *and* behaviorally radicalized),

radicalized thinkers (individuals who, while adhering fully or to a large extent to a radically violent ideology abstain from any violent action), and skeptical fighters (individuals who will perform acts of violence in the name of an ideology while remaining largely or wholly unconvinced of its validity). They argue that looking at the social context and life course of these individuals will allow researchers to discover a complex assemblage of cognitive, axiological, and instrumental reasons which explain, in the last analysis, the radicalization paths and transitions taken by these individuals throughout their life. Using methodological individualism, then, we may profitably reconstruct the intriguing phenomenon of radicalization. One must first realize, however, that "radicalization" is not a singular phenomenon and cannot hence be understood without decomposing it in an internally consistent typology. Then, by focusing on individual motivations and contexts over time, researchers can reconstruct the phenomenon and understand real-world events.

An illuminating example of an analysis of what McLaughlin and Robitaille have later called the "radicalized warrior" in their typology of radicalization can be found in an interview conducted with a former member of the Italian Red Brigades who spent more than 30 years in jail (Orsini 2013). Orsini, the author of this study, calls this type of radicalized individuals "terrorists by vocation," that is, individuals who commit violent acts as a result, not of any desire to obtain personal gain or reward, but of a profound belief in the truth and value of the ideological cause they adhere to (ibid., 672–673).

Once again, using Boudon's work as a theoretical means of interpretation, he provides insightful remarks about the life course and social positioning which led the interviewed individual to adhere so deeply to a cause as to commit violent actions on its basis (ibid., 682). The interviewed man, who ended up going to jail for his cause, had a modest childhood but was surrounded by wealthy kids who treated others with contempt and arrogance (ibid., 674–675). Perceived injustices, both at the level of his personal life and at the national level, gave him reasons to resent the wealthy and to adopt an anti-capitalistic mentality. He became so committed to this mentality that he ended up joining the Red Brigades after abandoning his family (thus reducing the personal cost of fully committing to this ideology). The ideological goals became his life purpose and were rooted in values, not in personal gain.

These elements are quite common for members of the Red Brigades, an organization based on both a reinforcement of values due to close proximity with other members *and* a reduction of personal costs to act on the basis of these values due to a strong incentive to cut ties with other social groups. It hence provides its members with a social environment conducive to full commitment to the cause (ibid., 674).

Boudon's typology of rationality is hence very helpful to make sense of how the life course and social contexts of individual actors provide them with reasons to believe or act on the basis of an ideology; it can also solve the paradox of believing in a violent ideology without acting on it (and vice versa). One can immediately see, in light of the above considerations, how his social theory can help in constituting a relevant and original research agenda. More studies could be done using this framework by focusing on the other types of radicalizations put forward by McLaughlin and Robitaille (2021).

Conspiracy theories

Boudon's work often attempted to clarify what many social scientists believed to be non-understandable. He took side with Weber and Durkheim against Lévy-Bruhl to explain magical beliefs and attempted to provide an account of these beliefs based on his own typology of rationality (Boudon 1993). What Lévy-Bruhl termed the "primitive mentality" can actually be understood as the result of rational thought processes. Rain dance rituals are not performed because they are the result of a different mentality, but rather because the social and cognitive context in which those who perform them are situated is such that these actions *make sense to them*.

Likewise, many contemporary beliefs seem completely non-understandable from the typical social and cognitive context of middle-class, highly educated, and by-and-large system-trusting intellectuals. As such, many scholars describe beliefs in, for instance, superstitions or conspiracy theories as the result of irrational or pathological considerations. But other scholars who have adopted Boudon's perspective of asking oneself not *if* a belief is rational, but rather *how* it is rational, have been much more successful at explaining adherence to these kinds of beliefs. Indeed, in light of the complexities related to the definition and the methodological approach to understand conspiracy theories from a sociological point of view, Boudon's methodological individualism proves to be a useful starting point in particular to make sense of the believers' reasons to adhere to conspiracy theories (Nefes and Reche 2020, 98–99).

Taking a stance against various irrationalist social theories or typical media and political portrayal of conspiracy theorizing as pathological, Reche and Nefes (2020) use an approach based on Max Weber and Raymond Boudon's sociological theories to make sense of the instrumental and axiological reasoning processes behind adherence to conspiracy theories. They emphasize that conceiving of conspiracy theorizing as pathological logically implies an unacceptable dualism (ibid., 15). On the one hand, there would be rational human beings who, although they can make mistakes, generally use *proper* thinking and can reach truth. On the other, there would be irrational human beings whose thinking is flawed from the outset and can hence never reason toward any truth statement other than by mere accident.

But stipulating a thinking disorder because the content of thoughts is deemed inadequate is far from providing a proper argument in favor of its existence. Indeed, this polylogism requires proof: *what* specifically is the distinguishing characteristic between those who think properly and those who think pathologically? Moreover, how can we explain the change in those whose thinking becomes "cured" over time (i.e., those who *stop* believing in false conspiracy theories) or in those whose thinking becomes "sick" (i.e., those who *start* believing in them)? The truth is, there is no real evidence that their thinking is in any way pathological. The mere fact that conspiracy theorists believe in things most people find odd or appalling is certainly not sufficient to demonstrate this.

According to Reche and Nefes (2022), there are various reasons that can explain both the *adherence* (why would someone *believe*) and the production of (why would someone *create* or *perpetuate*) conspiracy theories. Some conspiracy theories *are useful* even if false: the authors provide the example of those selling homeopathic medicine for profit (ibid., 19). Certainly, these sellers benefit from the conspiracy according to which modern medicine is corrupt and based on lies (ibid.). But this very statement, as the authors aptly point out, can *itself* become a baseless conspiracy theory. One cannot infer from the fact that one benefits from a lie that this is absolute proof that there is any kind of attempt at willfully manipulating buyers. It may very well be the case that these sellers are sellers *precisely because they do believe* that they are helping the public against the evils of modern medicine.

While asking *cui bono* certainly provides some evidence in favor of the instrumental-utilitarian rationality of spreading lies, it is not sufficient to establish it. Indeed, many conspiracy theories themselves suffer from this weakness of resting solely on speculations about who benefits from the alleged crime or lie. One must pay closer attention to the actor's social context in order to understand how the complex combination of values and interests entered into the actor's choice to believe. In fact, Reche and Nefes argue that two of the main aspects characterizing beliefs in conspiracy theories found in the literature, partisanship and religiosity (ibid., 23–24), are, respectively, examples of the presence of both instrumental thinking (I wish my political group to win or my religion to become more widespread, so I push a conspiratorial narrative, or accuse my enemies of being conspiracy theorists, to make them look bad) and axiological thinking (the strength of my political values or my faith provides me with values which make me more likely to accept that my opponents are evil). In other words, my *a priori* framework (in the Simmelian sense) of how I see morality and interest provides me with good reasons to integrate the conspiracy theory in my own set of beliefs or in my own line of argumentation.

In addition to this evaluation of the literature, Nefes (2015a) has also conducted empirical work on the reception of conspiracy theories involving a secret Jewish ruling class in Turkey promoting capitalism and globalism vehiculated through a famous local book series. Using Boudon's theory of rationality to make sense of his data, he finds that the political inclinations of the readers shape their understanding of the conspiracy, with leftists being more prone to read the book as a conspiracy based on class distinction and rightists focusing their attention primarily on racial elements (ibid., 559). Based on the interviews he made with readers of the books with heterogenous political stances, he argues that beliefs in conspiracy theories are the result of a combination of instrumental and axiological thinking processes (ibid., 570–572).

From left to right, conspiracy theories can strengthen one's political opinion by providing clear, additional support to it. From the left's perspective, a secret group of global capitalists causing the exploitation of the working class is consistent with prior beliefs, even rendering them more strongly connected than before, thus providing good reasons for leftists to adhere to the particular conspiracy under analysis. From the right, a small ethnic group attempting to erase the country's majority in order to consolidate their power and wealth can likewise strengthen one's already held political views about the loss of tradition and national identity, once again providing good reasons for right-wingers to incorporate the conspiracy to their set of beliefs. In other words, reflecting on how the conspiratorial narrative fits within an actor's set of values and instrumental political goals can cause the actor to adhere to the conspiracy theory in question. Boudon's typology of good reasons to hold a belief hence proves once again useful to understand adherence to conspiracy theories.

There are other angles researchers can take in studying conspiracy theorizing. Indeed, conspiracy theories have at times been part of the governments' official narrative. Nefes (2017) studied the case of the Turkish government framing protests in 2013 as the result of a secret group of both foreign enemies and local traitors plotting against Turkey's ambitions toward economic progress. The protests were initially about expressing opposition to the destruction of a park to build a mall but then became much wider in scope, culminating with a coalition of supporters for various leftist causes (environmentalists, anti-capitalists, homosexual activists, etc.) issuing a number of eclectic demands. The government's conspiracy theory was then elaborated to turn public opinion against this eclectic coalition (ibid., 612).

By analyzing a website which serves as a popular forum for Turkish people to discuss current political events, Nefes used Boudon's theory to understand what the participants' reasons were to adhere (or not) to the government's conspiracy theory about the protests (ibid., 615–616). He found that a pro-government political perspective increases the likelihood of considering the conspiracy theory to be true (ibid., 617–618). This suggests that political views play a role on whether or not one believes in a conspiracy theory; they provide axiological and instrumental reasons to accept (or reject) it, as this acceptance (or rejection) is seen as consistent with both the values and the political interests of the individual accepting (or rejecting) it.

Nefes (2014) similarly studied an online forum to understand the case of conspiracy theories on the attempted murder of the President of Taiwan in 2004, finding once again that adherence (or non-adherence) to conspiracy theories is linked with the values and interests of political views. He also used the same Boudonian theoretical framework to make sense of online antisemitism in Turkey (Nefes 2015b).

Shifting our attention to the mechanisms which contribute to the *dissemination* of conspiracy theories, some work has been done on the role of increasing access to technology as a contextual element favoring the proliferation of such beliefs. Using insights that Boudon has put forward in his theory of beliefs, Bronner (2015) studied how conspiracy theories relating to the case of the terrorist attack on *Charlie Hebdo* are the results of a complex network of actors cognitively motivated to bring forward simplistic, yet plausible, explanations to a public which does not have the time nor the abilities to investigate things further.

The juxtaposition of these motivations and the speed at which information can be propagated through technological advances would provide a plausible explanation for the rapidity and success of such theories. Directly inspired by Boudon, Bronner (2016) explains how the internet contributed to increase the competition between providers of information and how, having limited time to get information, users tended to choose information providers most likely to provide them with information which consolidated their prior beliefs (in particular in conspiracy theories) (ibid., 6, 15–17). This competition provides an instrumental incentive for information providers to become more "shocking" in order to stand out, thus making it more attractive to put forward information based on conspiracy theories (ibid., 20–21).

Moreover, it is often the case that scientific claims are more complicated to grasp than pseudo-scientific claims; the latter may even seem more intuitive to the uninitiated. There are hence good reasons for the observing public to believe in pseudo-science and conspiracy theories when the alternatives seem *prima facie* less convincing. The general public has no time to investigate each topic in detail; it is hence rational for people to use their own background knowledge and intuitive logic to determine the plausibility of statements presented to them. Supporting his thesis with a wide variety of recent examples, Bronner (ibid., xvi–xix; 2015) concludes that conspiracy theories are hence both more accessible to newcomers and are consolidated in the minds of those already believing in them (due to the combined effects of science being more complicated to grasp and at times less intuitive than pseudo-science) *and* of the internet facilitating access to these highly profitable, "shocking" statements. These effects combined provide good reasons for people to increasingly adhere to conspiracy theories.

In a very thorough article, Renard (2015) explicitly uses Boudon's framework of the actor as having "good reasons" to believe in what they do to understand beliefs in conspiracy theories. Indeed, social scientists must pay attention to the various *a priori* frameworks characterizing the individual believers' social and cognitive contexts to then be able to make sense of the thought processes leading to belief in a particular conspiracy theory (ibid., 72). He invokes some general themes which can be helpful to understand adherence.

Indeed, let me add to this discussion that it may very well be difficult, at first, to explain why some individuals still believe in, for instance, the flatness of the Earth. But once one realizes that this belief is probably *not* the *first* conspiracy an actor holds, this belief becomes more understandable. Indeed, if we know an individual holds many conspiracy theories as true, then we are less surprised to become aware that this individual *also* believes that the Earth is flat. Why are we less surprised? Renard (ibid., 73–75) explains that the *loss of trust* in official institutions and their representatives (experts, politicians, journalists, etc.) provides good reasons to adhere to conspiracy theories.

We can easily come up with a simple and illuminating example. A mother is convinced (rightly or wrongly) of the innocence of her son in a crime he has been convicted of. She has good reasons, given her social context and life course shaped by this event, to believe that the State is corrupt. If the State is corrupt, then all beliefs taken for granted by her because they were consolidated by Statist institutions (such as the education system) can be put into question. Indeed, if she can't trust the State to administer justice properly, why would she expect it to administer education properly? Hence, everything she learnt in school is up for questioning. Since she is unlikely to be a natural scientist who has access to the proper instruments to refute the idea of the flatness of the Earth, she could be convinced by arguments which merely sound plausible or intuitive and which are held by individuals who agree with her on how corrupt the State is. Then, it becomes easy for social scientists to see that her belief is *not* irrational but is rather the result of her specific social context affecting the manner in which she reasons.

Renard, like Bronner, mentions that technology does facilitate access to alternative sources to the traditional media and educational system (ibid., 75).

For a person who is not trained in the topic of interest, both traditional news and alternative news may seem equally plausible, or the conspiracy adherent may even find alternative news more convincing (i.e., truth may require complex thinking whereas falsehoods may be easy to grasp and more intuitive).

Moreover, it is undeniable that official experts and traditional media often *do* have biases and *do* make mistakes. It is equally true that, at times, some unofficial sources *do* provide better (less biased, more truthful) information to the public. In such a context, it is little surprise that, for those individuals who are confronted to official mistakes or biases which matter a lot to them (given their singular social context), alternative sources become more reliable.

I have been mentioning above a few particularly relevant articles from the same journal issue (i.e., *Diogenes*'s special issue on *Conspiracy Theories Today*, originally published in French in 2015, but with English translations now available). In fact, most articles from this issue (Campion-Vincent and Renard 2015) can be seen as participating in the expansion of the application of Boudon's theory of rationality to the topic of conspiracy theories. For example, to mention one last study, Delouvée (2015) argued that we should modelize adherence to a conspiracy theory as a spectrum rather than as a binary dichotomy of "believers" against "non-believers." Focusing his attention on the *transmission* (rather than the production) of conspiracy theories, he shows that there are often subjective good reasons for one to propagate such theories (even if the belief is weak), such as when an individual develops a sense of belonging to a social group.

One can see here that a topic which is often treated as a social phenomenon beyond the scope of any theory of rationality can be studied intelligibly using Boudon's social theory. Future studies on various aspects of conspiracy theorizing or superstition could hence profitably use parts of Boudon's insights to enhance their analysis.

Conclusion

We have seen above that a wide variety of topics have been treated with great originality and insight using, partly or fully, Raymond Boudon's social theory. I have also suggested many paths forward for future research. It takes little imagination, from reading the above, to see how most social phenomena could be studied using this general theory. As a result, I venture to argue that Boudon's theory has initiated a general research program. However, and this is mostly an advantage for researchers, it remains at a relatively early stage of development. There are hence many opportunities open for early career (or even established) scholars to contribute to our understanding of society by widening or specifying this general research program. It was my hope that this chapter, by providing a commented review of the literature using Boudon's theoretical framework since his death, will contribute to initiate more applications, criticisms, or refinements of this framework for the rational study of society in the future.

References

Arifin, M. H. (2017). The Role of Higher Education in Promoting Social Mobility in Indonesia. *European Journal of Multidisciplinary Studies* 2(6): 234–242.

Becker, B. and Tuppat, J. (2013). Unequal Distribution of Educational Outcomes between Social Categories: "Children at Risk" From a Sociological Perspective. *Child Indicators Research* 6: 737–751.

Berger, J. and Diekmann, A. (2015). The Logic of Relative Frustration: Boudon's Competition Model and Experimental Evidence. *European Sociological Review* 31(6): 725–737.

Besnard, P. (2003). *Études durkheimiennes*. Genève: Droz.

Blossfeld, P. N. (2018). *Changes in Inequality of Educational Opportunity: The Long-Term Development in Germany*. Wiesbaden: Springer.

Boudon, R. (1967). *L'Analyse mathématique des faits sociaux*. Paris: Plon.

———. (1971 [1968]). *The Uses of Structuralism*. London: Heinemann Educational Books.

———. (1974 [1973]). *Education, Opportunity, and Social Inequality: Changing Prospects in Western Society*. New York: Wiley.

———. (1982 [1977]). *The Unintended Consequences of Social Action*. London: The Macmillan Press.

———. (1989 [1986]). *The Analysis of Ideology*. Cambridge: Polity Press.

———. (1993). L'explication cognitiviste des croyances collectives. *Cahiers de recherche sociologique* 21: 143–162.

———. (1994 [1990]). *The Art of Self-Persuasion: The Social Explanation of False Beliefs*. Cambridge: Polity Press.

———. (1995). *Le juste et le vrai : études sur l'objectivité des valeurs et de la connaissance*. Paris: Fayard.

———. (1998). Limitations of Rational Choice Theory. *American Journal of Sociology* 104(3): 817–828.

———. (2001). *The Origins of Values: Essays in the Sociology and Philosophy of Beliefs*. New Brunswick: Transaction.

———. (2003). Beyond Rational Choice Theory. *Annual Review of Sociology* 29: 1–21.

———. (2004). *Pourquoi les intellectuels n'aiment pas le libéralisme*. Paris: Odile Jacob.

———. (2006). *Renouveler la démocratie: Éloge du sens commun*. Paris: Odile Jacob.

———. (2007). *Essais sur la théorie générale de la rationalité*. Paris: Puf.

———. (2011). La théorie générale de la rationalité, base de la sociologie cognitive. In: F. Clément and L. Kaufman (eds.), *La sociologie cognitive*. Paris: Maison des sciences de l'homme, 43–74.

———. (2012). "Analytical Sociology" and the Explanation of Beliefs. *European Journal of Social Sciences* 50(2): 7–34.

Bourdieu, P. and Passeron, J.-C. (1990 [1970]). *Reproduction in Education, Society and Culture*. London: Sage.

Bronner, G. (2015). Why Are Conspiracy Theories Doing So Well? The Case of *Charlie Hebdo*. *Diogenes* 62(3–4): 8–16.

————. (2016). *Belief and Misbelief Asymmetry on the Internet*. London: Wiley.

Bulle, N. and Morin, J.-M. (2015). Raymond Boudon, a Classical Sociologist. *Journal of Classical Sociology* 15(3): 286–292.

Bulle, N. (2016). A Method of Measuring Inequality within a Selection Process. *Sociological Methods & Research* 45(1): 69–108.

————. (2019). Democratization of Educational Systems, Inequality, Opportunity, and Selection Process: A Re-Examination of the Case of France. *School Effectiveness and School Improvement: An International Journal of Research, Policy and Practice* 30(4): 432–454.

Campion-Vincent, V. and Renard, J.-B. (eds.) (2015). Conspiracy Theories Today [Special Issue]. *Diogenes* 62(3–4), 1–158.

Ceron, F. I., Bol, T. and van de Werfhorst, H. G. (2022). The Dynamics of Achievement Inequality: The Role of Performance and Choice in Chile. *International Journal of Educational Development* 92, article 102628, 1–11.

Coleman, J. (1986). *Individual Interests and Collective Action: Selected Essays*. Cambridge: Cambridge University Press.

Delouvée, S. (2015). Repeating Is not Believing: The Transmission of Conspiracy Theories. *Diogenes* 62(3–4): 56–63.

Demeulenaere, P. (2022). À la recherche de l'unité de la sociologie: Boudon interprète de Durkheim, une mise en perspective. *L'Année sociologique* 72(2):333–363.

Durkheim, É. (1951 [1897]). *Suicide: A Study in Sociology*. New York: The Free Press.

————. (2001 [1912]). *The Elementary Forms of Religious Life: A New Translation by Carol Cosman*. Oxford: Oxford University Press.

Ferejohn, J. A. and Fiorina, M. P. (1974). The Paradox of Not Voting: A Decision Theoretic Analysis. *The American Political Science Review* 68(2): 525–536.

Green, A. and Kaye, N. (2022). The Effects of System Type and Characteristics on Skills Inequalities during Upper Secondary Education: A Quasi-Cohort Analysis of OECD Data. *Research Papers in Education*.

Labrosse, J., Gaudreault, M. and Picard, F. (2017). School Choice Options Limit Access to Higher Education for Various Groups of Students in Quebec. *European Journal of Higher Education* 7(1): 56–77.

Leclair, J. (2023). Parameters of Action in a Context of Legal Pluralism. In: G. Otis, J. Leclair and S. Thériault (eds.), *Applied Legal Pluralism: Processes, Driving Forces and Effects*. London: Routledge, 64–160.

Leroux, R. (2014). Autour de Tocqueville: Raymond Boudon et la rationalité du politique. *Journal des économistes et des études humaines* 20(2): 79–90.

————. (2019). Raymond Boudon, lecteur de Weber. *The Tocqueville Review* 40(1): 105–117.

————. (2020). Boudon's Interpretation of Dukheimian Sociology. *Durkheimian Studies* 24(1): 175–184.

Liu, Y. (2019). Choices, Risk and Rational Conformity: Extending Boudon's Positional Theory to Understand Higher Education Choices in Contemporary China. *Higher Education* 77(3): 525–540.

Marlière, É. (2022). Radicalization Analyzed by Social Sciences: Can the Medium-Range Concepts Already Mobilized on Urban Riots Explain Radicalization Processes in France? *International Journal on Criminology* 9(1): 49–75.

McLaughlin, G. and Robitaille, C. (2021). Radicalization toward Violent Extremism: A Typology Based on a General Theory of Rationality. *Behavioral Sciences of Terrorism and Political Aggression* 16(1):21–43.

McLaughlin, G. (2023). *Radicalisation: A Conceptual Inquiry*. London: Routledge.

Mises, L. (1998 [1949]). *Human Action: A Treatise on Economics*. Auburn: Ludwig von Mises Institute.

———. (2008 [1956]). *The Anti-Capitalistic Mentality*. Auburn: Ludwig von Mises Institute.

Nefes, T. S. (2014). Rationale of Conspiracy Theorizing: Who Shot the President Chen Shui-bian? *Rationality and Society* 26(3): 373–394.

———. (2015a). Scrutinizing Impacts of Conspiracy Theories on Readers' Political Views: A Rational Choice Perspective on Anti-Semitic Rhetoric in Turkey. *British Journal of Sociology* 66(3): 557–575.

———. (2015b). *Online Anti-Semitism in Turkey*. New York: Palgrave.

———. (2017). The Impacts of the Turkish Government's Conspiratorial Framing of the Gezi Park Protests. *Social Movement Studies* 16(5): 610–622.

Nefes, T. S. and Romero-Reche, A. (2020). Sociology, Social Theory and Conspiracy Theories. In: M. Butter and P. Knight (eds.), *Routledge Handbook of Conspiracy Theories*. London: Routledge, 94–107.

Olson, M. (1971). *The Logic of Collective Action: Public Goods and the Theory of Groups*. Cambridge: Harvard University Press.

Orsini, A. (2013). Interview with a Terrorist by Vocation: A Day among the Diehard Terrorists, Part II. *Studies in Conflict & Terrorism* 36: 672–684.

Otten, K. (2020). When Upward Social Mobility Leads to Frustration: Boudon's Game-Theoretic Model of Relative Deprivation and Experimental Evidence. *Research in Social Stratification and Mobility* 65: 1004401–1004413.

———. (2022). The Logic of Relative Frustration Revisited: Theoretical Revision of Boudon's Competition Model and Experimental Evidence. *European Sociological Review* 39: 630–645.

Overbye, E. (1995). Making a Case for the Rational, Self-Regarding, 'Ethical' Voter… and Solving the 'Paradox of not Voting' in the Process. *European Journal of Political Research* 27: 369–396.

Patok, M. (2019). Free Movement of Workers and the EU Integration Processes: Experience of the Polish Immigrants in France. *European Journal of Transformation Studies* 7(1): 19–48.

Reche, A. R. and Nefes, T. S. (2020). The Rationality of Conspiracy Theories: An Approach Based on Max Weber and Raymond Boudon. *CENTRA Journal of Social Sciences* 11(2): 11–30.

Renard, J.-B. (2015). What Causes People to Believe Conspiracy Theories? *Diogenes* 62(3–4): 71–81.

Robitaille, C. (2020). Simmelian Elements in Raymond Boudon's General Theory of Rationality. *The Tocqueville Review* 41(2): 121–135.

Savard, A.-C., Tremblay, J. and Turcotte, D. (2015). Problem Gambling among Adolescents: Toward a Social and Interactionist Reading. *International Gambling Studies* 15(1): 39–54.

Savard, A.-C., Turcotte, D. and Tremblay, J. (2018). Problem Gambling in Adolescence: An Analysis Conducted from the Actor's Perspective. *Deviant Behavior* 39(5): 587–602.

Schoeck, H. (1987 [1966]). *Envy: A Theory of Social Behaviour*. Indianapolis: Liberty Fund.

Simmel, G. (1971). *Georg Simmel on Individuality and Social Form: Selected Writings*. Chicago: University of Chicago Press.

Thompson, R. and Simmons, R. (2013). Social Mobility and Post-Compulsory Education: Revisiting Boudon's Model of Social Opportunity. *British Journal of Sociology of Education* 34(5–6): 744–765.

Tocqueville, A. (2000 [1835/1840]). *Democracy in America*. Chicago: University of Chicago Press.

Valdés, M. T. (2022). Unequal Expectations? Testing Decisional Mechanisms for Secondary Effects of Social Origin. *Social Science Research* 105, article 102688.

Weber, M. (2019 [1921]). *Economy and Society: A New Translation*. Cambridge: Harvard University Press.

Will, G. and Homuth, C. (2020). Education of Refugee Adolescents at the End of Secondary School: The Role of Educational Policies, Individual and Family Resources. *Soziale Welt* 71(1–2): 160–200.

INDEX

Milton Keynes UK
Ingram Content Group UK Ltd.
UKHW020007300424
441951UK00003BA/29